HOW TO WIN AT NINTENDO® GAMES 4

JEFF ROVIN

ST. MARTIN'S PAPERBACKS

How to Win at Nintendo® Games 4 is an unofficial guide, not endorsed by Nintendo®.

HOW TO WIN AT NINTENDO GAMES 4

ISBN: 0-312-92721-5

Printed in the United States of America

St. Martin's Paperbacks edition/October 1991

10 9 8 7 6 5 4 3 2 1

CITIZENS OF *ALL* THE MOST KNOWLEDGEABLE PLANETS THINK JEFF ROVIN'S *NINTENDO GAMES* BOOKS ARE AWESOME!

"There has never, in the history of the galaxy, been a book as monumental as *How to Win at Nintendo Games 3*—except for #s *1* and *2*, of course."

—Barnard's Star Media Syndicate

"With these incredible guides in your hot little hands, you might very well soon be winning lots of friends, gaining incredible manual dexterity and having never-to-be-forgotten adventures in other dimensions."

—*The Wolf-359 Times Book Review*

"FAR OUT!!!"

—*The 61-Cygni Review of Books*

"Jeff Rovin's latest achievement, *How to Win at Game Boy Games*, is practically guaranteed to make you among the best Nintendogamers within five parsecs. I hear his next effort is *How to Win at Nintendo Games 4*. I can't wait!"

—*Beta Pictoris News*

St. Martin's Paperbacks titles by Jeff Rovin

HOW TO WIN AT NINTENDO GAMES
HOW TO WIN AT NINTENDO GAMES 2
HOW TO WIN AT NINTENDO GAMES 3
HOW TO WIN AT NINTENDO GAMES 4
HOW TO WIN AT NINTENDO SPORTS GAMES
HOW TO WIN AT SUPER MARIO BROS. GAMES
HOW TO WIN AT SEGA & GENESIS GAMES
HOW TO WIN AT GAME BOY GAMES
THE UNAUTHORIZED TEENAGE MUTANT NINJA TURTLES QUIZ BOOK
SIMPSON FEVER!

CONTENTS

Introduction	1
Bart vs. the Space Mutants	3
Batman	9
The Bugs Bunny Birthday Blowout	18
Castlevania III: Dracula's Curse	25
Chip 'N Dale Rescue Rangers	35
Double Dragon II: The Revenge	43
Double Dragon III: The Sacred Stones	47
Dragon's Lair	50
The Dream Master	55
Final Fantasy	62
Godzilla	77
The Legend of Zelda	83
Mad Max	101
Mega Man 3	104
Ninja Gaiden II	113
Nintendo World Cup	128
The Punisher	133
Silver Surfer	139
Spot	150
StarTropics	153
Super Off Road	175

Teenage Mutant Ninja Turtles II—
The Arcade Game 181
Tetris 191
Total Recall 197
Zelda II: The Adventure of Link 202
Ninten-Dos and Don'ts 216

INTRODUCTION

Want to know the *best* way to describe this latest book in our *How to Win at Nintendo Games* series?

Classic Nintendo meets New Nintendo. A book of great old games and spectacular new ones.

From your letters, you've told us that you wanted complete guides to *The Legend of Zelda* and *Zelda II: The Adventure of Link*—so here they are, from start to finish. We've also covered other proven crowd pleasers as well as exciting new games, with tips to help both beginners and advanced players.

Each entry is broken down into descriptive categories designed to give you a complete overview of gameplay and strategies. There's also a meaty selection of tips at the end of the book for a few zillion games not covered up front.

As always, your letters are welcome, and we'll be happy to answer those which include a stamped, self-addressed envelope.

But . . . you didn't pick up this book to hear us *yammer*. In fact, we could *swear* we hear the mighty voice of a brave warrior admonishing extraterrestrial invaders to eat his shorts. . . .

BART VS. THE SPACE MUTANTS

Type: Science fiction shoot-'em-up . . . sort of

Objective: Extraterrestrials have infiltrated the town of Springfield, home of the Simpsons. Only one young boy can defeat the aliens as the game begins . . . meaning that the future of Springfield rests in the hands of Bart Simpson. To beat them, Bart must destroy and/or disable a specified number of Objects—innocuous as they may seem—for these are the secret tools of the invaders.

Layout: The screen scrolls horizontally as Bart makes his way through various sections of the town. There are five levels in all.

Heroes: At the beginning, Bart can walk, jump, use X-ray Spectacles to reveal aliens, and bounce on certain objects for added height. Each time he leaps onto the head of an alien who is disguised as a human—but revealed to Bart by the Spectacles—he earns a letter in the name of a Simpson family member. When he collects them all, that parent or sibling will show up to help Bart at the end of the level (their participation is not necessary, but desirable). Coins are collected from many beaten foes and hidden locations; these are used to get extra lives or items in the Springfield stores. Hidden coins only remain on the screen for a few seconds. Bart can also acquire temporary invincibility by finding the Head of the statue of Jebediah Springfield. These, however, are rare.

Enemies: There are many different kinds of extraterrestrials. These range from aliens disguised as humans to extraterrestrials that roam the streets in their natural, spidery forms. Most of these creatures tend to slide from side to side or to hop. Other foes include Dogs (level one), huge rampaging Candies (level two), and so on.

Menu: Only one player can be Bart.

Scoring: Bart earns points for collecting Coins, exposing aliens, and performing other tasks. Bart plays against a timer.

Strategies: In the first stage of play, the first level, purple objects must be covered, painted, or otherwise nullified. Jump up to the Krusty portrait by using the Trashcan. Back on the ground, stop-and-go under the aliens, leap left from the top of the Window beyond the creatures to get the Spray Can; push right on the controller after you nab it so you don't land on the alien as you drop. Turn left and paint the *Space Mutant 4* poster—stand in the poster's purple border, on the right, to make sure your paint reaches. Go *left*, back to the first Trashcan, and paint it. When you reach the clothesline, hop to the top and walk across the clothes hanging there. They'll fall and cover the purple objects below. Jump from there to the Window on the right and keep hopping right to get the Spray Can up there. When you reach the second trio of bouncing aliens, you can't walk under them as you did the first group; leap each one when it's starting on its way down. You'll get a Coin from the Bushes above the first two. At the Wet Paint Awning, go to the Window on the right, jump off its lower sill to the Awning, and hop from there to the top of the Tool World Window. Jump up and spray the Flower

Pot, standing on the right and facing left. Spray the Hydrant in front of the shop, then go inside and buy a Wrench and Key. Use the Wrench to open the Hydrant on the left and spray the Awning, changing it from purple to red. At Mel's Novelty Shop, get one Cherry Bomb and as many Rockets as you can afford—you'll need a lot of them, especially if you're just starting out: it's tough learning their range. Jump from the Window to the left side of the Door, leap to the top of the Window—careful not to hit the alien—face left and spray the Flower Pot. Walk under the alien to the rightmost Window for the 1–Up. *Don't* go into Toys 'N' Stuff: the Magnet is useless on this level (though you'll find it useful in the third stage), and you can live without the Whistle—it'll summon Dogs, something you definitely don't want. Jump from the toy store Window to the left side of the Door to spray the Flower Pot on the Window above—beginners are advised to stand as far to the left as possible on the Window before leaping to the Door. Over Candy Most Dandy, leap to the Windows and spill the paint over the Awning. (You can also kick the Ball up there to accomplish this.) Leap to the leftmost Window, drop to the Awning, face right and jump up to spray the Flower Pot. Use a Cherry Bomb to scare the Bird from the Cage at the Pet Shop—you can do this from outside the store—but stand on the Window sill to do this, since a Dog usually comes by (it runs back and forth once) and could pose a problem if you're on the ground. Hop from the Trashcan—which you should first paint—on the left in order to reach the Flower Pot above the Bird; you can also get this Flower Pot first, by leaping from the rightmost Window of the Candy Most Dandy shop. When you reach the Park, get a Coin from the Bush before the "Keep Off" sign. Make sure you get up on the Grass by that sign and walk to the right. In a moment a police officer will come along: come down behind him and spray his purple uniform *or* rush ahead of him, turn and spray, then continue walking left until he disappears off the bottom of the screen. In any case, if you miss him you're in trouble: he only appears once, and you can't complete the level without dying his clothes. At the statue of Jebediah Springfield use a Rocket, from the left, to chase off the Bird. (Fire when the Bird is just to the left of the right edge of your screen.) Pay attention to what ol' Jebediah tells you here: he's not just talking to hear himself! Get on the Skateboard—collecting the Coin from the Bush beside it—and be prepared to hop four packs of Dogs in a row. Stay on the top of the screen and leap the aliens—grabbing the Spray Can while you go—and dodge the Skateboarding Kid (keeping an eye peeled for the 1–Up in the Bush when the Kid starts chasing you). After you negotiate the crowded sidewalks, spray the Fountain and continue past the Bowling Alley . . . pausing to spray its sign by Rocket. When you meet the second group of aliens, run under them all in a single burst; watch when they're all airborne, and *hurry!* A Bee often attacks after you pass the parking lot, so be on the lookout. There's a Coin in the Bush over the two aliens before the Kwik-E-Mart. Paint the Fountain after the Kwik-E-Mart, fire Rockets at the purple shades of the Retirement Home, and you'll be ready to face the level boss—a bully of a Kid who chucks things at you. You must throw projectiles back, *or,* if Maggie has arrived, catch the Bowling Balls she rolls. Heave them at the Kid and he's a goner.

What about the Key you bought in the Tool Shop? You can use the Key to enter Moe's: from there, you'll warp to the Retirement Home.

Meanwhile, what did Jebediah mean about getting "ahead"? Simply that when you find his Head, you'll be granted a short stretch of invincibility.

To find the first Head—which is in the second level—when you jump across the second Cement Pool, leap up from the last Candy to get the Head. Other than that, this level's pretty merciless. You only have one chance to knock the Hats off passersby, and it'll take some skill to grab the free-floating Hats between various Candy Ledges over the Cement. When you cross the Pool, find a Krusty in the Ashtray. When you reach the two aliens with a Marshmallow between them, run under the first two when they're aloft and *over* the third one . . . all in the same, swift move. The alien mini-boss—a man with a Hat—has to be hit three times in the head: once to dislodge the Hat, and two more to ferret out the alien. Go up the Escalator: the Sneakers come in pairs (just as you'd expect) and are easily leaped. The boss at the end of the Mall is the Simpsons' mean Babysitter, who hurls Suitcases at you. If Marge has arrived, she'll help by disarming the Babysitter, *to a degree*. Bart must still leap on the Suitcases, which will cause them to rebound back at the nasty teen.

Tips for later levels: In the third level, you'll find Jebediah's Head by going to the High Dive Board in the Teddy Bear display. Shoot the guy who's dropping bombs, jump to left to the Springboard and ring the Bell: your prize will be the Head. Also, if you acquired the Magnet at the level one toy store, select it at the Wheel of Fortune and hit the Start button. Thanks to the Magnet, whatever number you choose on the Wheel will come up! When you have to face Sideshow Bob here, it's a good idea to have Lisa: she'll drop Bowling Balls on his head. In any case, you've got to jump on Bob's feet four or five times—without him stomping on *you*—in order to beat him.

In the fourth level, you must jump on each Case *three* times to open it. There's a mini-boss and a boss here. The mini-boss is a Tyrannosaurus Rex. You've got to leap on its head three times to defeat it—but the trick here is that you must get *off* the head after each jump! Go to the Ledge on the monster's left, leap onto its head again, and repeat. Shortly after you defeat the behemoth, you will fight the shock-therapy Radio Talk Show Host. He's actually easier: again, you've got to pounce on his head three times.

The fifth level is tricky because there are Doors to enter, and you can't do that without the passwords. Get those from Lisa, then stand under the Control Panel beside the door and push up to access the input mechanism.

Rating: B–

The people at Acclaim have created a clever, novel game. The *big* problem with this cartridge is that you go back to the beginning when you lose. And there's only one warp area (Moe's), which will quickly become frustrating . . . and boring. It's too bad: considering how terrible most licensed games tend to be—witness *Ghostbusters* and *Total Recall*—this is otherwise a much better game than you might have expected!

Challenge: C+

Graphics: A– (the Groening graphics are wonderfully recreated, and the de-purpled bowling sign in the first level is *perfect)*

Sound Effects: C (good music and voice synthesis, but not enough effects, per se)

Simulation: B–

BATMAN

Type: Superheroic shoot-'em-up

Objective: If you saw the flick, you know the scenario. The Joker is plotting to terrorize Gotham City during its 200th anniversary celebration, and it's up to the Dark Knight Detective to stop him.

Layout: The game scrolls horizontally as the Caped Crusader makes his way to the Joker's hideout. The brawl sprawls through five stages.

Hero: Batman has three lives, his powerful fists, and a Utility Belt full of Weapons: the Batarang, which functions more or less like a boomerang; the Spear Gun, which has great range and strength; and the Dirk, which covers a wider range than the Spear Gun. (Why is this Weapon called that when "dirk" means "dagger"? Beats us!) Bonus items that Batman collects as he goes are additional points, Hearts (restores a portion of your life), and Pellets (adds bullets to your dirk; 99 is the most the hero can carry). Batman's most amazing ability, however, is his Wall Jump, a wall-climbing skill that is more Spider-Man than Batman but is cool nonetheless.

Enemies: In addition to various goons and automatic Weapons that he turns against Batman, the Joker has five sub-bosses working for him (based on the comic books, not the movie): Killer Moth, Machine, Electrocutioner, Dual-Container Alarm, and Firebug. These attack at the end of each level, and will be discussed at the appropriate time.

Menu: There's just the one-player game.

Scoring: Points are awarded when Batman beats foes and acquires power-up items.

Strategies: Spend a little time in 1–1 working on your Wall Jump. When you've got that perfected, here's what you can expect stage-by-stage.

Stage 1–1: The game begins in the streets of Gotham City, with nothing too challenging here: thugs who you can punch out, Mobile Trackers you can blast, and Heatwaves you can hit by standing just beyond the reach of the flames, then moving in when they die down. Heatwaves can be chilled-out with basic punches.

Stage 1–2: A construction site is the setting now. You can't leave here unless you're at the top of the structure, which can be accomplished one of two ways: you can proceed to the right to the half-Girders, and climb; or, right before you get to them, you can execute a Wall Jump between the two Walls that go up to the third story. The foes here aren't much more dangerous than in 1–2 . . . until you get to the top of the structure. That's when the Enforcers make their debut. The first will arrive as soon as you pass the first upright steel Girder on the top-left side of the building. Jump back behind the Girder and, when you can, stand and blast the Enforcer with the wide-angle Dirk. A pair of direct hits will stop the flying gunman. Roughly six uprights later another Enforcer will pay you a visit; the upright here isn't as high, but it will still afford protection as you blast the jetpacking killer. When you reach the end of this section of the building, drop to the ground—what's a four-story fall to a superhero?—and either rush the sword-swinging flunky ahead, decking him before he can lop off your cowl, or hang back and begin shooting with the Spear Gun, edging forward as you fire. (The run is more of a challenge, but the other approach *is* safer!)

Stage 1–3: Killer Moth will flutter down now, flinging Fireballs at the black-clad hero. Despite his flamboyant entry—make that *flame*boyant—he's easy to beat: watch where the Fireballs land. There's one safe spot on either side. Simply note where that is, then move in with your Dirk.

Stage 2–1: The action shifts to the Axis Chemical Factory. Here, the initial danger is from both Heatwaves and dripping Gluk, a lethal chemical. The Gluk leaks from overhead pipes, and if Batman isn't careful, he'll get dripped on. Use the Ledges and Pipes here—nothing too difficult *yet*. Use the Batarang liberally in this stage, since most of the enemies have to be hit more than once, and the Batarang usually strikes twice with each toss.

Stage 2–2: This is sort of a make-or-break level for you: Batman *has* to make Wall Jumps here in order to proceed. To start, you'll be crossing "Ledges" which consist of Electric Coils; you must jump and land *with precision*, or you'll be fried batcakes. Head right to begin, jump up to the long Ledge to the left, and stop beneath the second overhead Coil from the right. Now, you *can* continue left if you want, but a smarter move is to leap to the right side of that second Coil. Grab on to the right side at the bottom and Wall Jump to the Coil on the right. Otherwise, you'll have to go well to the left and do a lot more leaping. Whichever way you choose, cross, next, through the opening on the right and continue on until you reach the stack of Coil Ledges rising straight up to the right of a Wall. You're going to have to Wall Jump to the top, going from the left side of each Coil to the Wall and back again until you reach the top. When you get there, rush at the enemy waiting for you and punch him. The next section is even tougher in terms of Wall Jumping: go to the right side of the Coil you're on—the topmost Coil of the stack you climbed—and lower yourself so you're clutching the bottom right side of the Coil. Make a big Wall Jump to the upper right—not to the Coil *directly* overhead, but to the one beyond. You've got to catch that Coil on the right side in order to continue. Once you're there, you'll have to perform a similar maneuver. Drop to the boxlike Ledge to the lower right, hop to the next one, climb down its right side, and Wall Jump to the Coil in the upper right just as before. Let yourself down to the Pipe below, walk right, and exit.

Stage 2–3: You're in the processing section of the Plant with its sharp, crushing Gears. An overhead bomber known as a Drop Claw awaits three Ledges down: punch its projectiles for bonuses. If you stand to the side and bop them repeatedly, you can stock up with all kinds of items. Follow the Ledges down until you reach the Conveyor Belt. Get off the Belt at the Wall, Wall Jump to the Ledge *above* it, continue to the right, drop onto the next Conveyor Belt, then avoid the Gears under the next Ledge by Wall Jumping on top of it. *Carefully* jump down the Pit on the right: Gears line both its sides, so make sure you drop down the center. You have to get to the Conveyor Belt on the left now, but it isn't an easy leap. Climb onto the left side of the Wall projection you're on, hang onto the edge so that the tips of your pointy ears are equal to the top of the projection, then leap to the left. Go left on the Conveyor Belt; the Drop Claw at the end won't be as easy to milk for goodies as the one above, but it *can* be done. Anyone who's ever walked up a down elevator and stayed in the same spot will know how! Get onto the Ledge just below the Belt on the left side, but *don't* go down to the Gear Ledge below: it's a dead end . . . literally! Hop up to the small Ledge on the left, go over that Wall down another Gear-lined Pit, and head right. Hop the two Conveyor Belts ahead, go down to the floor and continue right, and leap over the Gears to the Conveyor Belt above them. Exit to . . .

Stage 2–4: The Machine Intelligence System stage! The first order of business here is to eliminate the Cannons on the right. Duck when it shoots high, leap when it shoots low. Your Dirk or Spear Gun will take it out . . . or, if you're feeling brave (stupid?) you can run across the Conveyor Belt and punch them out between bursts. Once they're gone, get to the Ledge above them, then hop up and fire to take out the Current Controller on the left. With that gone, the Wall to the right will open and you'll be eye to eye (literally) with the Nerve Center. In order to beat it, the cowled crimebuster should kneel just below the blue Orb. When it shuts down, guns will emerge . . . but they can't hit Batman here. When the Orb opens, Batman will be ideally situated to leap up and punch it. Ten hits will do the trick.

Stage 3–1: Batman has to make his way through the underground passageway, an abandoned laboratory that leads from Axis to the Joker's lair. Moments after you leave the brick Walkway, you'll be attacked from the shadows by Jader. He'll pounce all over Batman unless you destroy him before he can move. Proceed cautiously, scrolling the screen slowly: a portion of Jader will appear on the screen, and though he won't move yet, the bounder is vulnerable to your fire. Three volleys should put him away. There's another Jader ahead at the fat, vertical Pipe that hangs from the ceiling, and a third after the brick Column ahead, just before the first Coil on the ground. Before you reach the third one, though, you'll have to do a Wall Jump onto a small brick Ledge; otherwise, you won't make it across the deadly Pit ahead. You'll have to repeat this maneuver at the next set of three brick Ledges; fail, and you'll be a hero . . . a ground bat-beef hero sandwich! Hit the Drop Claw's bombs at the end to power-up.

Stage 3–2: You'll begin at the top of a maze of Pipes, Ledges, and Coils. Head right, using the little Ledges after the first Waterfall—or is it a Glukfall? When you reach the second Waterfall, jump down . . . but fall to the right so you land on the upright Coil there, then hop to the small Coil on the left. (You can *try* for the small Coil when you jump off the Walkway—but if you miss, you'll be ground round!) Head left along the brick Walkway and take a mighty leap to the left to the small Coils there. Hop to the right, go down the Waterfall, and be ready to fight the Jader there at once. Continue right, hop to the small Coil at the end of the Walkway, then to the larger Coil to the right, and from there to the Walkway above. Go left, under the Coils, to the Waterfall; power-up at the Drop Claw there, then go right, leaping from Coil to Coil to the upper right. You're now on the final and most difficult leg of your journey: you must Wall Jump up the narrow Pit in order to get to the next level. Go from the last Coil to the bottom of the Coil above and left; Wall Jump to the right and so on.

Stage 3–3: Batman must climb through a heavily protected cavern now, guarded by Electrical Emitting Vehicles, Mobile Home Mines, and various goons. Head right and avoid the Mobile Home Mines by landing near them (thus activating them) then hopping back to where you were while they detonate. The Mobile Tracker beyond is easily destroyed with the Spear Gun, but the EEV at the far right should be destroyed with your fists. When you see it, rush over and begin punching. Most aggressive players actually take *less* damage than if they stood their ground and shot it! Go up and left. The next EEV will appear midway through your passage—after you take two steps down onto a low-lying stone Ledge. When it appears, duck to the right to scroll it off, then double back to the left: more often than not, the EEV will be gone. If not, run over and beat it as you did before *or* duck below the Ledge it's on and, between its shots, jump up and blast it with your Spear

Gun. You can power-up at the Drop Claw a little further on. After rising another level and traveling to the right, you'll have to take a steep climb up a narrow Pit. There are Heatwaves and Gears here, so don't rush things: stay put and wait until a Heatwave is dormant before continuing up and attacking it. When you reach the top, move to the left *slowly:* there's an EEV just on the other side of the Wall.

Stage 3–4: This is where you meet your third sub-boss, the infamous Electrocutioner. He fires an electrical beam that will toast you: when you arrive, get onto the overhead Ledges and always stay *behind* the killer, facing the middle of the screen and punching the Electrocutioner in the back when you can.

Stage 4–1: Hereafter, you won't face anything of consequence that you haven't dealt with before. Hence, we'll concentrate on the highlights. This stage is another laboratory. Don't be misled by the clownlike decor: the place is deadly. The layout is straightforward and obvious; as for foes, you'll face Jaders, Heatwaves, Mobile Home Mines, and Drop Claws. Treat them all as you have before.

Stage 4–2: Again, there's nothing new. The only real difficulty here is the series of overhead Pipes and plates that need to be skillfully Wall Jumped.

Stage 4–3: Fall all the way down, watching out for the Rail Runners, and refill your Utility Belt at the Drop Claw. Leap along the Ledges and forget about using your fists: Dirk and Spear are your best friends here. The Conveyor Belts are smaller than the ones you used before, and you'll have to be careful when you jump: land too far to the opposite side and you'll be conveyed right off before you can jump again. While you leap, you'll also have to take out Mobile Trackers. There are no real surprises . . . just the need for excellent timing and shooting. You'll face a few EEVs at the end, along with easy-to-whip Nightslayers; try to lure the second of the two under the Drop Claw. It's more fun to outwit him than to outpunch him!

Stage 4–4: Okay, *now* you've got a new challenge, the Dual-Container Alarm. Before entering their chamber, power-up at the Drop Claw. When you walk into the Alarm Room, do a Wall Jump to the left side of the Ledge in the middle. Crouch, facing left. As the deadly duo arrives, *punch* them rapidly and repeatedly. They'll take up positions on different sides of the room to catch Batman in a crossfire; thwart them by jumping down. When they move, get back to the middle Ledge and resume your attack. After one of them has been destroyed—probably the first—the other will begin a relentless fireball assault, firing away at you as it shifts back and forth on the floor. Leave your post and drop to the far *left* side of the chamber. Shoot at it and, when the vehicle nears, punch it.

Stage 5–1: Climax time! You've tracked the Joker to the Cathedral—but to reach him, you must climb from Ledge to Ledge while avoiding huge Gears grinding away between them. Wall Jumps aplenty will be required here. Most are upward-moving Wall Jumps, except for the Drop Claw region. You'll have to Wall Jump down to get to it . . . and get to it you must, since only a fully-powered Batman can hope to triumph.

Stage 5–2: Use Wall Jumps to go up the left side of the screen, Wall Jumping to the right when you reach the Gears. The big danger in this screen, however, is the Firebug—mightiest of the sub-bosses. This flaming fiend flings fissionable fire (say it ten times fast), and he'll run at you the instant you reach his chamber. Hang to the far left of the room and attack with your Dirk. This will cause the Firebug to halt, though it won't stop him from hopping up and down and chucking Fireballs. Leap these, shooting the Firebug when he alights. Dirkless? Use the Spear Gun. Don't have one? Use the Batarang. You can even beat the humanoid inferno by edging toward him, leaping the Fireballs, and punching him when he lands.

Stage 5–3: Finally, a face to grinning-face showdown with the Joker. He's armed with his infamous extendo-gun, so you'll have to jump his shots as you did with Firebug. The difference here, though, is that while you can mount a shooting attack as you did against the Firebug, the chances are better that the Joker will hit you back—and not just with his gun. He can also order Lightning to strike from above. What to do? Leap in an arc and land as close as possible to the Joker. Kneel and punch the Clown Prince of Crime: he and his lightning can't attack while Batman's fists work him over. When he tries to flee, crowd him and continue pummeling him. Au revoir, Joker.

Rating: B–

This is a good game, though it wouldn't have gotten much attention if it were about Joe Hero instead of Batman. And it might as well have *been* about some other character since it doesn't really utilize elements of the Batman mythos other than his haymaker punches and the Batarang. Visually, the game is as dark and forboding as the movie—fun to watch, even when the action lags.

Challenge: B–
Graphics: A–
Sound Effects. C+
Simulation: B–

THE BUGS BUNNY BIRTHDAY BLOWOUT

Type: Cartoon quest

Objective: It's Bugs's fiftieth birthday, and you must guide him safely to his party.

Layout: The screen scrolls horizontally.

Heroes: Bugs can walk, climb, jump, or swing his Hammer. He acquires Hearts (lives) as he goes by hitting Fireballs, and also collects Carrots (see *Scoring*).

Enemies: In addition to the other Looney Tunes characters who are jealous of Bugs's celebration and are out to get him, there are numerous "Contraptions" that Bugs must destroy or avoid. Most of these are pictured in the instructions. Note: Bugs can ride many of his foes. He can also stand on their heads and hit them out from under him—a good way of staying safe while getting rid of them!

Menu: Only one player can take the part of Bugs.

Scoring: Points in this game take the form of Carrots. The more you get, the better your luck will be in the Bonus Bingo rounds.

Strategies: Here's the game, a stage at a time.

Stage One, Round One: No surprises here. Make your way through, collecting Carrots. The foes here are easy to beat. Jump down the Well at the end, get the Big Carrot on the other side, and after dealing with Daffy—Hammering him, or ignoring him—you'll be spirited to the Bonus Bingo round.

Stage One, Round Two: Another field. There's a Jumping Telescopic Bullet Sprinkler directly ahead, so don't climb the Ladder until it's gone. Stay on the upper Ledges, or the Stop Light Worm will get you. After the Elevator (the white platform) takes you down, head right, across the Waterfall. Go down the Well when the Boulder's gone. When you emerge, go to the top WB sign and take a big leap to the Ledge hanging in the sky: that's the only way across. Enter the Well, and when you emerge go down the one on the right. It will lead you to the one on the left. After you've cleaned out all the goodies, emerge and go right. Go down the Well at the end. When you come out, Tweety will attack, so whack the bird unconscious and you'll be rewarded with a Carrot and another Bingo round.

Stage One, Round Three: Watch for the Boulders that start falling shortly after you begin heading right—immediately after the third Worm. Enter the Well in the chamber ahead, then go right through the Wall, then *left.* Go right to get to the Well, another showdown with Daffy, and the Bonus round. (If you want to go left, use the See-Saw to vault to the Elevator, but be careful—the white platform comes and goes!)

Stage One, Round Four: Go down the Well, collect the goodies, and emerge using the Well in the lower left. Cross the Waterfall quickly—the Elevators vanish—then jump into the Well between them. Collect the goodies and head right. Watch out for the Boulders here: not only do they fall, they also roll when they hit the Ledges! Go right, up the Hill, to the Well there. When you emerge, enter the Well on the left. Gather the goodies and leave using the same Well. Take the Well on the right and leave, heading right. Cross the Waterfall using the Elevator, then exit via the Well at the end. It's Coyote time: he hops all around then walks a bit. Run up to him after he hops and hit him while he's walking. Play Willy the Weasel, earning points for each one you clobber.

Stage Two, Round One: Boulders start falling after you leap the first Pit in this desert setting. You'll also have to jump the Columns ahead by waiting *between* them while the Worms coil overhead. Watch out for the Quicksand ahead —you can get out if you land near the edge and walk fast— followed by a Bullet Sprinkler. No other surprises until you cross the green Ledges over the Quicksand: they disintegrate, so cross quickly! Daffy pesters you at the end, but he has no special abilities and is easy to club.

Stage Two, Round Two: Go to the Treetops to avoid the Bullets, but cross quickly or you'll have to deal with an army of Time Bombs as well as occasional attacks from Twisters. Keep a sharp eye peeled for the Well in the air, with its wealth of Carrots. When you emerge, a Boulder will fall at once; after that, stay on the green Ledges to avoid the succession of Bullet Sprinklers below. Enter the Well at the end, then cross carefully to the Well on the left. When you emerge from that one, you'll be greeted by a Bullet Sprinkler. Go right, take the Elevator up at the end, and go left. Enter the Well and fight Tweety.

Stage Two, Round Three: Walk slowly to avoid the falling Boulders. Use Elevators and Treetops whenever possible on this level, since the ground is full o' danger! Smash the

Sphinx to get the goodies below. Watch for the overhead Well; lotsa Carrots inside. Whack your way to the Big Carrot at the end of the round and you'll be ballooned to . . .

Stage Two, Round Four: There's a Well way up in the sky, accessible by an underground route. Stay on the ground and drop into the Pit—you'll see a hint of Carrot sticking up. Get the goodies underground. The Well here takes you to a region where you can go up or go down. When you emerge from the lower Well, go right. Hopefully, you haven't destroyed the entire Sphinx and can use its head to vault to the Ledge and cross the Quicksand. Enter the Well. Go right to the next Well and you'll come out in the Sky. Stay in the Sky and go left. The next Well will take you to Yosemite Sam, who'll be shooting at you: hit him between volleys, which consist of three Bullets each. Another Weasel game, and then . . .

Stage Three, Round One: New foe here: Poisonous Frog, who not only can hop you to death, but whose breath is lethal. Leap these guys before they move. The rain of Boulders can be dangerous, but not nearly so much as the Comets. Shortly after you pass the Well in the Sky—it contains four Carrots—you'll come to a pair of Lava Pits: after these, the Comets will begin rocketing up from the Lava-free Pits. After these, you'll be attacked by Frogs on ground that collapses under your feet; obviously, stay on Ledges wherever possible! At the end, ride the Elevator up to a bout with Daffy and a Bonus Round.

Stage Three, Round Two: The One Ton is introduced here; the Ledge it's on will crumble beneath your feet, so get on and off *pronto!* Hitch a ride here on Soap Bubbles, as necessary; when you reach the red Mesa with a ladder, go down the Pit to its left. Head left across the Lava Pits and enter the Well at the end. Cross to the Well on the right and go right when you emerge. The Volcanoes here spit Fireballs, which can not only hurt going up but coming down. *Don't* ride the Bubbles here: these are from Red Soap Boxes, which are your enemies. Enter the Well, go left, and beware of more collapsing Ledges. Collect what you want here, return to the Well, exit, and go left in the sky. Enter the Well there and attack the Net-throwing Elmer when his back is turned.

Stage Three, Round Three: A lot more Lava and a lot less land, but nothing else substantially new here. The Bullet Sprinklers return so don't rush ahead! Daffy stalks you at the end.

Stage Three, Round Four: Like the last stage, only tougher . . . with almost every foe you've faced to date! Make sure you Hammer through the ground where the two Frogs are —before the Volcano—and go left to the Well. A skateboarding Sylvester Jr. followed by a skateboarding Sylvester Sr. will keep you busy at the end of the level. Leap them when they attack and bop the tips of their tails from behind. You'll know you've connected when they lurch ahead a bit.

Stage Four, Round One: An underground world! Watch out for the Waterfalls that pour suddenly from above—only over Pits in the beginning and, later, only when you see big holes in the wall. There are also falling Stalactites, and darkness that appears whenever an Oil Drum explodes. When the Oil explosion flashes after the first Waterfall, get to a safe place—an outcrop of rock—and stand still until the lights come back on. Daffy's your foe at the end of this round.

Stage Four, Round Two: A Ghost comes flying at you immediately, then turns and attacks again after it's passed. That may force you to rush ahead—right into a Waterfall —so don't tarry when these fiends appear! Another explosion-darkness hits when you reach the first Well. As for *good* news, Geysers can be used to hitch a ride to the top of the screen. When you reach the red Boulders in the ground, smash 'em, go down for the goodies, then ride the Geysers or use the WB signs to get back up. At the end, watch out for Tweety. the room *seems* empty, but the jealous little canary is hiding behind the Rock on the right!

Stage Four, Round Three: Darkness for starters, followed by all of the underground foes and a few from above as well! But you've seen it all before. Bugs vs. Daffy at the end.

Stage Four, Round Four: You'll face darkness before the collapsing Bridge, more *after* it, and then it's underground mayhem as usual. Tangle with the skunk Pepe LePew at the end: this guy has to be hit from the *front,* since he leaves deadly clouds of skunk smell behind him.

Stage Five, Round One: Bugs is in a forest. Climb the Trees for goodies—be aware of what's under you at all times, 'cause some limbs fall when you step on them—and jump *high* on the Vines (if you're low, you'll have trouble getting to the next one). The Well's in a Tree Stump at the end, and tenacious Daffy is on the other side.

Stage Five, Round Two: A lot of Worms here, and Brick Walls that need to be climbed, but otherwise it's the same as the first round. After you enter the Well, watch for the Spider to descend from above. Elmer Fudd is just beyond the next Well.

Stage Five, Round Three: The Frogs are back, and the Vines are farther apart; there are also *more* Vines than before. The Elevator at the end of the forest will take you to the Treetops, where you'll have a pretty easy time of it until the Boulders begin to fall . . . and roll toward you. The Blocks up here crumble when you walk on them, so be careful. At least there's no Looney Tuner waiting for you at the end!

Stage Five, Round Four: Climb the Tower to the sky, go right, and ride the Elevator down. Go right, staying on the upper Ledges as much as possible—the lower ones break and are more thickly populated with enemies. At the end are Foghorn Leghorn and Henery Hawk. Hit Henery first (he's on top) by standing on the left Wall and Hammering him. Beat Henery and Foghorn will drop!

Stage Six: You're inside a house and, improbably, face most of your old foes, including falling Stalactites. The new enemy here is a series of Conveyor Belts: if you don't get off these quickly, you'll be conveyed to your doom. The Wells in this stage are urns. After the first round you'll fight Daffy, then Elmer, then Daffy again, then the Tasmanian Devil—you've got to Hammer his projectiles back at him. Beat the Devil, and Bugs can finally attend his party! (Stick around for it . . . and the "surprise" ending!)

Rating: B

Not as delightful as the last Bugs game, but young children will find it entertaining through Stage Three, Round One, after which it gets a little too difficult . . . and more experienced gamers can take over!

Challenge: B
Graphics: B (some image breakup)
Sound Effects: B
Simulation: C

CASTLEVANIA III: DRACULA'S CURSE

Type: Horror shoot-'em-up

Objective: You've whupped 'im twice before, but does that stop Dracula? No way! Especially since this game takes place a century *before* the others! A forebear of Simon Belmont, Trevor Belmont, must make his way through the Castle to destroy the infamous vampire.

Layout: The screen scrolls horizontally or vertically, depending upon the locale. There are 17 shriek-inducing levels in all.

Heroes: Trevor starts the game with a Whip and the ability to walk, jump, crouch, and climb Stairs. As he goes along, he acquires various power-ups which are described in the instructions; once uncovered, these remain on-screen for four seconds. Trevor also has the ability to summon help in the form of Grant and Sypha (see instructions). Many power-ups don't work unless Trevor has Hearts, which must be collected from Candles and from most slain foes. Note: if you have a strong weapon, you may not want to replace it —for example, the Pocket Watch when you face the Clock Tower Medusas. Thus, always hit Candles but *don't* automatically grab what falls until you see what it is.

Enemies: Every kind of ghoul and monster imaginable is present: see *Strategies* for details. The farther you progress in the game, the more hits enemies tend to take to destroy them.

Menu: The game's just for one vampire-hunter.

Scoring: Trevor earns points for killing monsters—as low as 50 for the Marsh Monsters in the first level, and moving on up. He also earns points for any Bonus Bags he uncovers. Points are important: they provide 1-Ups when you reach certain plateaus. Each level has a timer; if you fail to complete the level before the clock runs down, Trevor loses a life.

Strategies: Level by level, here's how to make your way to and through the Castle.

Nothing daunting and no surprises to start. You'll fight Skeletons, Bats, Bone-Throwing Skeletons—move away when they throw, then rush in for the kill—Medusas (they weave up and down as they approach; back off or move in, if need be), and Marsh Monsters. At the end of the level, force the Skeleton Warrior into the right-hand corner and kill it there. Take the path to the left.

Make sure you know how to walk up the Stairs—stand at the foot of the lowest step and push up on the pad; *don't* push up and left/right. If not, you'll be falling to your death a *lot* in the Clock Tower. Note that you can—and often must—stand on Gears here. Easy going, at the start; leap the Pit on the right and whip the Wall for a Heart. The Knights you'll encounter each take two hits to kill, but they're plodding fellows, so don't sweat. When you reach the very top of the Stairs where the Pendulum is swinging, go *left:* climb the Ledges and jump onto the Pendulum when it's near. When you're on it, walk to its right side (you won't fall) and ride it right. Leap onto the Wall, hop to the next Pendulum, and take that to the right. That's the only way you'll get across here. To cross the next passageway, you'll have to ride on the *Teeth* of the Gear. (Beginners: make sure you straddle it—and all future Gears—so that your left leg is on the left side. Otherwise, you'll slip precipitously!) Hop off to the right, and after you pass the Skeleton here *be on guard!* Once you ascend and the screen scrolls, and you begin climbing the Stairs, Medusas fly at you. If you haven't got a Pocket Watch to freeze the hideous heads, just get up the Stairs as fast as you can. Be careful when you're on the Gear on top: a Medusa will fly along and knock you off if you don't whip her first. (If you want, you can duck, and after you're hit, try and fall to the right. You'll lose energy and look like a clod, but at least you won't die!) The serpent-lady assault will end *briefly* when the screen scrolls again. After you've cleared this area and passed through the door in the upper right, ride the Gear and hit the Wall above the Ledge on the other side to uncover the power-up—a Big Heart . . . unless you get the Dagger first (see below), in which case it'll be a II. Whip the Candle on the top, and if you have no other powerful weapons, collect the Dagger. Next screen the Medusas resume their raids. When you reach the end of this level, you'll reach a screen with a Sword-swinging Skeleton; go to the right Wall, over the Ledge, and eat the Leg of Werewolf to restore your power. Next, you'll fight Grant. An Axe or Sacred Water work best against him; jump his Dagger and leap over him when he charges to the right. Defeat him and he'll be your companion! Make your way back to the beginning of the Clock Tower to continue.

The next route starts with an Owl attack. You can see their eyes before the birds attack: either rush ahead or wait until they materialize. When they appear, they hesitate for a moment before taking flight; that's the time to kill them. If you allow two or more to collect, they'll flock and do you in! You'll acquire a Boomerang from the fourth Brazier: use it to destroy them en masse. The Red Skeleton in the ruins beyond regenerates after a few seconds, so don't hang around. Boomerang or Whip the two Stone Dragons on top—leaping or whipping its Fireballs—and keep going right. After descending the Stairs, continue right. When faced with a choice of routes—there'll be a map screen overhead—stay on the upper level if you want to take on a different partner, Sypha. Watch out for the huge Crow here; it'll swoop off the screen to the left then *return* to claw you a few moments later. Get an Axe from the Brazier on top. The Spores on the next level down are worse than the Medusas ever were: they open and split into smaller fiends after a few seconds, or else when hit. Each part must be dealt with separately. If possible, leap or duck the parents rather than hit and break them up. Below, the Whip Skeletons take only one hit to destroy. Look out for the Spiders, which descend suddenly: not only do they rush down on a strand of web, they spit little Spiders at you—*and* they regenerate quickly! *Wait* at the right side of the first Pit and leap the Baby Spider fired by the big Spider on the right; otherwise, the Spider on the left will knock you into the Pit. Wait at the foot of the Stairs until the Spider on the left has come and gone: otherwise, its Baby will hit you as you climb. These crimson crawlers also have the ability to pass through the ground as if it weren't there, so don't think you're safe just 'cause you're in the subterranean passage up ahead—the one with the two Candles. When you're at the bottom of the level, go right to the statuary. There's Leg of Werewolf in the lowest Block on the left, but *don't* get it yet: you'll need the Ledge for your attack. Go to the Cyclops on the right and get in a few licks at its head. When it comes to life, run to the left, crouch on the Leg of Werewolf Ledge, and whip its head. Retreat to the Ledge to the *left* of the Leg of Werewolf Ledge to get out of the way when the monster is near, then descend again when it backs off and resume your attack.

You'll go to the Ghost Ship now; if you didn't bother to get Sypha, Grant can help you get through here quickly. On the first deck you'll fight Ghost Pirates. Go left down the steps quickly—skip the Lanterns up here; you can go back for them. If you hurry, you'll be able to get down, turn, and fight the Pirate while it's still well to the right.

The second Lantern to the right on this level contains Invisibility. When you pass through the door on the next level, beware: the slightly yellowish sections of floor will crumble if you stand on them too long. Get past the Ghosts down here as swiftly as possible, or you'll take a fatal plunge. (Ghosts take two hits to destroy.) Next up are two of those self-rejuvenating Red Skeletons, another Ghost, and a Bone-throwing Skeleton. This one'll leap the Pit to your Ledge, so hit the bonester *fast*. Beyond the door are Elevators. cross the two of them when they're both *high*, otherwise you won't get across to the opposite Ledge. The next set of Elevators is a foursome: take the first three in a row, wait till the third rises slightly, then leap to the fourth and across. When you reach the Medusa here, stand on the ground and toss your weapons into its chest. Duck to avoid the shafts and rays of the creature. (You can also get in close and whip the snake-headed fiend, but you'll take hits in turn). There are more Ghost Pirates beyond, with crumbling floors. At the end of this corridor, you'll go up on the right: hit the Wall on the top level for Leg of Werewolf. (You might want to go ahead a bit and clear out foes before dining: if you take any hits while clearing out the hall, you'll be able to come back and restore all your health.) When you're back on deck, you'll see a Pole: there was one just like it when you started the level. It works like a seesaw, and you've got to hit near to the middle, slant it down to the right, cross, and leap off to the next Pole without sliding off either side. Pair o' Crows on the other side—the Watch is best to use against these plucky birds—another Pirate below, then in a lower level a Ghost and Bone-thrower. Jump down *fast* to confront the Skeleton on the long Ledge just left of center, then rush to the far right of the screen, turn left, and slay the Ghost. In the Tomb Room, you'll face a pair of Mummies: stay to the left of the left Ledge—on the ground, *not* on the Ledge—and, crouching, whip the first of the bandage boys, then chase down the second. Then, from the rightmost coffin . . . it's Cyclops! Beat as before, by whipping its head from the right Ledge. If need be, leap over the Cyclops to avoid its hammer, then lure it to the left by running that way. You can make a stand on the left Ledge then, or jump it and return to the right. The ship will take you to the Castle . . . and you've taken a shortcut that will save you having to go through several levels!

Inside, walk over to the Stone Dragon—you don't have to crouch here—and leap up between Fireballs, which come in threes. If you have no weapon, get one from above and to the left of the granite lizard. Another Dragon follows: crouch to whip its first wave of Fireballs, then squat on the left side of the Pit and whip both it and its second wave of Fireballs. Gargoyle monsters fly at you on the next level, but are easy to beat with a long Whip or weapon—in most cases, make your stand on the Stairs rather than the Ledges; the monsters are easier to hit there. Upon reaching the top of the Stairs, you'll face a Knight on the left. He'll toss an Axe, but fear not! Walk left so you're snug against the Ledge he's on. Wait till his boomerang Axe has returned to him, then jump up and whip him. A few hits will do the trick! (You can also whip and destroy the Axe, just in case you get caught standing when it's thrown.) The door's up and to the right. Next room has Fuzzies that drift about their Ledges. They move in steady, rectangular patterns: jump them and run past—the best you can do with a weapon is paralyze them. It would be a good idea to use Sypha here, since he can collect an Ice Spell from the Candle on the right over the lower Fuzzie. If you remain Trevor, you'll get Sacred Water. The Knights above don't throw Axes (phew!), so you won't have much difficulty with them. What *will* give you a pain here is that the screen begins to scroll automatically in nasty, thunking chunks. Leap where you can, or take the Stairs, only *keep moving*! If you're Trevor, you can make all the jumps here, but it will be necessary on some to stand with your toes hanging off the Ledge as far as they'll go. Suffice to say you won't mind the Gargoyle beasts that attack when you're out of this section! When you've climbed the long set of Stairs on the right—after the screen's stopped scrolling—head up and left, past the Gargoyle monsters. (Look for the Boomerang and 1-Up in this corridor!) Pass through the door and face an Axe-throwing Knight: get to the Ledge underneath him, and go all the way to the left, facing left, to cause the Knight to go to the right. Climb the Stairs and when the Knight's on the right, poke your head up the *instant* his Axe returns to him. Begin whipping so you destroy both the Axe, when thrown, and the Knight. Up above: squat to beat the lower Stone Dragon and Fireballs —note that the Fireballs come in twos now—leap between flames to destroy the one above it, and go up the Stairs. Stop with your upper foot on the eighth step, lower foot on the seventh: after the Dragons to the left spit their two Fireballs, go up *one* step, whip the next wave, then rush past the head above after its wave. Race past the heads on the right and pause in the middle of the next set of Stairs (there's a head on the left): stop and go up the last screen, whipping any Fireballs you can't stand between. You're now in the realm of the Frankenstein Monster. After killing a pair of Crows, you'll be attacked from the left by the Frankenstein Monster. Every time the monster stomps his foot, Stones fall from the ceiling: you'll be safe from these on the upper right ledge—but you can't stay put because Frankie will also throw Stones that'll hit you there. You'll have acquired an Axe in the previous room, and it's the perfect weapon to heave at the monster from here and from the left when you have to vacate. If you have under 30 Hearts, you'll have to resort to some in-close fighting with your Whip.

The next stage, set on a Bridge, spotlights Trolls and Axe Knights. The former take long hops—you've seen them before—the latter must be destroyed by kneeling in front of them when they throw low, or simply standing when they toss high. When you pass through the door, the Fish people will attack: look for them as they swim toward you, through the water, and whip them before they can attack. If you still have Grant, he'll be helpful in the next phase:

he can climb the big Wall ahead to save you a lot of aggravation. No new foes here, just tougher versions of the old ones. Sacred Water is best here. When you reach the Bridge, you must hurry across or it'll crumble. Leap or rush through the Crows here; losing some energy is preferable to forfeiting your life! Climb down the long Stairs at the end and you'll face the twin Dragons. They rise and sink into the River, breathing flame when they emerge. The key to beating them is to stay behind them and use your Whip to hit them in the back of the head . . . or your special weapon to hit them in the head, front, or back, when you're too far to use the Whip. The Dragons will emerge in a recognizable pattern: start on the far right Ledge, facing left, use your special weapon, then get on the center Ledge —in front of the dark archway—and face right. Crouch to avoid the flame of the nearest Dragon, hit it, return to the left Ledge to strike from behind, and repeat.

Where you end up depends largely on the paths you've taken to date. Regardless of your route, you will eventually end up on the sixteenth level—the realm of Dracula. Start out by heading left and battling the three Crows; beyond the Red Skeleton is a super weapon, if you need it. Go down the steps and you'll face one of the toughest screens in the game: the screen scrolls up as you descend, but it's far more difficult than previous scrolling screens. To get past the Gears, wait on the Ledge above them and *don't* leap on the first of the Teeth to come by. Wait for the second. Jump down when it's at the nine o'clock position, turning clockwise—if you jump down right away, a Medusa head from the right will hit you back, and you'll be scrolled off the top and killed. Drop off the Gear—you can fall between them without being hurt—to the Ledge, then wait till the one below scrolls up and drop to it. Stay to the right on this Ledge (the one beneath the horizontal golden Gear): it *looks* stable but will begin to disintegrate when you step on it. Stand your ground there and fight the Medusa heads that drift over. Wait until the Ledge below the silvery Gear scrolls up. Drop to that one—*not* to the Ledge to the right of the Gear. When you can get to the Ledge under the Candle to your right, do so. Go next to the long Ledge below it, to the left. You'll be battling Medusas all the while; if you have the Mystic Whip—courtesy of the first Candle on the right at the very beginning of this stage—you'll be okay. From this Ledge, jump down to the small Ledge on the right . . . though you'll have to hop up and down on it, because it'll begin to fall apart. You want it to remain there until the Gear to the left scrolls into view. When it does, hop onto the Teeth and cross to the left—you must move *against* the clockwise-turning Gear—to the Ledge there. Go down the Stairs, where you'll face Bats, Stone Dragons, and other familiar foes . . . including, eventually, Dracula himself. As ever, there's no "safe spot" from which to fight the vampire: you'll have to have as many Hearts as possible, and Sacred Water or Boomerang is the recommended weapon.

Perhaps the most important strategy for beginners is this: on the name screen, type HELP ME (hit the right-pointing arrow between the P and M). You'll begin the game with ten lives in reserve! Codes that will get you along in the game are as follows. Use the HELP ME name, and plug in the following, from the left.

Code One:
Top row: Whip, Heart, blank, blank
Second: blank, Heart, blank, Whip
Third: blank, blank, Heart, blank
Fourth: blank, blank, Whip, blank
Code Two:
Top row: blank, Whip, blank, blank
Second: blank, blank, Heart, Whip
Third: blank, Whip, blank, Cross
Fourth: Heart, blank, Cross, blank
Code Three: (start of the third level)
Top row: Cross, blank, blank, Whip
Second: blank, Heart, blank, Heart

Third: blank, blank, Whip, blank
Fourth: all blank
Code Four:
Top row: Cross, Heart, blank, Whip
Second: blank, Cross, blank, Whip
Third: Heart, blank, Heart, blank
Fourth: blank, blank, Whip, blank
Code Seven:
Top row: blank, Heart, blank, Whip
Second: Heart, all blanks
Third: blank, Whip, Whip, blank
Fourth: blank, Whip, blank, Cross
Code Sixteen: (instead of inputting HELP ME, just hit "end"—meaning you only get three lives)
Top row: blank, Whip, blank, Whip
Second: Whip, blank, blank, blank
Third: blank, Heart, Heart, Blank
Fourth: Cross, Cross, blank, Whip

Rating: B

Fans of the earlier *Castlevania* games will have a fine time with this one. The new elements are clever—such as the ghostly aides and the fact that you can take different paths to your goal—though the look and feel of the series is getting a *wee bit* creaky.

Challenge: B
Graphics: B
Sound Effects: B+
Simulation: B−

CHIP 'N DALE RESCUE RANGERS

Type: Cartoon quest

Objective: Mandy, a neighbor of the Rescue Rangers, can't find her kitten. Chip (and Dale, in the two-player mode) sets out to search for it . . . only to find that enemies are everywhere!

Layout: The screen scrolls both horizontally and vertically, depending upon the phase of play.

Heroes: The chipmunks can walk, leap, and throw objects they find—Crates, Apples, Steel Boxes, and Bombs—at foes. Steel Boxes can also be piled one atop the other to form ladders; moreover, when a bottom or middle section is removed and placed on top, the other levels stay put! Crates and Steel Boxes can also be used for protection—the chipmunk hides inside—though the Crates are blown away after the foe strikes. Chip and Dale also acquire 1-Ups by collecting Stars and Flowers; Acorns restore any lost energy. Treasure Chests conceal power-ups, most notably Zipper: the Fly briefly renders the hero(es) invincible! But don't charge ahead until the little Fly is fully formed: you'll be vulnerable until then.

Enemies: From Mechanical Dogs to evil Toys to Cats, Rhinos, and even windy Electric Fans, you'll face all kinds of foes! More details in *Strategies*. A few notes. Pelicans will eat your Crates and spit them back unless you hit them from behind, from below, or in the legs. Racquet Roos take two hits each to discombobulate, while Warts can hop and may leap your Crate. Hawk Bombers won't charge you, and only drop their explosives straight down; Hopping Crates are slightly redder than normal Crates, so you can spot them before they leap up.

Menu: For one or two chipmunks (simultaneously).

Scoring: When you amass a certain number of Flowers or Stars, you earn a 1-Up; see instructions for details.

Strategies: As a rule, move everything you find: you never know where power-ups will be hidden. (For example, right at the beginning you'll find four Flowers in the quartet of Crates to the right of the Pole, and a Star in the Crate to the right of the first gap in the Fence.) When you get to the time-restricted Bonus Stages between each zone, move *quickly* to the top to uncover the power-ups there; the 1-Up is usually located top/center.

Zone O: The beginning is a cinch. Just carry a Crate at all times to bash the Mechanical Dogs. When you reach the Pole on the right, climb and go left on top. Zipper is in the red Treasure Chest ahead. Stay on the upper Wire instead of dropping down to the middle one or to the roof. You'll get the most Flowers there. At the end of this Wire, drop to the roof. A Mechanical Dog will attack; repulse it with a Crate from the right. You'll find an Acorn here. Continue left. At the top of the next Pole go right. Draw the Robotic Rat over, then rush left and jump on the Transformer to avoid it—you can also duck under the Steel Box *or* carry a Crate up from the Pole. Lure out the second Rat, use the retreat or Steel Box maneuver, then go ahead. When you find the one Steel Box at the next Transformer, hide in it to escape the Rat there—or jump to the topmost Transformer on the left. At the end of the Wire, leap to the Transformer quickly to avoid the Mechanical Dog. After you pass a row of four Crates, watch out for the Buzzer. Carry along one of those Crates and toss it to the right to beat the Bug. Leap the last Dog and enter the lab. Get a Crate, draw the Rat from the right, and go left. Turn and fire your Crate. You can stand on the rim of the Beaker to get the Flowers above; ditto the Pencils. Carry Crates around to clobber the Rats, and you'll have no trouble here. Enter the Hole after the Mouse steals your Cheese. To beat the Brush boss, heave the red Ball straight up at the green Bulb on top. It'll take five hits; run to the sides to escape the Brush's crossfire as necessary.

Zone A: You're up a tree—literally. The key to surviving here is to carry a Crate at *all times,* and duck underneath it as you climb. You'll be attacked by Flying Squirrels here—sometimes two at a time, and once from different sides simultaneously—but if you stay under the Crates, they're easy to avoid. Enter the Hole above and fight the Owl boss exactly as you battled the Brush boss, avoiding its falling (and deadly) Feathers.

Zone B: You can skip this level and go to Zone C if you wish. If you'd rather not—use the Steel Box to reach the Chest on top. Cross the Counter, fighting the Rats; switch from the top to the bottom to get the Flowers. Enter the Hole. Popper Mouse here tosses a trio of Balls at you and comes twice; just stay out of reach. When you reach the Faucets, jump on each one three times to shut it. After the Apples, a Buzzbomb will attack from the right—as soon as you step on the Pot handle. Make sure you're carrying a Crate! Stay on the Knobs over the Pots, or you'll perish. After the Hole: leap the Buzzbombs when they charge as you cross the Pots. Notice that you don't have to jump to the rightmost Knob over each Pot; you can jump all the way to the handle. Ditz puts in an appearance next; this creature is only confusing in a two-player game, since Ditz assumes the likeness of one of the chipmunks. Several Ditzes show up in a row. The Ship-boss flies over, dropping spidery death: five hits'll ground it.

Zone C: Roos are situated on the lower and middle shelves here, so proceed cautiously. You can leap over the lower ones; to beat the upper ones, leap up while holding a Crate and let it fly! Go to the Packages at the very top left of fourth Roo for a hidden Star. When you climb after the fifth Roo, you'll face a Roo on the left. You can only carry up one Crate, so you can't dislodge it that way; worse, if you leap and are hit by a Ball, it'll knock you off the Ledge and cost you a life. You have to get to the Ledge and jump ahead *at once*, then get behind the Roo. You may take a hit on the second leg of your jump, but at least you won't fall. Above, you don't have to squat to attack the Roo on the right. Get the Hawk Bombers beyond by *always* carrying a Crate ahead. After you go through the Hole, drop through the Ledge to the one below while *holding* a Crate. Use it on the foe dead ahead; stop-and-go to get through the Hawks. When you reach the Treasure Chest, make sure you check the Crates below it first; once you get Zipper, you'll want to tear ahead! Leap from Lamp to Lamp to the Hole.

Zone D: It's easier to kill the Hopping Crates from below, but they're not too tough to nail from the sides either. One hit will destroy each one. Ditto the Jack-in-the-Box heads. When you reach the Bobbing Toys, hit them with Crates to make them spin: that will prevent them from dipping left and right, thus enabling you to pass beneath. In the next room, you should jump over the first Rabbit—it'll run —then go left and collect the Flowers. Rabbits on the tiers ahead can't get you if you're standing on a Crate, so carry one and be prepared to leap on the nearest one behind you if you see one. Big Birds also attack here, but one Crate will do them in. (You can also change tiers to avoid both the

Rabbits and Birds.) Toss Crates at the Switches ahead to turn them off; if you happen to turn one back on by mistake, hit it again by getting under it and throwing a Crate up. In the following room the Purple Blocks will explode after a moment, so just run past them; familiar (and cinchy) Bobbers and Hopping Crates ahead. The boss is a Robot who rains Balls on you. Hit the Robot in the lights on its chest; when the Balls fall, simply find an opening in the rain and stand there, letting them fall harmlessly around you.

Zone E: You can skip this one too. If you're up for an adventure, though—hit the Hives with Crates, and watch out for the different-colored sections of Fence; they'll not only hurt you when you step on them, they'll also collapse. After the Fence, a Beetle jumps from the right; Crate it, or leap to the Fence to avoid it. Watch for the eyes that indicate another Beetle in hiding . . . though be careful! While you're watching that one, another will attack from the right. The Hoppers are no sweat after the Hole. The Chest gives you a Boat; on the other side of the water take the Hammer, hit the Wall down, and use the Hammer on the Hoppers. Next Hole: carry a Crate into each Sand Pit to hit the enemy down there; Buzzbomb attacks you as well in the second Pit. The Chest contains a 1-Up. When you fight the Big Fish boss, stay out of the corners. Get ahead of it, fire when it's overhead, then get the Ball and run the *opposite* way the Fish is moving. Repeat five times.

Zone F: Time your jumps so the Balls don't crush you. More Big Birds, then a tough section indeed: you've got to climb a chamber with disappearing Ledges. Go to the right and stand on the Crate; it, at least, won't vanish. Go left, then right again, then stay on the left to climb the last four Ledges. Problem here is that the topmost Ledge doesn't always appear with the others . . . meaning that you may get dumped to oblivion a few times before getting to the solid Ledges above!

Zone G: Warts are here, but one hit will kill them. There's an invisible Star after the first Steel Boxes; climb the Stool to get it to the right of the first Crates above, on the Counter. Don't be in a hurry to leave: there's a second hidden Star right above it. Incidentally—it's a good idea to take one of those Steel Boxes and carry it at all times for protection. After the Counter, Rollers keep you from the Flowers above; use the Steel Boxes to climb up. After the Hole, Rhinos attack. Go down, to the right, get a Crate, and throw it left at the charging brute. There's a 1–Up in the Chest above, and a hidden Star ahead, on the ground, before the Stool with the Bomb. Carry a Steel Box to fight the Rhinos and a slew of Buzzbombs that follow; kill the stationary Bugs on top by heaving Crates from below—watching out for Rhinos that thunder in from the right—then go up and get the goodies there. There's an invisible Star above/between the two Stools at the end. Next up: drop through the Ledge *with* a Crate to kill the Rhino, and get under the Steel Box to protect yourself from the Rhino that rushes at you from above. Again, carry a Steel Box to fight the Rhino and Buzzbombs that you encounter. Get the 1–Up from the Chest on the Lamp, and build a ladder across the final pit using Steel Boxes. When you face the Fat Cat boss, leap the Spikes on the left *fast*—before the Balls start to fall—and shoot your Ball up at the Cat. Draw its fire over to the left by edging over that way—still staying to the right of those Spikes—then scoot back under the Cat and fire again. Five hits and he'll flee.

Zone H: Kill the Crab Robots with one Crate each. These creatures wait a moment, then spray Eggs downward; they can't hurt you, therefore, unless you're beneath them. Make sure you pick up the one Steel Box you find: you'll need it to climb to the Flower garden at the top of the screen. When you scurry up the Pipes at the end of this area, take a Crate with you: duck under it when the Flying Squirrel attacks. Even though you'll be under the Crabs here, you'll have a few seconds to get to a Crate, climb, and hit the Robots from the side. At the Ledge before the Hole: use Steel Boxes to build a wall, then jump off the top when you cross. You'll get a hidden Star. After the Hole, a Ditz attacks. When the two Ditzes come at you, go to the upper Ledge to get Crates to bash them. The Popper Mice won't stop you here, and there're a *ton* of Flowers at the end.

Zone I: Watch for the familiar Beetle Eyes as you clear the two stacks of Cups; there's one Beetle in each. Hit the first two Pelicans in the legs. Then: trouble. A Fan blows to the left; get right up to it, jump straight up, and push the pad to the right. Then put on the brake *fast* to stop. Leap the Tacks between this fan and the next, which is blowing to the right. Leap off that second Fan, then push the pad left, to keep from being blown into the Tacks ahead—you can get an Acorn in the Crate beside the second Fan, if you need it. Hop over the Pelican ahead, then drop through the Ledge behind it, scrolling the screen as little as possible. Why? Because there's another fan to the right. If you scroll it on now, it'll blow you to the left and off the Ledge. Take a Crate down with you, jump up behind the Pelican and bop it. Move ahead, taking a Crate with you: when you reach the Fan, get right up to it, jump, toss the Crate at the Pelican's legs, and get to the top of the Fan as before. Repeat when you reach the next Fan/Pelican combo. More Robot Rats on the other side of the Hole: go to the top of the Lamp and get the Rat on the second Lamp, then stay on the ground, carrying Crates as you clobber Rats. There's a Zipper in the Chest, which will bring you to the Scales: make *sure* you carry a Chest as you leap from Scale to Scale. Buzzbombs will attack, and that will be your only protection. When you fight the Caterpillar boss, throw your ball up then *stand right under it.* Yes, the ball hit you. The Caterpillar will break into pieces and attack you; it's virtually impossible to escape all its parts. However, if the Ball hits you, you'll be stunned—and thus invincible—until the Bug reassembles. Get your Ball, attack again, and let it hit you again. As usual, five hits'll do the trick.

Zone J: This level's for lunatics only! It's full of Conveyor Belts that run in different directions. Start by leaping to the Belt ahead, using the left Crate to hit the Buzzbomb, then rushing ahead with the next Crate to kill the Rhino. Leap to the center Belt ahead—pressing hard right on your pad, since the Belt scrolls left—then jumping to the top or bottom (both of which scroll right) and back again to avoid Rhinos. The game moves too fast here for tips to be of any use: just *keep moving,* or you'll be conveyed to the end . . . fast.

Rating: B+

Challenge: B+ (this one's not quite the "breeze" that seasoned players might expect, though new players will enjoy it a *lot*)

Graphics: A (remarkable detail and animation)

Sound Effects: C (music is good but not diverse enough; sound effects are too sparse)

Simulation: A (you'll know just how it feels to be a chipmunk!)

DOUBLE DRAGON II: THE REVENGE

Type: Martial arts quest

Objective: In the postwar world, the merciless Black Shadow Warriors have turned the streets into a jungle. You—Billy (plus Jimmy, in two-player games)—must destroy the Warriors and their infamous leader.

Layout: Play is horizontal, except for noncombat climbing areas. There are nine levels of play.

Heroes: Your Double Dragon Warrior can walk, jump, squat, climb Ladders, kick, and punch. He can also employ several special moves which are described in the instructions. By causing a foe to drop a weapon, you can pick that weapon up and use it . . . but only for as long as that group of enemies is on the screen. After that, the weapon vanishes.

Enemies: Most of your foes are common street hoodlums; these and the bosses will be discussed in *Strategies*.

Menu: For one or two players, alone or simultaneously. Players can also select the difficulty level.

Scoring: Your warrior's success is measured solely by his progress and the amount of energy he has.

Strategies: There are two important tactics which, if applied, will make it pretty difficult for you to lose this game. First: to begin the game with double the amount of men, select a two-player B game. Have player one attack player two: each time player two dies, his life is added to the count of player one. Second: continue on missions one through three by moving the pad up, right, down, left, then hitting A, B during the Game Over screen. To continue on missions four through six, do up, down, left, right, B, A, A. There's also a trick that will give you unlimited lives, but it's like getting to the –1 World in *Super Mario Bros.*: extremely difficult. Reach the Train in Mission Five with one life and only one energy bar remaining. Leap to the second Pipe of the three on the side of the Train as it's moving *backward*. You'll fall to the Tread on the left and lose your last energy bar . . . but not for long. Like Dracula, you'll rise after a few moments and be immortal!

If you'd rather play a more conventional game of *Double Dragon II*, here's what to watch out for on each mission . . .

Mission One: Piece of cake until you get to the masked bruiser on the rooftop. Jump kick is the most effective attack; try not to let him pin you in the right corner, or he'll pummel you senseless.

Mission Two: When you climb to the third rooftop, move right with extreme caution: a Helicopter will attack *after* its bullets strafe the rooftop. You'll be hit if you don't hop to the left as soon as they appear. Between waves of bullets, get to the right of the gun and let the whirlybird move to the left. Stand to the right of the door and knock the thugs off the roof as they emerge. As you head right, more enemies will pour from the RS-11 chopper ahead: take them out as they arrive.

Mission Three: Inside the Helicopter, stand under the left green window and knock enemies toward the door so they'll be sucked outside when it opens—just make sure *you're* not the one who goes air-walking. This is particularly important when you face the last enemy, who's *extremely* big and powerful. Keep punching him to the right to weaken him *and* edge him toward the door.

Mission Four: After going down the Elevator and dispatching the first wimpoids, go to the right and start punching right: you'll want to get in as many hits as possible against your next foe. After he's on the screen, regular kicks will do him in. Watch out for the Claws that extend from the ceiling when you move on. Again, after you beat the easy guys here, stand on the right and punch in that direction to take some steam out of the hulk who comes along. Don't bother kicking him: only punches work on him. Cross the Conveyor Belts and exit the door on the left.

Mission Five: Cross the River on the top Ledge; stand with one foot *off* the right side to make the leap. Climb the green Poles, but be careful: the enemies who come from the door carry Dynamite. It'll explode after a few seconds, so don't hang around it . . . or, if you pick it up, throw it quickly. Beat the big guy by punching him as before.

Mission Six: Watch the Braziers above: when the first Flame falls from the second Brazier—after two Flames have dropped from the leftmost Brazier—jump to the left. Don't stop, even if there's nothing to stand on: a Ledge will appear to save you. After a few fights you'll come to more disappearing Ledges. Wait until the big Ledge materializes directly under the door. Leap on it, jump to the left three times, right once, then into the door.

Mission Seven: The opening Conveyor Belts are a snap. Fight your helmeted foe with jump kicks as you did before, but beat him quickly: the Ledge beneath your feet is shrinking—if you push him to the left, he'll fall onto the Spikes below. In any case, stay on the right so you'll have something to stand on. In the Gear room, jump to the first Gear after the first Spike is fired, and duck it as it drops again. Leap to the Ledge after the Spike is launched there, but stay on the left to avoid it when it falls. Rush to the next Gear, then jump to the Ledge on the right after the Spike there has fallen back. Climb the Ladder: on the top, wait on the Ledge to the right of center until the Spike has come and gone—or leap it; it doesn't go all the way to the top—then continue. More Dynamiters on a disappearing Ledge await in the next room *and* on the rooftop. Punch the last guy and stay out of the corners, or he'll beat the tar outta you.

Mission Eight: It's an old foe reunion until you have to fight yourself. It's a Billy clone, and he's most susceptible to high jump kicks. Thing is, if he gets back inside of you, he'll do some fiery damage . . . not something you want. Four solid kicks should do him in.

Mission Nine: This mission only appears in the Supreme Master mode, and consists of a battle with the leader of the Black Shadow Warriors. Spinning Cyclone and Hyper Uppercuts are your most effective attacks here. But this is a defensive battle too, 'cause you've got to stay out of the winged warrior's way: each blow *he* gets in will sap a lot of energy. And we do mean a *lot!*

Rating: C+

This one is *so* much like the first that many players will feel cheated. On the other hand, if more of the same is what you want . . . you've got it!

Challenge: B
Graphics: D+ (no detail and crude animation—okay the first time around, but we expect more now!)
Sound Effects: C (ditto)
Simulation: C

DOUBLE DRAGON III: THE SACRED STONES

Type: Martial arts quest

Objective: Young Marion has been kidnapped, and the only way to rescue her is to find three Sacred Stones, which have been scattered around the world. (And yes, we know—alphabetically speaking, *Double Dragon III* should come before *Double Dragon II*. But that'd look weird!)

Layout: Horizontal scroll with trouble-free climbing areas. There are five missions in all.

Heroes: The characters can walk, run, punch, kick, or use a variety of nifty martial arts moves. These are described in the instructions. They also begin the game with two weapons apiece, and can pick up more as they tour the globe. Most useful of all, though, are two fighters who join the heroes later in the game: Chin and Ranzou. Once you've linked up with them, you can *become* them and use their incredible powers.

Enemies: As ever, the world is overpopulated with ordinary thugs and bosses, who will be discussed below. By the way, whenever you fight bosses, make sure you *vary* your attack styles during each encounter. These guys are smart—well, smart for lowlife slugs, anyway—and they'll figure out an appropriate defense after you've used the same kick, punch, etc., twice.

Menu: Billy and Jimmy can play on alternate turns, or they can fight on the same screen.

Scoring: The only barometers of your success are energy and a pile of slain foes!

Strategies: Ready for the mission-by-mission lowdown?

Mission One: After you fight your way from the room, it's *Double Dragon* business as usual in the streets, rooftop, and inside the building. Nunchuks will help you whip the Hulk Hogan lookalike who attacks when you reach the end of the building.

Mission Two: Another one of Billy's favorite locales: a forest. (So what if it's in China? It looks like all the other martial arts forests!) When you reach the Shack, be ready to jump: the killers who attack you here can slide at you. Inside, wait to the left of the door and start Cyclone Spin Kicking the foes who emerge. That alone won't stop them, but it's a good start. When you face Chin, it'll take five hits from your weapon and seven kicks of any kind to knock him down. Keep your distance, move in for the hit, back away, and repeat.

Mission Three: Your arrival in Japan is heralded by a Ninja attack. Players are divided about whether Chin or Billy is best; the consensus, though, is for Chin. Keep your distance when you fight them: they can slide at you, but most often rely on the Katana or, if the battle drags on, on Throwing Stars. Be prepared to jump the latter or move up or down on the screen to avoid them. Inside the house, pairs of poles jab up through the floor. Jump past the first two sets quickly, then slow down, wait for the next pair to emerge, and go ahead when they retract. There are more Ninjas inside, and you might want to switch to Billy here so you can use the Cyclone Spin Kick to keep the crowds down. Upstairs you'll find more of the same, only the Throwing Stars may enter the screen *before* the Ninjas that throw them. When you fight Ranzou, use the Nunchuks and you'll defeat him in short order.

Mission Four: Italy and its majestic ruins. But no time to sightsee. Use Billy to fight the musclebound duo who attack, followed by enemies you've known and hated before. Use Ranzou below, in the statuary, as his Ninja Blade will be most effective. Mix up your attack on the boss, relying primarily on Mid-Air Somer-Assault and the Blade.

Mission Five: You'll know how to beat the Little League flunkies: the challenge here is to beat the lady who's running the show. What you have to do is play Billy and hit her with a side kick. That will cause her to lean forward, making her a perfect target for a Nunchuk hit. Do this a total of five times and she'll call it a day.

Rating: B−

The same kind of game and basic challenges as the first two adventures but—mercifully!—there are some new settings and plot twists.

Challenge: B

Graphics: C (animation's considerably better than in the second game, but still no detail)

Sound Effects: C

Simulation: C+

DRAGON'S LAIR

Type: Fantasy shoot-'em-up

Objective: Princess Daphne is being held prisoner in Mordroc's Castle: as Dirk the Daring, you must fight your way through the Castle to rescue her.

Layout: The screen scrolls horizontally as Dirk hacks or blasts his way through seven different regions of the Castle.

Heroes: Dirk walks, leaps, crouches, and has an unlimited supply of Daggers to toss. During the game, he can trade these in for other weapons by leaping onto letters which appear in his path: A (Axe), D (Dagger—the same as the one with which he begins the game), and F (Fireballs—three times as powerful as Daggers). He can also pick up E (Energy—to replenish what he loses every time he's hit by an enemy), L (1–Up), P (extra points), G (Gold), and C (Candle). Weapon letters always *supplant* the weapon Dirk was using before he picked up the new one. When Dirk loses a life and goes to the next one, he always keeps whatever weapon he had in the previous life.

Enemies: There are not-so-dangerous foes like Pteranodon Bats, which sap a little energy and are easily killed, to Snakes that slither from the walls and spit fireballs—one hit from a Fireball will kill Dirk—to the evil dragon Singe, which guards the princess. See *Strategies* for details on Dirk's foes.

Menu: One or two players can tackle the Castle on alternate turns.

Scoring: Dirk earns points for killing enemies and collecting Gold.

Strategies: You'll begin your adventure on the Drawbridge. Fling some Daggers ahead to kill any Pteranodons, walk forward, and leap to get the Gold. Beware the breakable section of Drawbridge below it, though. When you get past that, *immediately* turn and jump back to the left: a Dragon will emerge on the right. Squat while you're still on the Drawbridge—so the Dragon won't shoot Fireballs—and crawl to the left. Still squatting, face right. Stand up, just to the left of the leftmost number in the "lives" monitor above—otherwise, your Daggers will fall short. This will draw the Dragon up. Throw a few Daggers as it rises, then squat quickly again so the Dragon's Fireball misses you. It will take ten direct hits to kill the Dragon. Leap where you grabbed the G—to avoid the collapsing section of Drawbridge—fire some Daggers ahead (to kill any Skeleton Pteranodons ahead), and enter the Castle. Each of two Prisoners inside throws a pair of Bombs and then retreats. Either rush ahead or wait till the first one chucks his two projectiles, then walk past. Wait between the doors for the next one to throw two bombs, then stride by. Stand so you're covering the knob of the second prison door and open fire at once to kill the Snake that will appear. Destroy it quickly (it'll take three Daggers): its projectiles are deadly. Stand there a moment longer and slay the Royal Specter that comes drifting your way. (You'll know it's coming because all the other foes suddenly vanish! There's also a puff of smoke on the far right side of the screen.) Hit Start to reveal the A before the Stakes, then squat and crawl under the two Stakes. A P will appear when you reach the right side of the second Stake and press Start. Kill the Snake beyond before continuing to the E, and watch out for more Specters. (A note about the Snakes: if you can't get off three shots before they get off one—killing you—you can always back away to the left. Dirk is able to stand out of Fireball range, though his weapons will still reach.) To deal with the Prisoner beyond: trigger it by walking ahead, double back, then jump up and get the E. Go left, wait for the Prisoner to throw again, then walk past. Hit Start right after the door and you'll get an F. These Fireballs will work well against the Pteranodons that pour from the drain beyond . . . and, despite what the instructions say, are a better weapon for this level. There's a Prisoner next, with a D on the floor beside it. A little hop will get you over this—since you do *not* want to trade down from your Axe to a Dagger! Another Snake appears after the Prisoner, and the Pteranodons will turn and pursue you. Crawl ahead, shooting backward until the winged creatures' drain has been scrolled off the screen. Stand on the very edge of the platform: you'll face one more Snake before the next rising-and-falling Spikes. Kill the serpent, then—if you didn't get the Axe or want it—hit the Start button and get the A overhead. Move through the two Spikes by remaining upright and walking under the first one. Stop, take a short hop over the Pit, and walk through the second Spike—if you crawl here, you're going to run smack into the Prisoner beyond. When you've cleared the Prisoner, you'll face another Pteranodon drain. One more Prisoner follows, with a G right before the cell and an F after. Get the F here: it's better for the slithery climax to this level. Next up: a Pteranodon drain, and then one Snake . . . followed by an *army* of Snakes! They come out of the walls everywhere; stay in the middle and turn—and/or jump, since they slither from the ceiling as well—to meet all eight. Obviously you don't want to back away from one and hit another, so try to polish them off as they appear! The Snakes appear in different positions from game to game—though they usually start with one on the right, one on the far right, then one on the left.

A ride on the Elevator awaits: jump onto the first Ledge on the left. Pteranodons attack first; no sweat! Crawl through the first Piston; there's an invisible C and E above. Two side-by-side Pistons follow: stop-and-go your way through. You'll also face Red Pteranodons which behave like the first, but are slightly more lethal. Walk right across the moving Ledge next; there's an invisible A before the G ahead. When you come to the two moving Ledges—again, just walk right across 'em. When you reach the Dragon's Breath, wait till it's gusting just above the level of the platform, then B button your way over. There's an invisible L (1–Up) on the other side, so don't climb ahead without getting it. There are a lot of G's ahead, along with a Ledge that extends and retracts; just walk to the right as it moves in that direction. Two moving Ledges follow—different from the first in that the lights tend to go out here! If you happen to be on a Ledge when it goes dark, keep walking *slowly* ahead—the Ledge moves slower, by a bit, than Dirk normally walks. After these, you'll come to a pair of Mining Carts with a Troll in each. Walk to the right to expose the first Troll, then go left. Stand with your heels hanging over the cliff; jump up and throw your weapon. It will reach the Troll and kill it. Move forward until the projectiles of the second Troll are just reaching the toes of your boot. The projectiles come in pairs: after the second, move forward, scroll the Troll onto the screen, then go left again to where the blasts are just touching your toes. Jump up and kill the Troll as you did the first one. After they're dead, the level's complete . . . almost. Take the Elevator down to the next exit on the left and you'll face the Royal Specter—in the flesh! This ghost cannot die, so knock the creature over to the right, get on the Throne, keep knocking your foe right, then drop to the ground, crouch, and crawl under the spirit. You're now behind it. Turn to the left and use your weapons to knock the Specter to the left side. Push it as far over as you can, then return to the Throne, do a high jump, and reclaim your Gold. When you've done that, go back to the left and exit the way you came in. You *can't* leave without your Gold, so keep your distance from the Specter . . . and keep firing!

Another short trip on the Elevator, this time to the second exit on the right and the Hall of the Grim Reaper. The tactics here are pretty obvious. What you need to know are the locations of the invisible power-ups, so: there's a G before the first Pendulum, an E after the second, an A after the sixth—you'll want to get this and *keep* it, now—and a P just before the seventh Pendulum comes into view.

The last level, Singe's Cavern, has *no* invisible power-ups. The minor foes are all killers, but the dragon is a *real* pain. Flashes will announce the serpent's arrival. When the creature appears, take three steps to the left, then turn and face Singe. The creature will unleash Baby Dragons at you both high and low; you must duck the former and leap the latter. The monster will *also* breathe Puffs of smoke. These, too, must be jumped. When you leap them, toss your Axe at the *highest* point of each jump. It will take between 20 and 25 hits to kill the beast.

Rating: A–

Spectacular graphics and tough gameplay make this a superior, almost Genesislike cartridge. The one drawback: because the animation is so detailed, Dirk tends to move a bit slowly. He's also a little large, which makes him awkward to handle in spots. Still, these minor drawbacks won't detract from your enjoyment of the game.

Challenge: B+
Graphics: A
Sound Effects: A
Simulation: A

THE DREAM MASTER

Type: Fantasy shoot-'em-up

Objective: The evil King of Nightmares has abducted the benevolent King of Slumberland. Nemo's mission: to rescue the good king and bring peace to the realm of dreams.

Layout: The screen scrolls horizontally.

Heroes: Nemo can walk, crouch, or jump. He also possesses the ability to transform himself into various creatures he meets (see the instruction booklet) or to ride them. Becoming or mounting them, Nemo acquires their powers. For instance, as the Frog he can jump on top of enemies to beat them; as the Lizard he can walk up Walls; as Gorilla he can sock them insensible *and* climb up Walls; as a Hermit Crab he can pincer them to death (note: Hermit Crab can't swim, so make sure you turn back to Nemo when you leave underwater Ledges); as a Hornet he can fire little Stingers; as the Mouse he carries a Hammer that can bang holes in certain Walls, and he can also climb Walls just like the Lizard. Nemo also has Candy which, when thrown at enemies, paralyzes them. As he travels, Nemo must acquire various Keys to get through locked Doors. He will also discover power-ups, the most important of which are Medicine—it will give him back a life bar—and 1-Ups. If you lose a life at any point, whatever power-ups you claimed will be there when you return.

Enemies: These range from Army Ants to Float-Fiends to Flying Fish to treelike Stumpers. More on these and other foes in *Strategies*. Note: if you don't become or ride one of the good animals, it will become an enemy and attack you!

Menu: For one player only.

Scoring: There are no points; Nemo loses "life" when hit.

Strategies: Slumberland is divided into different "dreams," which must be visited in turn.

Mushroom Forest: Head to the right and become the first Frog you see. Jump up to the big Mushrooms on top; there's a Key over the blue one and Medicine under the Mushroom. Continue right on the bottom, watching out for the flying Army Ant (Air Force Ant?). Climb the Stairs on the lower ledge, then head left on top to get the Key over the blue Mushroom there. Go right, get more Medicine, and snatch the Key from over the big red Mushroom. Become the Mole ahead and dig straight down for the fourth Key. Dig left, then drop down through the void for the next Key. Continue burrowing left: at the Wall, dig down. Go right at the bottom and ride the Lizard right. You'll be back on the surface right before the Mole. Stay with the Lizard, head right, cross the Waterfall—the Lizard can cling to the sides of the Ledges when you jump—and climb to the very *top* of the Wall on the other side. The next Key is there. Medicine is beyond if you need it. Go right to the doors, open them, and head to . . .

Flower Garden: Travel right and cross the water—if you drop down *through* the water, you'll come to a tunnel and a little green creature who will tell you to be sure and get the Lizard. Mount the Gorilla, head right, and climb the Tree to the top. Become the Lizard, get the Key, and leave—you can drop right down the center of the Tree. Go right on top, get on the next Gorilla, leap the Pit to get the Key in the middle, and drop down the center so you aren't impaled on the Spikes! After you pass the two Spike ledges, skew to the left so you can get the Key there *and* grab the Wall. If you fail to grab hold, you'll die. Exit via the Tunnel on the left as soon as the Hornet moves left . . . then become the bug! Fly back to the right, get the Medicine on the Ledge, and continue right, watching out for the Buzzards dropping Eggs! Cross the Flowers and fly up for the next Key. Drop down, become Nemo, and submerge—avoiding the Stumper on the bottom. Get the Key on the right. Falling Boulders drop down the side-by-side Pits after you get the Key, so time your jumps with care. On the surface, go right and return to the water to the right of the Flowers. Dive in, get the Medicine from the bottom/right, and swim up. Become the Lizard on the Ledge to the left—wait till the reptile comes right, from under the overhang, so you can feed it—climb the Tree for the Key, and exit the Garden.

House of Toys: Climb the Tower on the left for the two Keys, then continue right along the rooftop. The third Key is on the Block to the right. Continue right, get on the Train, and hang to the left so you'll be able to fall back to avoid the dive-bombing Planes. Watch for the Medicine and 1-Up after the Bomb-dropping Balloons first appear. (Get the Medicine and drop back down to the Train, then hop *left* onto the 1-Up Block. If you stay up there after you get the Medicine, you'll be scrolled off the left.) Stand on the second car of the Train, over the last window, to avoid the Presses—you'll have to shift back and forth a little, but this is still the best place to be. Move forward in order to leap the two Bunnies that attack, then stay to the left as the Train begins to sink: there's another Plane/Balloon assault up ahead. After the first set of Spikes, be on the lookout for the next Key: you'll have to run to the right and jump for it! The next two Keys come at you almost immediately. The Train rises suddenly, into a roof of Spikes, so watch for the niches in the roof and slide under those: otherwise, you'll be impaled! Run along the tops of the Spiked Blocks that follow, or crouch under them; then be prepared to do some fancy footwork as you continue to duck Spikes while dodging Planes—stand on the middle car again, so you'll be able to dash in either direction as well as jump up. Another 1-Up and two Keys await one after the other when the Train rises. The exit is right after that.

Night Sea: The first Key lies just ahead, in the water. Ride the Hermit Crab beyond it, dig into the sand for a power-up, emerge, go right, get the Key on the left side of the Ship, and burrow under the derelict vessel. Dig all the way down and enter a Tunnel: pincer the Stumper for a 1-Up, exit to the right, and you'll be on the Ship; continue right. Enter the Tunnel near in the *upper* Tunnel of the cliff beyond. Go right, become the Frog, then get the Key and Medicine. Backtrack, exiting to the left, and swim down to the next Tunnel entrance. Enter, swim into the *upper* passage, and hit the right Wall: you'll pass through. Swim up, collect the 1-Up, get the Medicine on top, head right and then down, and get the Key. Exit to the right. Swim to the right, avoiding the Squids that rise suddenly from the bottom, emerge at the top, and go right as Nemo. Avoid the projectile-spitting Plants on the right, then mount the Crab on the sea floor. Dig down for a Key, go right, climb the Stairs, become Nemo, and get the power-up from the Ledge on the left. Back in the water, move quickly to the right; two Black Fish will attack—Candy them or hide behind the Coral—and when you emerge, a Flying Fish will zoom at you from the left; another will attack from the right. Be ready to jump both! The exit is to the right.

Nemo's House: Climb the Blocks to the Banister, go up and head left for the Frog. Return to the Banister, go up, then hop to the left on the lower Ledge to get the first Key.

Go right, up the next set of Stairs, and once you pass the Chandelier, get the Medicine then drop into the Pit to the left. Go right, then left at the Plate-throwing Monkeys, and drop down the Pit between them. Go left, drop down again, and go right under the Presses to get the Lizard. Ride the reptile left and climb the Wall to get to the 1-Up and the Key. When you've got them, leave and go to the top of the Key chamber; switch your Lizard for the Hornet there, and fly back to the Monkeys. Go up to the Ledges over the Monkey on the left, grab the Medicine overhead, and head right flying along the top. Exit at the right and fly left. Leave via the first opening on top, and follow the Pole up until you reach the roof. Go left of the Chandelier for the next Key. Continue left until you come to another Key —right above a Monkey. Fly up through the opening to the right, then up through the one to the left. Head right through the Presses and hitch a ride on the Mouse. Double back to the left, drop down the Pit, go right to the Pole—past the opening above the Chandelier—and whack it apart. Get the Key, go right, and Hammer away the Blocks at the next opening. Drop through, go right so you'll note where the Bed is (the exit is to its right), then head left, get the Hornet, fly up, turn left—passing over the Crates but staying within that corridor—then fly down through the opening above the blue Door. Get the Key from the left of the door, then return to the Bed and leave this level.

Cloud Ruins: Go right, and on the second group of moving Clouds, *don't* get on the one that comes down at you diagonally, from the upper right. You have to use the lower ones to reach that. Ride it up to the roof and become the Hornet, get the Medicine on the right, and continue to the right. After the next building (the one with the red roof) there's a Cloud: fly straight up from it and you'll reach a 1-Up. Keep rising, past the Buzzards, until you reach a large Cloud platform: head right and you'll find the Cloud Ruins. Cross the Clouds, moving to the upper right, then get off at the building, go right, and turn into a Frog. Go up to the rooftop of the gray building and trade the Frog for a Lizard. Head down, then right across the lower gray rooftop, then under the Brick Wall. Become Nemo again, and cross the Clouds, descending gradually. Stay to the left side and grab the 1-Up as you go down. Go right at the bottom, and you'll find all the Keys in a row at the very end of the level!

Topsy-Turvy: Go right, past the vertical Ledges, to the first Key. Go back to the Ledges, climb, go left, get the Frog, and jump up to snare the Key over (or is that *under*?) the window. Go right, become the Hornet, fly right, and get the Key from behind the Monkey—you can also come at the simian by flying up, over the Mouse, and down. Head for that Mouse now, get the Key above it to the left, switch helpers, and Hammer through the Wall to the right. Go down and left for the Keys. Go right, become the Frog, continue right, go up, and become the Hornet. Keep going right for the 1-Up and Medicine, hop off the Ledge and fly up through the opening. Shoot the Monkey to your left, get the 1-Up, exit the way you entered, then fly up the opening on the right. Bash the Monkey and get the Key, then exit where you came in. Fly right, follow the short Wall maze, and get the last Key from under the doors, to the left.

Nightmare Land: Mount the Lizard, and instead of using your newly acquired Beam to blast foes as you go, simply hop your foes. You'll face Lava Geysers after the second Lizard (time your hops); climb the Tree for Medicine, descend the Stairs on the other side, cross the Lava Sea on the Ledges—wait until Lava Geysers shoot before proceeding—and continue right until the Penguin spins down like a top. And *what* a Penguin it is: King Penguin hops from side to side, spitting deadly bubbles and unleashing little Penguins. To beat it, start close and get in a few shots early before it begins ejecting death. When that happens, back up and concentrate on hitting the small Penguins. When

King Penguin changes sides, move over and hit it fast several times with your Beam, then turn on the small birds again. Repeat: it should take eight direct hits on the Penguin to kill it. (Don't automatically rush to the opposite side when King Penguin gets ready to switch: sometimes he comes back to the same side!) When it evaporates, climb the purple Ledges and mount the Lizard in the upper right. Drop back down for a 1-Up, and reclimb the Ledges. Climb to the left now, doing stop-and-go when you reach the green Ledges that spit flame. Float-Fiends are plentiful here: kill them as you encounter them, or they'll hector you as you try to make it through the triple-flame segments—you've got to rush through three bursts at once: stop-and-go won't work here! When you reach the Nightmare King, fire at his head while dodging the red Blobs and Lasers he fires at you.

If you want to jump to specific dreams, do the following. During the title screen, push up, select, left, right, A, A, B. Use the A button to go to the dream of your choice, then hit Start to go to that dream.

Rating: C+

The game tries hard to be *Super Mario Bros.* and occasionally succeeds. Overall, though, it lacks the diversity of other cartoon style classics. (Capcom also gets a big raspberry for failing to credit artist Winsor McCay on the box and/or instructions. McCay created the *Little Nemo in Slumberland* comic strip, which was published between 1905 and 1911, upon which *The Dream Master* is based. The character may well be in the public domain, folks, but McCay deserves a tip of the hat nonetheless.)

Challenge: B–
Graphics: C
Sound Effects: B
Simulation: C–

FINAL FANTASY

Type: Medieval quest

Objective: There was a time when Coneria was a splendid place to live, thanks to the four Orbs of Power that kept the elements in balance. But then the wicked knight Garland and his equally evil accomplices caused the light of the Orbs to disappear, and corruption filled the land. Garland also abducted the Princess Sara, just to make things *really* unpleasant. Now, four heroes, the Light Warriors, set out to right these wrongs in a sprawling adventure. . . .

Layout: The view is from above as the heroes travel through the seven Chapters of the game, while battles are presented in profile.

Heroes: The Light Warriors build up their combat abilities as they move through the game. The health of an individual Warrior is indicated by Hit Points: the more he has, the more punishment he can endure from a strong foe.

Enemies: These range from easy-to-beat foes like Wolves and Imps, to tougher enemies like Werewolves and Red Bones, and so on all the way up to Phantoms and Iron Gol and the bosses. These will be discussed in turn, but keep in mind some basic weaknesses. Fire and Harm work especially well against Zombies and other members of the undead, as does the Light Axe. Lightning and the Coral Sword are potent forces against water dwellers. Also, when you enter Treasure chambers, not every monster inside one will attack: if it fails to charge at once, edge around the perimeter of the room and it/they may not attack at all!

Menu: There's only the one-player game.

Scoring: The Warriors earn Experience Points and Gold when they're victorious in battle.

Strategies: Chapter by Chapter, here are the maps, items to look for, and traps you'll find. While these are presented in order, you may wish to try and tackle some of them *out* of sequence in order to acquire the Weapons and Items available in later Chapters. Bear in mind, however, that you can't always do this: for example, it's not possible to reach the lands of Chapter Five unless you've first obtained the Airship in Chapter Four.

Chapter One: "The King's Quest"

If you consider the Castle as the center of a clock, you'll find the Temple of Fiends in the eleven o'clock position; Matoya's Cave at one o'clock; and Pravoka at three o'clock. These, and the town of Corneria in which the Castle sits, are the five main areas you must negotiate in this section. In the Castle, there are locked doors; behind them, from the right in the room on the right, are a Silver Knife, Sabre, and Iron Staff; from the right in the room on the left, TNT, an Iron Shield, and Iron Armor. Unhappily, you won't be able to enter the rooms without the Key, and you can't get it until Chapter Two. So, all you can do at the moment is talk with people in the Castle and get information. Go upstairs to the King and have a chat with him. When you're finished, strike up a conversation with the Sentry outside and to the left of the chamber. Return downstairs and get a history lesson from the Wise Men outside the Treasure Vaults—you'll find them by going right from the main entrance—then visit the Queen's chamber on the left side of the floor and heed what Queen Jane has to say. While you're there, search for the Invisible Man behind a brick wall above the Queen's room. The message you get will prove helpful. Then it's time for the talk to end and the action to begin—which means you must take a trip to town.

Outside Coneria, fight the weaker foes in order to build up your Experience Points. The magics you're looking to acquire are Cure and Harm from the White Magic Shop, and Fire and Lightning from the Black Magic Shop—Garland is particularly vulnerable to Fire and the Sleep spell, though the latter isn't as useful all-around as Lightning. These stores are located in the upper left corner of the village. In the Item Shop to the right of the center of town, you can get Heal Potion, Pure Potion, or a Tent; Heal is the cheapest and best buy—and the most useful, especially when you face Garland. As for traditional armaments, the Armor Shop and Weapons Shop are right below the Magic shops. They offer a wide array of things from which to choose: if you're low on funds, buy what you can afford, use those Weapons to go out and earn more money, then purchase more. Build up your entire arsenal in this order: Weapons and Armor, magic, then items. By and large, the Weapons and Armor are considerably less expensive than other goods; moreover, with them you can acquire greater wealth to purchase whatever else you want. Of them all, the Rapier is most recommended for the Fighter. Other places to be aware of in Coneria are the Clinic in the upper right and the Inn in the lower left. When you've attained Level Two, head to the Temple of Fiends . . . though it would be unwise to battle Garland before you've tackled enemies in the surrounding terrain and reached Level Three. At that level, you're sure to whip him.

The Temple consists of several important sections. Princess Sara and the Black Orb are located in the center. In the upper left is a Cabin and Heal Potion; in the lower left is a Cap. The doors to the upper and lower right are locked —but, when you do get inside (that Key mentioned above . . . remember?) you'll find a Were Sword and Soft Potion up top, and a Rune Sword on the bottom. The latter is particularly valuable in that it works against the powerful magicks you'll confront. To beat Garland, the most effective tacks are to have the Mages employ Fire up to three times, then let your Fighter move in and use his Rapier. When Garland falls, Sara will reward you with a Lute— which won't be used until the last Chapter—and will take you back to the Castle. There, the happy King will reward you by building a Bridge so you can travel to the farthest reaches of the realm. Prior to setting out, be sure to talk to the Conerians again: they'll have some fresh information for you!

Your next stop is Matoya's Cave, named for the Witch who dwells there. Slipping around her table, you'll discover that your next mission is to find her stolen Crystal. Also, have a chat with the Broom, and read what it tells you *backward*. Needless to say, the creatures you'll fight to and from the Cave are, on average, twice as powerful as the ones you've battled before—so arm yourself accordingly!

From there it's off to Pravoka—which you also learned about in Coneria. The town lives in fear of Pirate raiders, and they're your main foe here. Like Coneria, Pravoka has many places you must visit. Go first to the Inn, which is straight ahead at the twelve o'clock position, moving clockwise from there, you'll find the White Magic Shop, Clinic, Black Magic Shop, Weapons Shop, Potion Shop, Armor Shop, and the headquarters of Bikke the Pirate. In the White Magic Shop go for all but the Lamp; in the Black Magic Shop buy the Ice and Slow magicks. As for Weapons, go for the Scimitar or, if you can afford it, the Short Sword. You should also pick up some Armor, if you have the money: the nine Pirates aren't terribly strong when hit, but they're ferocious on the attack. When you battle Bikke and his ugly lot, make sure you have Heal Potion to restore individual members of your band, just in case the Pirates gang up on them. After beating the sea dogs, you'll be given Bikke's Ship, and will also find the people of Pravoka more than happy to talk. Listen to what they have to say!

Chapter Two: "The Sleeping Prince"

When you're on the boat, hold down A and start tapping B. Your friends and family may think you're nuts, but be persistent: after you've hit B 55 times, the title screen will return with a puzzle for you to solve! Slide the numbers around using the A button until they're arranged in order from 1 to 15. Your reward for this is nothing, absolute zippo, but you'll have a good time! To return to the game, hit the B button.

Your destination is the land below, and the objectives there are the Marsh Cave in the lower left, the Castle of Elf in the lower right, the Northwest Castle in the center, and the Dwarf Cave near the top. Start out by going to the Castle of the Elf, where you'll find a locked door in the upper right—behind which are, from the right, a Copper Gauntlet, Gold, even more Gold, and a Silver Hammer. The Elf Prince is located in a room in the upper left, and he has the Key we spoke of earlier. But he's asleep, and to wake him you must get the Magic Herb from Matoya. Alas, she won't give it to you unless you get her Crystal back . . . which you can only do by beating the Dark Elf of the Northwest Castle: he's the baddie who stole it! To reach *him*, however, you must first get the Crown that is found in the Marsh Cave. So, guess where you're headed next?

No, *not* the Marsh Cave. Some level-boosting and conversation are first on the agenda. You're going to visit Elfland, the town in which the Castle of Elf is situated. The layout is as follows. Just left of the town center is the Item Shop. Below the town center is the Clinic, while the White Magic Shop is to the right of town center just above the Black Magic Shop. In the upper left region of Elfland are another Black Magic Shop (far left; it's Level Four) and White Magic Shop (just to its right, also Level Four). Just above the bottom of the town are an Armor Shop on the left and a Weapons Shop on the right. The Inn is located a short walk above the Weapons Shop. The White Magic you'll want to get here are the Second Cure and Fire protection; the Black Magic to buy are the Second Fire and the Second Lightning. Level Four White Magic you should get are Pure and Ice protection; Black Magic Level Four purchases should be Fast power and Second Ice. Items worth acquiring—they all are, but these most of all—are the expensive House and Pure Potion. If you can afford Soft Potion, that too is worth getting. As for Weapons and armor, the Silver Sword is way overpriced, all things considered; the Sabre is a much better buy. If you've got Gold to burn, use it on Houses. Also, upgrade your Armor here. The regions to the right of Elfland are particularly fertile grounds for Red Ogreslaying and Creep-bashing: they'll enrich you, but they can also take a serious toll on your Hit Points. Make sure you return to the Inn if your power begins to flag!

Next up on the schedule is the Northwest Castle. King Astos sits in his throne room; to the lower left is a chamber—with a locked door, of course—in which, from the right, are an Iron Gauntlet, a falchion (called a falchon in the game, it's a short, curved sword), and a Staff of Power. Talk with the King; he's not to be trusted, but don't hesitate to get his missing Crown, as he asks. Build up to Level Nine, stock up on Heal Potion to the limit, then trek out to the dangerous Marsh Cave. Don't try to get through it in one trip; when your power wanes, return to the Cave entrance and recuperate in one of your Houses. At Level Eight you may have to do this three or four times.

As a rule, use the following powers against the monsters you meet: Harm and Fire against the Undead, Second Lightning against Scum and Mucks, and Pure against the toxins of poisonous creatures. The entrance is equidistant from the exits to two other levels of the Cave: the doorway in the upper left leads you to a room of Treasure Chests, while the one in the lower right brings you to that *and* the entrance (at the top center) to another room filled with Treasure. The three doors at the bottom of this room are sealed, but there's enough on top to make the trip worthwhile . . . especially the Crown! It's located to the lower left of center, and you will have to slug it out with Wizards in order to claim the prize. Use Second Lightning and Mute, and you should be able to triumph without too much trouble—he said laughingly!

With the Crown in-hand, go back to Northwest Castle and your showdown with the Dark Elf, a.k.a. Astos, the king. Second Fire and Fast are the keys to victory here. Once you've defeated the Dark Elf, you'll possess the Crystal. Go back and see Matoya again, swap it for the Magic Herb which will awaken the Elf Prince, and get the enchanted royal out of bed. He, in turn, will give you the Key that opens all those locked doors. Before you collect all those goodies, talk to the denizens of Elfland, then head to the Castle in Coneria and Northwest Castle, in turn, to get to the Treasure Chests. Finally, make your way to the Dwarf Cave. There are a great many Treasure Chests here along with a Blacksmith (at the top) who you'll be returning to later. Most important, however, is that you visit Nerrick near the bottom of the Cave: give him the TNT you've just collected, and he'll use it to blast a tunnel through which you'll pass to continue your adventure.

Chapter Three: "The Rotting Earth"

The title may not be very appealing, but the mission sure is. The new region in which you'll find yourself consists of the town of Melmond in the top left (where the tunnel leads), the Earth Cave on the bottom right, and Sarda's Cave on the bottom left with the Titan's Tunnel above it. Explore the town of Melmond and talk to its superstitious denizens. The landmarks here are the Armor Shop at the top of the town, Dr. Unne in the top right, the Weapons Shop below and between them both, the Inn just to the left of the center of the village, the White Magic Shop just below the town center, and the Black Magic Shop in the bottom right. At the White Magic Shop, pick up Third Cure and Life; at the Black Magic Shop, get Third Fire and Warp. Proceed from Melmond to the Earth Cave. Here you must get the Ruby from the Vampire and beat Lich, the Earth Fiend.

There are four levels in the Earth Cave. The Hall of Giants will be to your left; below are treasures—880 Gold and Heal Potion. To reach them you must zigzag to the lower right, go left, then cut down. If, instead of going left, you went down to the right, you'd have found Pure Potion and 795 Gold. To the upper right from where you started is 1975 Gold. Due right, then down to the right, is the door to the next level. On the second floor you'll find Treasure in the bottom and in the upper right. To the bottom right is the door to the next level. (Note: the door room is located off two rooms that are connected to the main rooms of this level by a narrow vertical corridor. The entrance to this corridor is in the right center of the level. Don't miss it!) When you enter, you'll be at the six o'clock position of the third level: there are Treasures in the four o'clock, three o'clock, twelve o'clock, and nine o'clock positions. Visit them in that order; the Vampire is located down and to the right of the nine o'clock chamber. Use Second Fire to beat him. Defensively, Invisible works best. When the red-headed bloodsucker is defeated, claim the Ruby in the upper left. In a room above the Vampire is a Stone Plate; unfortunately, you can't move it just yet. Mark where it is, for you'll be returning!

Leave the Earth Cave and head for the Titan's Tunnel. Bribe the Titan therein with the Ruby—there is *no* other way to get by—then head down to collect the Treasure here. In the upper left is the passage to Sarda's Cave. Enter, and the wizened wise man will give you a Rod to pry up the Plate. Return to the Earth Cave, open the sealed entrance, and go to the fourth floor. Make your way to the room at the top center and another at the bottom left for Treasure, then head to the room in the upper left to access the fifth floor. There, in a chamber on the center left, you will find Nich—the fiend who has caused the Rot. Lich is by far the strongest foe you've faced to date. Your Fighting Warriors should use Fast, and both Fire and Fire Protection should be employed, as well as Harm. Don't enter unless your Hit Points are fully stocked. When Lich is beaten, touch his Orb and its light will be restored.

Chapter Four: "Warriors in the Sky"

This region consists of the Ice Cave at eleven o'clock, the Gurgu Volcano at nine o'clock, Ryukahn Desert at five o'clock, and Crescent Lake at four o'clock. Crescent Lake is your first stop. There, you'll find the Weapons Shop in the upper left, the Armor Shop below it, and the Item Shop below that. The Inn is at the bottom, the Clinic to its upper right, and the White and Black Magic shops in the upper right. Your best purchases here are Exit—this will be very important to you later on—and Second Invisible from the White Magic Shop, and Third Lightning and Quake from the Black Magic Shop. Located to the right of the town proper is the Circle of Sages. Talk with each of the Sages and you'll get earfuls of historical info. However, one of the Sages, Lukahn, will also give you something useful: a Canoe, which is the only way you can travel the River that weaves through this region. You'll also learn about your objective: to destroy Kary, the Fiend of Fire.

Kary dwells in the Gurgu Volcano, but before you attack him, you had best visit the Ice Cave to obtain the Ice Armor: nothing works better against fire fiends than ice Armor and Weapons! Similarly, when you face the ice creatures here, use Second or Third Fire and the Flame Sword —found on the third floor of the Ice Cave; you might want to go right to it. Mute and Soft Potions will also be required here. On the first level, you'll find the Ice Shield and ten *thousand* in Gold in the lower left. There are other Treasures here, as well as the Stairs to the next floor. Head to the lower left for the Stairs to the third level; Cloth and the Floater will be found near the Ice Sword. But there are holes in the floor, so how do you get to them? Easy. Step into the hole in the top left. That will drop you into a room full of Undead monsters. Fight or run your way to the Stairs; these will take you to another room with a single hole. Walk right in, and you'll find yourself beside the Chest with the Floater. Claim it, and the holes will no longer present a problem! When you have to battle the Eye here, use Fast and the Rune Sword. Exit the room in the upper right, take the lower set of Stairs on the next floor, and you'll find tons of Treasure, including the Ice Armor in the upper left and a whopping total of 40,780 Gold at the bottom!

When you've finished up at the Ice Cave, set up a House outside the Volcano and be prepared to return to it three or four times: every step you take on Lava inside drains your power. That's important, for you'll need all your energies to battle Kary. Be aware that one of the most potent weapons you can bring to bear against the fire monsters here is the Ice Sword in the upper left chamber on the sixth floor; you might want to go there right away. The first level of the Volcano should be crossed counterclockwise; you'll find the entrance to the next level in the eleven o'clock position. The second level is laden with powerful weapons and should be explored *in its entirety*; the region in the lower left is especially rich. In the very bottom of the left side is the entrance to the third level; you'll find no Treasure here, just the entrance to the fourth floor, located on the far right. Again, there are no goodies on the fourth floor, only the fifth-floor entrance, which can be found in the upper right. To reach the sixth floor, head to the lower right corner. There are Weapons, Armor, Magic, and other Items in every room of this level, so don't skip a single one. In the lower right is the entrance to the seventh and final level. This floor is shaped like a huge snowflake, and you arrive in its center. Visit *only* the chamber directly to the left for the Flame Armor—the other rooms contain nothing—then head to the lower left chamber to fight Kary. Thus far, your battles will have been with Gargoyles, Fire creatures, and the like; strong compared with what you fought in the other Chapters, but puny things when stacked against Kary. The Ice Sword is crucial, as is Fire Magic and the ice Weapons you acquired in the Ice Cave. Fire Protection and Second Invisibility are also extremely useful. When the wicked demon lady is beaten, the second Orb will reignite. Back in Elfland, you'll have heard rumors of an incredible Airship. Time to see if the legends are true! Anchor the Canoe at the mouth of the River to the right of the Ryukahn Desert, head to the middle of the sands, select the Floater from your arsenal, and—*voilà*! The Airship will emerge from the dunes.

Chapter Five: "Rewards of Courage"

The only two places of significance here are the Castle of Ordeal on the left side of the mainland, and the Cardia Islands to the far left. Go first to the Cardia Islands and talk to the Dragons there. Travel every inch of the Dragons' realm: you will need all the Treasure you can get. When you find King Bahamut, converse with him and he'll tell you what you're to do in the Castle of Ordeal. Land your Airship on the *light* green field at the bottom right of the mainland, packing three or four Houses so you won't have to return there whenever your powers flag. Head left to the Castle of Ordeal and enter. Cross to the upper left of the first floor to reach the second, get the Zeus Gauntlet here, then go to the lower right corner of the second floor to get to the third. This level is laden with Treasure—including, in the lower left, the Rat's Tail that King Bahamut sent you to acquire. Watch out for the Zombie Dragons here, against which Second Fire is a useful Weapon. When you have the Tail, sit on the throne and you'll be whisked back to the first floor. Go back to King Bahamut, who will reward your achievement by boosting the levels of each of the Light Warriors: Fighter to Knight, Thief to Ninja, Black Belt to Master, Red Mage to Red Wizard, White Mage to White Wizard, and Black Mage to Black Wizard.

Chapter Six: "The Sea Shrine"

Well to the right of the lands in Chapter Five is a mountainous peninsula in the middle of which you'll find the town of Gaia. Visit all the buildings, as usual, buying all the White and Black Magic you can afford, as well as the Protective Ring in the Armor Shop. Fill up on Heal quickly by pressing down the A button when you go to purchase it. The shops are located along the top, left, and bottom sides, and in the center. Unique to Gaia is the Fairy's Spring in the upper right. You can't obtain the magic Oxyale there until you locate the missing Fairy, and you can't do that unless you talk to the good people of Gaia and also in Onrac, your next stop. (Note: because you have the Airship, you don't need to stay at the expensive Inn here, but you can visit cheaper ones such as the Inn in Coneria.)

Fly left, past the Cardia Islands, to the middle of the right side of the next land mass. Onrac is situated there, and the only shop you need to visit is the Item Shop; the others offer nothing you need. Talk to all the people you can, and when you're finished here, take a hike to the shore, just below the River. You'll find a Submarine there, but you can't board it because only Oxyale can provide it with air! That means you've got to get the Fairy. You'll find her in the small patch of Desert above the great Desert to the left: she's the "guest" of a Caravan. Visit the Caravan Shop and buy the Bottle, despite the high price—50,000 in Gold!—the Fairy is inside. Take the Bottle back to the Fairy's Spring in Gaia, liberate the Fairy at the water's edge, and you'll be rewarded with Oxyale. Go back to the Submarine and board: it will automatically transport you to the sunken Sea Shrine. Have your Lightning at the ready—especially Third Lightning—to defeat the sea beasts. Conversely, the Zeus Gauntlet will protect you from enemy blasts.

You'll be deposited in the depths of the Shrine (floor three) with two floors above and two below you. Though your main objective here is to find and defeat the Kraken, it's also important that you talk to Mermaids and acquire the Slab, which will be of considerable interest to your old friend Dr. Unne in Melmond (see Chapter Three). You'll find this on the fifth floor, in the far right corner of the room in the upper right. Before we talk about the fifth floor, however, let's go back to the third. There are two Treasure Chests here, located in rooms below center right and above center left, both containing Gold. The entrance to floor two is in the upper left, to four in the upper right. Going to four offers a great deal of Treasure as well as an entrance to the fifth floor, located in the lower right. The fifth floor contains oodles of Treasure Chests. Take that route first, then return to three, go to floor two, head up to the upper right corner, and you'll be able to go to a different section of the third floor. This is a small room with no Treasure but entrances to another section of floor four—entrance on top. The floor four room leads—via an entrance in the lower right—to still another section of three, where you'll find two Treasure Chests and an entrance to an area of the second floor (in the upper left) which has a *lot* of Treasure—and, in the upper left, an entrance to the uppermost floor, home of the Kraken and another Orb. The tentacled beast resides in the uppermost left chamber of the floor: use Third Lightning to help slay the beast, and beware its blinding Ink.

When you're finished here, leave the Shrine and return to Onrac. From there follow the River up until you come to the Waterfall and enter the Cave: your task now is to investigate reports of a UFO you heard about in the village. The Cave consists of a relatively simple maze that works its way to the left: whenever there's an opening to the left, take it. When the corridors finally end in a vertical passage, follow that down. (Though the maze is easy, the foes are not: proceed with caution!) When you reach the Robot, use Fire against the Mummies. The extraterrestrial automaton will reward you with a Cube that you'll need in . . .

Chapter Seven: "Quest's End"

Return to Melmond and show Dr. Unne the Slab. He'll

be only too happy to translate it and teach you the Lefein language. Otherwise, you won't be able to understand the folks you visit when you go to the town of Lefein.

The village is located on a peninsula directly above the land where you experienced your Chapter One adventures. Talk to everyone to learn the glorious and tragic history of the town, go to the stores that line the top of the village, and take a trip well to the right of the town—by walking through a break in the wall, upper right—to the White and Black Magic shops. There, you'll pick up extremely valuable magic. Yet, the most important acquisition of all will come from the Lefeins, who not only give you a history lesson, but also the Chime. With this you can enter the mysterious Mirage Tower, which lies in the middle of the Desert to the upper left. Once inside, you'll be facing the last of your great adversaries, Tiamat.

When you enter the Tower, you'll find that it's full of Treasure. You can't carry it all, so be prudent in your selections! The place is also populated by Robots, but you won't learn anything new from them. Explore the first floor, then go to the second via the Stairs—you'll notice them as soon as you go in. There are more Treasures on the second floor, and an entrance to the third located up on the far side of the level. On the third floor you'll find the Transporter which will take you to the Sky Castle . . . but you'll also find a big Blue Dragon guarding it. Third Fire is recommended to fight the serpent. When you've whipped the Thunder-spouting beast, use the Cube to rev up the Transporter, and you're off!

The first floor of the Sky Castle is loaded with treasure to the left, right, and down. Up ahead is the entrance to the second floor. There are three rooms on each side of this level; the entrance to the third floor is straight ahead. If you're really ambitious, get Adamant from the room in the bottom left, bring it to the Dwarf Cave from Chapter Two, and let him make you the super-powerful sword Xcalber. On the third floor, you'll find Treasure in all directions, but the most interesting attraction here is the Robot by the square wall in the center room. Make sure you look out the window, as your mechanical friend suggests! The entrance to the fourth floor is located in a small chamber on the left below the big Treasure room. The fourth floor is a never-ending maze *unless* you do the following: head right to an intersection, then walk down (or left and up). That will get you to the fifth floor . . . and Tiamat. On rare occasions the entrance to Tiamat's chamber is guarded by a WarMech robot; if it appears, use Ice Armor on defense and Xcalber if you have it. As for Tiamat, fight the Hydralike beast using your most powerful weapons, employing Second Invisible for defense.

Now that Tiamat is destroyed, you would think the game is over. Not so! Go back to the Circle of Sages (Chapter Four) and talk to them again. They'll tell you about a time portal located in the Temple of Fiends (from Chapter One). Return there and fight through the eight floors—aided by the Lute you obtained from Princess Sara—battling each of the bosses you fought in the past . . . as well as a new one, Chaos. Before you fight the winged, superpowerful demon, be sure you get the sword Masmune; it's on the same floor as the second Tiamat. Also, don't face Chaos—on the floor after Tiamat—unless you're at Level 28 or above and Hit-Pointed to the max. When you finally do engage the creature in battle, arm the White Wizard with Wall so he's free to help the fighting men as their powers are depleted.

Rating: A

This is a great game, a true escape into another world! It's an extremely involved game—far more complicated than the Link adventures or similar quest games. Because of that, though, it's the perfect game for fantasy fans once they've mastered the enemies of Hyrule!

Challenge: A
Graphics: B
Sound Effects: B
Simulation: B+

GODZILLA

Type: Monster vs. monster game

Objective: In a videogame version of the Japanese movie *Monster Zero*, invaders from Planet X attack the Earth using giant monsters. To save itself, our world calls upon its two greatest monsters, Godzilla and Mothra, to battle their way through a series of monster-infested Ring Fields to destroy the Headquarters in each one.

Layout: The fight rages across eight planets. On each world there are two types of screens: the Hex screen, in which the monsters move like chess pieces across the planetary landscape; and the Battle screen, in which Godzilla or Mothra battles through that section of terrain, ultimately trying to get to the Headquarters.

Heroes: Each monster has its own unique power. Mothra can fly—though only halfway up the screen—and fires "Eye Beams" and drops sheets of Poisonous Powder. Godzilla not only can walk and breathe Radioactive Breath, he can jump, kick, and swing his Tail, all to destructive ends. Each creature loses energy when hit; this energy can be replenished by collecting Life Capsules. These are liberated from enemy installations when smashed, and travel slowly offscreen; once they've scrolled away, they're gone. The Capsules look like little, red Lunar Excursion Modules and are often difficult to see against the reddish scenery of some worlds.

Enemies: The giant monsters that guard each Headquarters are described in the instructions. The smaller enemy defenses—guns, ships, etc.—will be described in *Strategies*. (Note: the king of the Xian monsters is referred to as Ghidora in the instructions. That's the titan's Japanese name. In English, it should be Ghidra. Likewise, Moguera, from the film *The Mysterians*, is actually Mogella in English. We're stuck with the Japanese names to avoid confusion . . . though a little consistency would have been nice! After all, they don't call Godzilla and Mothra by their Japanese names—Gojira and Mosura!)

Menu: There is only the one-player game.

Scoring: The monsters earn from ten points to several thousand points for destroying enemies, and 50 points for grabbing a Capsule.

Strategies: It isn't sophisticated, but it works: many players find that Godzilla works best for them if they press the pad alternately down right while quickly, alternately tapping the A and B buttons. Try it and judge for yourself! Also, make sure that whenever you do Godzilla's Breath, you *advance* while using it. If you stand still, you'll only get whatever's before you; if you move ahead, you can very well incinerate two or more big foes. Other players take this tack, which works very well: send Godzilla forth to get rid of the monsters, then fly Mothra out to deal with the Headquarters. The big bug's the weaker of the two monsters, and this protects fleet Mothra from a premature death. In general, play Mothra to the left side of the screen, darting forward as necessary, then hurrying back.

On individual worlds, you'll have to employ slightly different strategies depending upon the order in which foes appear in the sections.

In any "Wilderness" setting, the best way to get Godzilla through is to have him either kick his way across or crouch and whack his way along using his Tail, jumping up to smash pinnacles whose bases have been knocked from under them. The latter is also the best way to uncover Capsules, which are often hidden in the *tops* of the peaks. (Make sure you smash the bases of the next mountain to the right as well, before turning your foot on the nearest peak: you'll hate releasing a Capsule, only to have the next mountain base to the right stop you as you chase it!) Mothra can fly over the peaks and shower them with Powder to unleash the Capsules. Aircraft can be dealt with using Eye Beams (Mothra) or having Godzilla Fire Breath them or jump and kick them—or even duck them; no dishonor in that.

"Sub-space" regions start out like the "Wilderness," then hit you with giant Mushrooms. To get Godzilla past these, use repeated jabs on the B button while holding the pad right . . . or just fry them! Mothra has an easier time flying by. There are variations—such as the huge vehicle on Mars—but you'll see at once how to fight these.

"Jungle" presents you with seemingly indestructible Towers. Godzilla must leap up and kick or Breathe Fire on their tops, while Mothra can simply Powder them into oblivion. The Vines are a problem to get over . . . but not *under*! Just don't get stabbed by the Needles they drop. Wait until they've been launched, then rush ahead. On Jupiter and beyond, you'll face golden plants that grow quickly and rather tall: Godzilla will have to use Breath on them or get across them before they grow. Kicking them takes time—time in which the reptilian hero might take hits from other sources.

"Volcanoes" pits you against the Firebirds, which are easy to beat: Powder 'em or use Fire; Mothra's Eye Beams can also down them, and, frankly, Godzilla can usually sneak right under them. The Tentacle screen is more difficult because there are all kinds of foes flying around: use your Powder or Breath, advance as you recharge, and repeat. (Godzilla can be particularly well-served by Breath here: Capsules are bound to be uncovered by cooking a crowd of foes. Better to waste the Breath than die, we say!) Mothra's at a particular disadvantage here, for if the bug loses Powder power, its Eye Beams will be of little use. Godzilla, at least, can kick or Tailswat enemies if he's Breathed-out. Powder and Fire Breath will both dampen Volcanoes to allow you to pass.

In the "Mecha City" phase, Mothra will do better flying on the ground than in the air, since most of the gunfire is aimed up. Godzilla can lumber through in his usual kicking, Tail-swinging manner—though the jump kicks will serve him best. The green guns set in the walls occasionally give you Capsules.

"Headquarters" is a lot like "Mecha City," only there's no low-flying for Mothra, since the guns fire everywhere and the insect will have to rise to get above the metal barriers that come jutting out—Godzilla has to kick them down. You'll need to do a lot of high-flying Powderdropping to get through. Godzilla's approach should be the same as "Mecha City."

Gezora: easily beaten by three Breaths from Godzilla, or a steady barrage of Powder from Mothra. This is the first monster you'll face. By the time you face Gezora on Jupiter, the dude's tougher . . . but still relatively easy to defeat.

Moguera: using Godzilla, Breathe Fire at once to weaken the robot, then pin it in the right corner using kicks; Tailswats don't do the trick here. Use A while pressing the pad right to keep the tinhead there; Godzilla's Breath will recharge meanwhile. When the meter's full, toast Moguera again and repeat. Three blasts'll do it . . . unless the big automaton chickens out and runs! Fighting with Mothra is tougher: Eye Beam–butt Moguera to the right, then keep the metal monster there by throwing Powder and, when that runs out, zapping Moguera with more Eye Beams.

Maintain a relentless attack, or the monster will recover and hit you hard. Back away or up/down slightly when the robot uses its own Beams—though they're difficult to avoid—then get in and mix it up again. (Note: Moguera has a habit of running from Godzilla when its energy is low. All Godzilla needs to do is step one Hex away, then come back to Moguela to resume the fight. The robot is the second monster you'll find on Earth.)

Varan: hit it with a burst of Breath or Powder, then push it back with kicks or more Powder, then Eye Beams. With Godzilla, press the pad to the right and quickly tap, alternately, A and B. That'll keep Varan pinned to the right and sap the purple one's energy. Varan first appears on Mars.

Hedorah: the Jupiter-based Smog Monster fires Smog projectiles and can stretch its gooey hands toward you. Again, use Godzilla's Breath to beat it back, then get in and kick/Tail-whip it. If the hands try to snare you, back off, use Fire again, and charge!

Baragon, Gigan, and Mecha-Godzilla are all stronger than the ones that came before . . . and if you don't have full Breath/Powder capacity, and aren't prepared to push these guys to the right wall and keep them there, you won't win. Still, as difficult as they are to beat, no one compares to . . .

Ghidora: when this scaled wonder charges, watch out—Ghidora has a truly staggering amount of energy and will pin you right against the left side. If you're Mothra, you won't be able to fly much, so throw your Powder at the three-headed beast; with any luck, one of the "spears" will hit the golden monster. A few such hits will drive Ghidora back a little, allowing you to get off the ground and drop more Powder. Godzilla will need to rely on Fire a lot, and Tail-swats the rest of the time.

As for passwords, N5RU8TSRB7 PKG07 will get Godzilla past the Gezora on Earth; F417XDP0MD 3H69 will give you Gezora and Moguela dead as fossils; Q012TRFW1U 5ND8 will take you to the Headquarters of Earth—prior to battle—and FEDSWHKCSH

QFY5QB8FSTU will take you to Mars. For a Mars mission with Moguera, Gezora, and Varan defeated: MEEM9F-W7BJ H7J5DPK. With Mothra at the Martian Headquarters: Y4R0ANBDY2 E1551P. To get right to Jupiter, with both monsters, input J1GY99W91S L38N1YW08M HLS. To get farther along on Jupiter: U1GMUXFRMR 2M3R80A5U3 B3N. But why monkey around with low-level codes? Want to battle Ghidora right off the Batragon? (A little in-joke, there, for you Japanese monster fans.) Input the code M0NSTER 0 (using the zero, since there're no letter O's in the game). If you simply want to get to the end of the game and observe the monsters without having to fight them—and read a rather inane message from Planet X—use the password START TO END. To hear Godzilla music, input SOUND.

Rating: B–

You'll get a good sense of what it's like to be a monster; the flight controls of Mothra are especially realistic. But the giants' fighting ability is much too tame and clumsy to appeal to fast-action fans. (They're also huge targets, which makes it difficult for them to avoid taking a lot of hits. There are a lot of Capsules around, but still—some gamers don't *like* being wounded!) In spite of the eye-popping graphics, the landscapes are all very similar. The one really glorious aspect of the game is the Hex screen, which gives you a chance to use some smarts and boosts what would otherwise be a C rating.

Challenge: B–
Graphics: A
Sound Effects: D (inappropriate music, and where's that famous Godzilla *roar*?)
Simulation: A

THE LEGEND OF ZELDA

Type: Fantasy quest

Objective: In thc long ago Age of Chaos, in the land of Hyrule, peace was maintained due to a wondrous golden triangle called Triforce. Unfortunately, the evil Ganon and his minions came along and stole it—abducting the beloved Princess Zelda as well. In order to rescue her and restore peace to the land, the heroic Link must locate the eight pieces of Triforce hidden in Hyrule. (Psst: he's going to find one in each of the first eight mazes of the Underworld!)

Layout: The view is from above as Link moves through the 128 screens that comprise the Overworld of Hyrule, and the nine mazes of thc Underworld.

Heroes: Link has the ability to move around, wield a sword, and pick up extra arms and magic as he travels. These include more powerful Swords, Arrows, Boomerangs, Bombs, Rafts, Ladders, Keys, Hearts (to boost Link's life force), and other items—such as a Magical Clock which appears on occasion and, when struck with a Boomerang, will paralyze every enemy on the screen. Link can also speak with people he meets, picking up valuable bits of information. Those who help Link during his adventure are the Old Man, the Old Woman, the Merchant, and Fairies, all of whom will be discussed in due course.

Enemies: There are many, ranging from the small, leaping Tektites to the arrow-shooting Molblins to falling Rocks—from which there is no protection except a well-timed run—to the centipede Lanmola to the magical Wizzrobe and many others.

Menu: There is only the one-player game, though there are two Missions for Link to undertake. If you wish to go directly to the second Mission, simply input ZELDA on the character screen.

Scoring: You don't play for points, but for Rupees, which appear when certain foes perish and are used to purchase weapons or goods. There are two denominations of Rupees.

Strategies: The trick to winning this game—apart from remembering to get your Sword in the Cave on the first screen!—is not just beating monsters in combat, but knowing where to find crucial items and hidden doorways. The first part is easy to learn; thus, we're going to emphasize the power-boosting objects and concealed passages.

A word about your foes. If you destroy every enemy on a screen, they'll be back if you recross that screen. Depending upon how you want to play the game—meaning, do you enjoy battling these guys—you can avoid this problem by killing all but one creature on a given screen. When you return, only that one beastie will be there.

To begin with, you can't win the game without making it through the Underworld, and you daren't go to the Underworld until you've fortified yourself as much as possible in the Overworld. This means obtaining a wide selection of items; here's what they are and where to find them. It's recommended that you draw a map in order to keep these directions straight: they can get complicated. You can do this easily by drawing a grid 8 squares tall and 16 squares across; that will cover all 128 screens. In order to follow the landmarks discussed below, label the grid as follows: under each square, from the left, write a number. The lowest, leftmost square will have a one beneath it, two to its right, three after that, all the way to sixteen for the bottom right square. Going up the left side, label the bottom left square A, the one above it B, and so on through H for the upper left square.

Getting under way in Mission One, you're going to get *money*. The enemies that will provide you with the most wealth can be found to the right of where you began (A8): skip A9 and go right to A10, A11, A12, and A13 for a goodly share of Rupees. You'll have to fight Tektites and other nasties for them, but they're easy enough to kill . . . and well worth the risk. When fighting Tektites, note that they rest for a relatively long period between leaps, thus giving you a chance to rush up and stab them. Another rich store of treasure can be found in square D11.

In addition to Rupees, you're going to have to acquire weapons and other items. Foremost among your immediate needs is a Candle. This can be found in the Store in B7 . . . the square diagonally to the upper left of where you began the game. Once you've got the Candle, head to square D14 and use the fire to torch a Tree in the bottom right. You'll reveal a Store in which you can purchase a Large Shield. This store has the *best* price in Hyrule for such an item: just 90 Rupees. Make sure you earn that much on the way over. (By the way, it's a good idea to make a list of what each Store has to offer. For example, you can only buy Bombs and Arrows in four of the ten Stores, Keys in four others, and so on.)

There is no way to survive the Underworld unless you have recuperative powers, and you can't get these unless you first get the permission of a special Old Woman. She is located in square H15. Medicine—that is, the Water of Life—can be found in any of the following locations: H14, D12, A9, H5, B5, and E4.

The other items of serious importance in the Overworld

are the Power Bracelet and the Blue Ring. You'll find the former in F5; though that screen is not in a remote area of the realm, you can only get to it by a circuitous route, heading all the way to the left side of the grid—the "1" column—along the B row, coming up to the E row, and cutting to the right. But the trip's worth it. The Power Bracelet can be yours by beating the Statue in the top right, and it will enable you to move the Stones that block entrances to Underground Shortcuts. These are located in four screens—F4, A10, D10, and G14—and will allow you to climb Stairs that will take you to the other three locations. As for the Blue Ring, it's expensive at 250 Rupees but worth every one of 'em since it enables Link to take a great deal more punishment than usual. The Blue Ring can be found in just one Store, located in E5. (There's a Store in the screen below, but you can't get the Ring in it! Looking for the Ring is sort of like seeking hot, new Nintendo games: only one place'll have it, if you're lucky.) Annihilate the middle Statue in the top row to gain entrance to the Store. (These rockheads are easy to defeat if you come at them from behind—that is, from the top part of the screen.) You can purchase additional arms and objects at the remaining stores, which can be found in screens D11, D14, B16, and H13.

Of less importance—but useful just the same—are the three gaming centers. Win here, and the game will be easier! These are located in G16, G7, and A13. One thing you'll definitely want to do before getting underway is move one screen to the left of where you started the game. If you have a Bomb and a minimum of ten Rupees, blast the wall which leads to the cave and pause the game (start on controller One). Using controller Two, hit A and up. This will permit you to save, continue or retry the game. Start again, enter the cave, play the game, and save your game *if* you earned money. If not, use the retry function and spend the same ten Rupees to play again. Save your game each time you win and rack up those Rupees!

In addition to the Old Woman, an important ally during

this phase of play are the Fairies, which give Hearts back to Link. While Fairies will appear at random, you can be sure of finding them on screens D4 and E10.

The only other locations you need to know in the Overworld are the entrances to the Catacombs, and we'll get to those in a moment. Fact is, you won't find them or *many* of the locales discussed herein unless you know how to get out of the Lost Woods and the Lost Hills. These begin in B2 and G12, respectively. The scenery will keep on repeating itself as you travel, unless you do the following. When you reach the Lost Woods screen, go up one screen, left, down, then left again and you'll be free. To get out of the Lost Hills, head up *five* times.

Before you head into the Catacombs, there's one thing to remember: make sure your Heart Containers are well-stocked. That will enable you to throw Swords, which is necessary because of the many enemies awaiting you within. Stand just within the doorway and heave weapons to clear the way; it will then be easier to move in and attack those foes who must be hit with stronger weapons.

The Catacombs should be taken in order. Their locations—in sequence—are: E8, E13, A5, D6, H12, F3, D3, B14, and H6. You won't have any trouble entering any but the last three: a Whistle is required to enter D3, you'll have to burn a Tree to get into B14, and H6 can only be accessed by detonating a Bomb.

Taking the Catacombs in turn, here is how to get through each of them, what you'll need to do so, and what you'll find as you battle your way through.

Catacomb One: You should have at least a trio of Heart Containers; weaponwise, you can get by with your basic sword. Moving to the right, you'll obtain a Key from one of the dead Stalfos. Head left to the complementary area on the other side of where you started and slay the Keese for another Key. Return to where you entered and journey ahead, killing your skeletonic foes; in the next screen up, you will be able to obtain a third Key. Go to the right: the dead Keese there will cough up a Compass. Return to the left, keep going left, kill the Keese, go up and decimate the Gel. Head to the right, kill more Gel, and obtain a Map here. Continue right, stabbing all the Goriyas so you can claim the Wooden Boomerang. Return to where you got the Map and continue ahead, slaying the Stalfos with blade and Boomerang. Get the Key and press ahead to win another Key. Timing your moves with care, head left, avoid the Spikes, and climb down the Stairs. Use the Boomerang to defeat—or more accurately, de-wing—enemies here and take the Bow. Return now to where you obtained the Boomerang and continue to the right. It'll take both Sword and Boomerang to get through this section of the Catacomb: if you win, you get a Key. If you lose, you're booted back to the front door! Upon getting through this area, move up and battle the Dragon: repeatedly stab it in the head and you'll kill it without too much trouble. After collecting the Heart Container, head right and get the section of Triforce. So doing, you'll be spirited to the exit. (If you take a different route—for example, if you want to enter the Map sector from the area below—it will be necessary to blast holes in Walls using Bombs. Be careful, though: not all Walls in the Catacombs are vulnerable to this assault.)

Catacomb Two: You'll definitely need the Power Bracelet here, so if you haven't obtained it yet, do so. You'll also have a much safer trek if you own the White Sword—check out the Cave in H11—and Large Shield. Make sure you have six or seven Heart Containers, a Candle, Water of Life, and the Blue Ring.

Upon entering, head to the right and kill the Snakes for the Key. Head up, defanging more Snakes, then go right and battle the Gel for the Compass. Retrace your steps to the left, fighting foes until you can go no farther. Prevail over the baddies here and you'll get a Key. Return to the right two screens and head up. You'll encounter Goriyas here; turn right, evaporate the Gel, grab the Map, then use a Bomb on the wall overhead. Slay the Goriyas in the region you've accessed, then snatch up the Metal Boomerang and depart quickly, exiting to the left. Get the Key here after defeating the Snakes, head up and beat the Moldorms for another Key, go right and use the Boomerang on the Keese, return to the left and head up, and slash away at the Snakes here. In the region to the right, cut up the Gel, head up, and check out this section of the Catacombs: there's information here pertaining to Dodongo. Come back down, left, and up: beat up the Goriyas, keep going straight ahead, and face Dodongo. In order to kill the beast, you must convince it to gobble down a pair of Bombs. This can usually be accomplished simply by placing them in front of the fiend, as an offering. After Dodongo is no more, and you've picked up the Heart Container, head left for the second piece of Triforce.

Catacomb Three: You'll need just about the same things you used to get through the last Catacomb—though it wouldn't hurt to pack about eight or nine Bombs for the trip as well!

Go left, stab the gooey Zol, take the Key, head up to fight more Zol and get another Key, attack the Darknuts in the section above—they can't be hurt by a frontal assault—turn to the left and beat back the Keese for a Compass, keep going left and dispatch the Darknuts, then take a turn *down.* Use a Bomb or two against the Darknuts here and rush to the Stairs: that's where you'll find the Raft. Leave and head up two screens; get the Key from amidst the Puffs and head right. In the next room, slay the Zol for the Key. Travel up, zapping more Zol, then move the Stone on the left. You'll find out what you already knew about the location of the White Sword . . . but what the heck? You needed the combat experience, and besides, you have to get to the screen on the left for another Key. Kill the Keese there using both the Sword and Boomerang. Go back to where you obtained the previous Key—one screen right, two down—then head right and get the Map after nullifying the Zol. Move down a screen, stabbing the Darknuts in the sides or back, then head right . . . right into a slew of foes! Surviving them, travel up and turn both Bombs and Sword on the Manhandlas. You'll be rewarded with a Heart Container. In the room above them, you'll find the third section of Triforce.

Catacomb Four: Go to F16 and, using the Raft, you can get an extra Heart Container. Travel to E10, then, to stock up on the Water of Life and raft out to the entrance to the next Catacomb. Upon entering, go left and kill the Keese for the Key. Return to the entrance and head up, bouncing the Vire to oblivion; then, Candle in hand, get the Compass from the sector to the right after killing the Vire. Go left one screen and up, getting a Key after slaying more Keese, then turn left, again using the Candle and battling the Vire. There's nothing to be won here, but your still-lit Candle will help you to beat the Zol and find another Key. Head up one screen, then right: kill the Vire and continue to the right. This screen serves up some nasty Like Like, which will snatch Link's Shield if they touch him. Kill these masticating monstrosities before they can do so—no kidding!—then push the left Stone aside and walk down the Stairs. Bat the Bats with your Boomerang, get the Ladder, and retrace your steps two screens to the left. Head up and fight the Vire, continue up and root out the Manhandlas, keep going up and get the clue—suggesting that you take a walk in the Waterfall at screen G11, which you will, in due course—then light a Candle and head right: there's another Key among the flock of Keese. Continue right, using the Candle to help you avoid the Spikes; then, with the wick still aglow, head down, fight the Vire, move the left Stone, and enter. Defeat the Dragon with a Sword thrust to its head, gather up the Heart Container, then travel up one screen to get the fourth section of Triforce.

Catacomb Five: Don't go directly to the entrance. Instead, earn money, travel to C16 for a Heart Container, go to the E10 Fairy for Hearts, purchase arrows at E11, and *then* go to H12 to enter the Underworld. Keep in mind, now that you have the Ladder, that you can use it to defeat foes like Darknuts: if you stand on it, you can hit at them while they can't get you!

Go right, shoot Arrows at the Pols Voices, get the Key, and double back to the entrance. Head up, Candle lit, and knock the stuffings from the mummylike Gibdo. Take the Key, head right for the clue—battle Digdoggers using the Whistle—go back to the left, blast a hole in the Wall on the left, go through, unwrap more Gibdo, Bomb your way through the Wall on the left and walk in, using Bombs and your Sword to fight the Darknuts. Shove aside the left Stone and descend the Stairs—let's call this area Screen A. You won't find any foes or goodies in this new chamber ("Screen B") . . . but you've just saved yourself a heckuva *long* trek! The next screen is super-important: head left, fighting off the Darknuts—they're plentiful *and* tough—then move the Stone, climb the Stairs, and claim the Whistle. Go back to the previous area—the one to the right of the Darknut screen—head down, undo the Keese for the Key, and blow a hole in the Wall on the right. Increase your Bomb capacity to a dozen, then retrace your steps to the left and up. Go back to "Screen B" and climb the Stairs that brought you to this region. You should now be back in "Screen A"—where you fought the Darknuts. Pass through the two holes you Bombed in the Walls, until you're on the screen *above* the one where you entered the Catacomb. Travel up on screen, using Bombs against your foes, then turn left. Kill the Zol for a Key, go back to the right, continue heading right—Candle in hand as you slay Zol—then go up. Slay the mummies, get the Key, go to the screen on the left, and use the Candle to help you find the Map. (You can also approach this screen from the one below if the going gets too hairy for you). Return to the screen on the right, go up, and light your Candle. Kill the Darknuts, get the Compass, continue up (still using the Candle), win the Key, turn left for a showdown with Gibdos and another Key, move to the next screen on the left—the Bow works best in here—go left one more screen and face Digdogger. The Whistle will break the big baddy into little ones, which are easily slain. Get the Heart Container and head up one screen for the piece of Triforce.

Catacomb Six: This would be an opportune moment to go to the F2 section of the Graveyard. Press against the Headstone in the center row, second from the right, for the Magical Sword. It's also a good idea to pick up more Water of Life before continuing your Underworld adventure.

That adventure resumes with a move to the screen on the right, Candle lit. The eerie Wizzrobes can't be hurt with the Boomerang, so you'll have to stab them all. Fortunately, your Large Shield will protect you from their spells. Claim the Key and return to where you entered. Go left and up: the Zols, here, will give up a Compass when beaten. In the screen above that you'll get a Key from the Keese; the Spikes will nail you in the next screen up unless you race through *quickly*. The next room up is tough, with no reward. Not only must you contend with Like Likes, you have to beat Wizzrobes and your old Bubble pals as well. When you've done so, move the left Stone to get to the room above. You'll face more Like Likes there; *hurry* through or risk losing your Large Shield. (Note: the Wall on the right can be destroyed by a Bomb, giving you access to the Catacomb beyond. *Don't* take it: there are items you need to get from above.) The next screen up pits you against a Gleeok, and it'll take several Sword thrusts to the head to do this baby in. When you've accomplished that, it's time to change directions by moving to the screen on the right. Get the Map and head down, fighting the Wizzrobes so you can reach the Stone on the left. Move it, and the Magic Wand will be yours! Go back down through the Map room to the screen below, use the Candle, and get the Key while killing or avoiding the Wizzrobes. (At this stage of the game there's no shame in avoiding confrontation. Your goal at this stage should be to acquire only what you need to win the game, not to add medals to your chest!)

Continue down, using the Candle for light and your Boomerang and Sword for combat. Head right and use the Magic Wand to kill the Like Likes and Wizzrobes here. Move the Stone and take the Stairs: this section of the Catacomb is *not* accessible any other way. Go down a screen, using the Candle, and get the Key. Travel left a screen, then up—pausing at the entrance for the Gohma to raise its eyelid so you can hit it with an Arrow. Get the Heart Container, go up a screen, and put another piece of Triforce in your pocket.

Catacomb Seven: Making sure you have at least 100 Rupees, use the Whistle to drain the Pond, and in you go! Walk up—fighting, natch—and blow a hole in the Wall overhead. Head up one screen ("Screen A"), go left one screen, then up. Use the Rupees here to buy a four-Bomb expansion of your explosive capabilities. Go down two screens—racing past the Spikes in the second screen—then down one more. Destroy the Snakes here and take the Key. Return to "Screen A," go up one screen and use Boomerangs against the Bats, go up another screen and defeat Digdogger with a one-two blow of tooting the Whistle, then attacking with Boomerang and blade. Use a Bomb on the Wall to the right, go through the hole and use the Magic Wand to destroy the Moldorm. Get the Key and go left two screens. Head up with your Candle, defeat your foes here, and get the Map; go to the screen on the right, Bomb the Wall on the right, and enter this crucial region of the Catacombs. Here, after beating back your adversaries, you should move the left Stone, descend the Stairs, and get the Red Candle. Leave by blowing an opening in the Wall on the right. Battle your way through this screen to the next one on the right, fight Digdogger as before in the screen beyond it, head up one screen, then Bomb the Wall on the right. Pummel your enemies here with Boomerang and Sword, making your way to the right Wall. Move the center Stone and climb the Stairs: you'll emerge in a screen that can only be reached via the Stairs. Defeat the evildoers there, blast the Wall on the right, slay the Dragon as you've done before, get the Heart Container, then go to the right one screen for the seventh segment of Triforce.

Catacomb Eight: Enter and go right, using a Candle. You'll get a Key after clearing the room of nasties. Go back to where you started, then move left one screen, killing the Manhandlas, and go left again. After killing the Darknuts and Gibdos, shove the left Stone to obtain the Magic Book, which strengthens the Magic Wand. Return to the Catacomb entrance and go up, beating the Manhandlas and using a Bomb on the Wall ahead. Attack the Darknuts for a Key, head left, break out the Candle, destroy the monsters here for another Key, continue to the left, and get a Key from the Darknuts here. Retrace your path two screens to the right, to the first of these three Key sectors. Journey up two screens, battling enemies, blast the top Wall and pass through, get the Map after beating the Manhandlas, continue up and slay Gohma as before—with an Arrow into its open eye. Go right: after slaying the Darknuts and Pols Voices here, move the left Stone and go after the Magic Key. The value of this is profound: this all-purpose Key makes it unnecessary for you to get any other Keys! Backtrack by going one screen to the left and two down—to the area where you blew a hole in the upper Wall. Go right and use the Stairs to reach to an otherwise inaccessible region of the Catacombs. Go left one screen, up one, blast the right Wall and go through, then head up. Here you'll find the last piece of Triforce!

Catacomb Nine: To enter, use a Bomb on the left Stone. This maze is extremely complicated. Head up two screens and left one. Use the Magic Wand on the Moldorm, then move the Stone on the left and enter. Upon emerging, turn the Magic Wand on the Like Likes and head right two screens. Kill the Patras here ("Screen A"), go down a screen and fight the Zol, move down again to face more Zol and Keese, then use a Bomb on the Wall to the right.

Enter and Bomb the Wall above, get the Map in the next sector and blast the Wall on top, kill the Wizzrobes here, then move the Stone and get the Red Ring. Return to "Screen A." Go up. Bomb the left Wall, attack the Wizzrobes in the room, then push the left Stone and use the Stairs. Fight your enemies when you emerge, then go left two screens—to "Screen B." Move the left Stone and take the Stairs; enter the new sector, blast the Wall on top, go through, fend off the Wizzrobes and other adversaries, move the center Stone on the right and take the Stairs to the Silver Arrow. Go back to "Screen B." Head up three screens, blow a hole in the left Wall and enter. You'll have to move the Stone here to access the Stairs—but you'll also have to watch out for the Spikes. Distract them by trotting over to the middle of the upper Wall, then making for the Stairs. In the new sector, Bomb the left Wall, enter, use your Magic Wand on the Like Likes, move the left Stone and go to the Stairs. Battle the Patra, head up, and it's time to fight Ganon. The boss is invisible, but you'll quickly pick up his orbit; he'll materialize when stabbed, after which you can slay him using the Silver Arrow. Head up, use your Sword on the fire in which Zelda is imprisoned, and your mission is at an end!

Now that you've rescued Zelda, it's time to undertake the second mission. Though the landscape is basically the same, the location of the entrances and goodies, and the layout of the Underworld, have all been changed!

Lay out a grid as before—for instance, H1 will be in the top left corner—and make a note of the following coordinates. The underground passageways are found at A10, D10, G14, and F4. As before, each will lead you to the others. This time around, the enemies that will give you the most Rupees upon their demise are located in A11, D11, A12, and A13. The Large Shield can be purchased cheap in D14, and the Blue Ring not so cheap in H16 (same prices as before). You can buy a Candle in B7, you'll find the Old Woman in G2, and Medicine can be found in A9 (torch the Tree on the left), F10 (toot the Whistle), E4 (use a Bomb between the Stairs), D12 (toast the Tree on the top right), and B5, H3, and H13; Stores are located in G3, D5, A5, F6, G6, B7, F7, D11, H13, D14, C15, B16, H15, and H16; the Power Bracelet can be obtained from the top right Statue in F5. Fairies are located at D4, E10, and H12; Gambling at B1 and G7. Using the Whistle in H7 will get you a Heart Container. Most important of all, of course, are the entrances to the Catacombs. In the order that they must be taken, these are found at E8, E5, E13, G12, D6, E1, B13, G10, and H1. You can't just walk into six through nine: you must blow the Whistle for E1, burn the Tree at B13, and use a Bomb on the top Wall for the last two.

You know how to beat most of the foes you'll face, so let's concentrate on the course you need to follow, and the items you'll find:

Catacomb One: Go left, get the Wooden Boomerang, double back to the entrance screen and go up. Get the Key, blow up the right Wall, and move the left Stone in the screen beyond to access the Stairs. Win a Key in the new room and go left, Bomb the top Wall, fight the Dragon, get the Heart Container and go right for the Triforce. There are other routes you can take—for example, straight up from the entrance screen—but this is the most direct. All you'll miss out on, besides numerous battles, is the Compass and Map.

Catacomb Two: Get the Power Bracelet if you haven't already, and another Heart Container. Stock up on the Water of Life as well, then go to the entrance of the next Catacomb. You can uncover it by pressing down on the top/middle Statue. Go up five screens, getting Keys in the first—that is, the screen above the entrance—and third. (Note: the screen between them is "Screen A.") Bomb the right Wall, get the Key on the next screen to the right, and return to the sector on the left. Go up, get the Key, go right, then come down to the screen where you obtained the last Key. Stroll right *through* the Wall on the bottom, get the Whistle here, then return to "Screen A." Head right, get the Compass, blast the right Wall, go through and get the Key. Head down a screen, get the Key, descend another screen and go to the Stairs. When you emerge in the new screen, head up, slay the Dragon, take the Heart Container, head up again, and you've got the piece of Triforce. Again, you didn't go to every room in the Catacombs—only those that let you acquire what you need!

Catacomb Three: Go up six screens, obtaining a Map in the third, a Key in the fourth, and a Metal Boomerang in the sixth. Return to the screen just above the entrance screen. Head left—you'll need to use Bombs here—and get the Heart Container, then travel down. Get the Compass, go to the right Wall, and shove the middle Stone. When you emerge from the Stairs, get the Key, head up, and get a little Meat action going to help you snatch the Triforce.

Catacomb Four: Before you enter, make sure you have at least 150 Rupees. Upon entering, go left with your Candle lit, get the Key, double back and go up. Head left, grab the Compass, go up with Candle in hand, head right, slay the Dragon in the next screen, and go right again. Walk to the left Wall, move the middle Stone, and claim the Magic Book. Walk *through* the Wall at the top of the screen and, in this sector, boost your Bomb capacity by four for 100 Rupees. Walk through the left Wall, exit to the left, then head up two screens, Bomb the Wall on top, enter the next screen, walk through the Wall on top, then go to the right Wall and walk through it—but *only* if you have 50 Rupees. That's what it'll cost you to make a transit here. After forking over the toll, head right and move the middle Stone on the left to reveal the Stairs. Go up, then up again. The Triforce is here, but *don't* claim it . . . yet. Walk through the Wall on top, continue up into the next screen, then up again into the next. Move the Stone that leads to the left, but *don't* enter. This is a one-way passage, and you'll have a heck of a trek ahead of you if you go through! Instead, head down the Stairs, get the Raft, and return to the screen with the Triforce. Get it now, and your business here is finished.

Catacomb Five: Enter, use your Candle, and go left—taking care not to get Spiked or Like Liked! Go down and take the Stairs ("Screen A"). Emerging, go to the left and move the center Stone. The new screen will give you a Key; enter the one below it to obtain the Bow. Return to "Screen A," where you first took the Stairs, head back up to the Spike screen and go left. Use the Candle and get the Map, then journey up two screens, watching out for the Spikes in the second. Go right and get the Compass, head up to the next screen, then right, then up. Take the Stairs and, when you enter the next screen, go left. After killing the Dragon and collecting the Heart Container, travel up to the Triforce screen.

Catacomb Six: Armed with as many Bombs as you can carry—and, it is strongly recommended, Red Water of Life—go to the next entrance: Whistle in the center of the Graveyard, facing left. Head up with a Candle, up again, then go left for three screens. In this last room, enter to activate the Spikes, leave, then reenter when they're on the way back. When you can get to the left, move the Stone and get the Ladder, then go back two screens to the right. Descend, get the Key, go back up one screen, right one screen, Bomb the top Wall and go up. Blast the top Wall here as well, go up and get the Compass in the next screen, go up, and move the left Stone in the middle row. Use the Stairs and, when you emerge, blast the Wall below you. Enter the screen, get the Key, and return to the room where you blew up the Wall. Go right and kill the Dragon, right again, and take the Stairs. When you emerge, go up two screens to get the Triforce.

Catacomb Seven: Go to the left of top-center screen, where the vertical row of Trees meets the clump on top; burn the leftmost of the two Trees. Enter and go right three screens. Take the Stairs in the third room ("Screen A"). When you emerge, head down. You'll get a Key here and, by going to the middle of the room and moving the left Stone, you'll be able to retrieve the Red Candle. Go back to "Screen A" and head right two screens—you'll need the Candle in the second—then up one (Candle also required here). You'll find the Map here. Head up four more screens, get the Key, and distract the Spikes so you can get to the Stairs. Upon emerging, go up, move the middle Stone, head right, pay the 50 Rupee toll, descend a screen, and in the second diagonal row from the left, move the third Stone from the top. Take the Stairs and, when you enter the new screen, head left three screens. You'll fight the Dragon in the second screen and find the Triforce section in the third.

Catacomb Eight: Armed with Meat, at least 150 Rupees, and a dozen Heart Containers—or more, if you can get them—cross the River with a Ladder, Bomb the Wall, and enter. Go up one screen and take the Stairs. Emerging, go down *through* the Wall, cross this screen, then go down another screen. Get the Magic Wand here, then head back up one screen and go one screen to the right. Take the Stairs and, upon entering the new screen, go up five screens obtaining a Compass in the fourth and a Key in the fifth. Go left two screens, blast the Wall on the left and enter, then go left two more screens. Get the Key here, then take to the Stairs. When you reach the next screen, go left, get the Magic Key, go back to the screen on the right, descend a screen (this is a one-way passage), move the middle Stone and head to the screen on the left. Walk right through the bottom Wall, go right two screens and take the Stairs. When you exit the Stairs ("Screen A"), use a Bomb on the bottom Wall, enter the screen, go down another screen and send the Dragon to lizard heaven. Go left, move the middle Stone on the right, enter the passageway and buy Bombs. Go back to "Screen A." Go up two screens and you've got the last piece of Triforce.

Catacomb Nine: This is it—a titanic tilt with the tilted tyrant! Enter and go up one screen then head left three screens. Travel up three screens, right one, and Bomb the top Wall to go up one. Go right one screen, up one, walk through the left Wall to the next screen, head left one screen, then up one. Walk through the left Wall and, on the next screen, obtain the Red Ring. Return to the screen on the right and take the Stairs by moving the left Stone. On the new screen blast the right Wall and go through, walk through the top Wall of the new room, move the middle Stone and use the Stairs. Go left when you emerge, blow up the top Wall of the next screen, enter and walk through the left Wall, and get to the Stairs by moving the Stone in the middle of the room. Claim the Silver Arrow and return to the room on the right. Go up one screen, left a screen, and move the left Stone to reveal the Stairs. When you emerge, go right—you're back at the entrance, weary traveler!—head up one screen, go left three screens, up three, right one, and Bomb the Wall on top. Enter the next screen, go to the screen on the right, walk up one screen, walk through the Wall to the left, go left again, then head up. Move the left Stone to get to the Stairs, go right when you emerge—through the Bomb hole—cross the screen and go right again. You've found Ganon: demolish him as before, then head up to save the captive princess.

Rating: A

This is a classic, an adventure game with charm and menace both! It also requires thought and inquisitiveness; the challenge aspect is actually A++, which more than outweighs its simple but not unpleasing graphics and disappointing sound.

Challenge: A
Graphics: B–
Sound Effects: C–
Simulation: C+

MAD MAX

Type: Road race and quest

Objective: The post-holocaust future is one in which people must fight for survival. In the roadway segments, Max must shoot down barriers and avoid collisions with enemy Cars to reach Rooms. There, he goes on foot to collect food and supplies; returning to his Car, he searches for Service Stations where he can swap food and water for fuel, ammunition, repairs, and an Arena Pass. In the Arena phase, Max must knock other Cars into Pits without being nudged there himself.

Layout: The view is from overhead in all stages. The screen scrolls in every direction Max is headed. There are three different levels, each of which consists of one Road segment and an Arena battle.

Heroes: Max's Car can bash other vehicles and hurl Dynamite at both Cars and impasses. It can brake and accelerate . . . and also run out of fuel. In the Room sections, Max can shoot a gun as he collects goods, which include Keys that open locked doors. In the Arena, Max's Car cannot fire, but can only hit other Cars.

Enemies: Enemy Cars on the road hurl Dynamite and also ram you, which does damage and causes you to waste fuel. The higher the levels, the more tenacious they become. Towers hurl Dynamite at you, which also doesn't do your paint job much good. In the Rooms, Mutants attack and sap your strength if they touch you. They can be shot or, in most cases, outrun—unless they surround you! In each Arena, not only is there a central Pit, but others that open and close suddenly.

Menu: One Max only!

Scoring: Power-ups, not points.

Strategies: The key to winning is to map each level. The instructions map the first level, where the Rooms should be taken in the following order: top center, bottom right, left bottom. Avoid the Room in the top right altogether. Begin the second level by driving up, left, up, left, up, right. At the Service Station, pick up two gallons of fuel, then go down, right, down, right (at the intersection), up, right, down, right, up, right, down, and to a Room where there's a *huge* supply of food and keys. You'll be well-equipped to find the other Rooms and Service Stations in this level. For the third level, start by going up, left, up, right, and up. On the right you'll see the Room with the Crossbow, which will be necessary later in the game. (You can also get there by going left when you start the level, then up till you can go no more, then right. However, you'll have to pass many Towers this way, and are sure to take some Dynamite damage.) You want to make sure you go into the upper right chamber with an extra Key: that's the only way you'll get the plentiful supplies of fuel to the right. When you leave, drive straight out and then down, left, and past the intersection to a Service Station. Return to the intersection and go up, left, and down: drive off the road at the bottom for another Room. Start by going all the way up here—watching out for the Pit in the top left—going right, and collecting a trio of Keys. Leaving, left, down, and right will take you to a Service Station. After you complete the third road, there's only the third Arena and the Ultimate Warrior to face.

In the Arenas, hang around the Pits, which open and close, so you can lure Cars to them. Avoid these Pits yourself by driving along the outside walls. This tactic is especially important when you've beaten all the Cars and are searching for the exit: it'd be a pity to whip them all and then fall into a Pit—or run out of gas. The number of Cars you face in the Arenas increases each time: in the last Arena, you'll be battling 50 Cars. When you begin here, you'll be in the bottom left of the Arena; when you win, you must make your way to the top right. After that, it's Ultimate Warrior time! Fight the goon by dodging and shooting. You can jump here . . . but there are also things you *can't* do—namely, pausing and replenishing your ammo. So don't squander it!

To help you get going in *Mad Max*, use the following codes: MMAX, WAST, and MAEL.

Rating: C–

The game is fun . . . initially. (It would have gotten a C, in fact, if it didn't send you back to the beginning of the level each time you died! *No* fun retracing old routes by rote.) Though each new level is more difficult, all are fundamentally the same. That makes things pretty boring once you've mapped the terrain. Also, the game is over much too quickly. The Arenas are always enjoyable—though, again, if you've seen one, you've pretty much seen 'em all.

Challenge: C
Graphics: C–
Sound Effects: A (*these* are terrific, regardless of the game's other failings)
Simulation: B

MEGA MAN 3

Type: Science fiction shoot-'em-up

Objective: It's a race between the superheroic Mega Man and the evil Dr. Wiley. All that stands between war and permanent peace are Energy Crystals located on a series of mining worlds. It goes without saying that Mega Man will have to battle through enemy hordes on each world in order to reach the evil scientist and destroy him.

Layout: The screen scrolls horizontally or vertically, depending upon the scene. Eight levels lead to the final confrontation, which consists of four levels with two foes from previous adventures on each.

Heroes: When the game begins, Mega Man can leap, slide, shoot, and climb. Along the way, he can gather power-ups which boost his energy; energy is *lost* when Mega Man is hit by foes. By defeating the bosses—the Robot Masters—Mega Man gains their extremely powerful weapons. Assisting Mega Man is his MegaDog Rush. Rush can be transformed into a variety of useful objects, as described in the instructions. Rush only appears when needed.

Important notes: If you want to execute a super jump, you can do so using both controllers. Press right on the pad on controller two, then press A on controller one. Not only will this enable you to leap high obstacles, but you'll be able to blast foes that would ordinarily be out of reach. More important is the ability to use the super jump to obtain invincibility. Do this by leaping into Pits at specific areas (discussed below), and waiting until your energy is nearly down to zero. The *instant* before it disappears, do a super jump from the Pit. Your energy will remain low on the meter, but it will be endless in practice. (Be patient when you perform this maneuver: your gauge may take a while to empty. When it *does*, it will do so suddenly—so be ready to leap!) Another important power is the ability to paralyze your enemies. Plug in both controllers and, while playing with controller One, push up and A on Two.

Enemies: The Robot Masters are pictured in the instructions; their numerous flunkies are reviewed in *Strategies*. As for the "surprise" bosses, consult previous books to see what the returnees were like!

Menu: You're on your own, Mega maniac! *Mega Man 3* is for one videogamer only.

Scoring: No points in this game—just energy.

Strategies: Note: regarding the passwords, all use *red* balls unless otherwise indicated. Here are the boss-by-boss tips you'll need to get through the game:

Magnet Man: The early going is easy. Climb down the Ladder at the right, shoot your enemy, slide under it when it attacks, and repeat. When it leaves, a door will open. The two gumdrop enemies below shoot Bombs but are easy to kill; on the level below that, jump and shoot as your foes climb down the Stairs, then leap them if they're still alive. You won't face any serious opposition en route to Magnet Man himself. The boss hides behind a magnetic aura, which he lowers briefly before leaping toward you, then flying into the air to drop Magnets on you. You must shoot him when his aura is down and he hops toward you. Stay to the right or left of center—opposite whichever side he's on—and get in your shots when the aura's down. When he's above you and firing his Magnets, dodge a step or two to either side to avoid them, but stay out of the corner. If you go there, the Magnets will rain down on you *hard*. The code to get past him is C5 F5.

Hard Man: Magnet Man's weapon works best against Hard Man, so he's your next objective. Run the opposite direction from the Hornets so they'll scroll away as quickly as possible; if they remain on the screen and drop their Hives, a bunch of bugs will emerge and you'll almost certainly take some hits. Slide across the green Jaws and leap the Bolo Man's Bolo while plugging away at him. The Monkeys above are easy to shoot. When you reach the Bulldozers, shoot them in the head while you back away—or simply stay out of their way until they turn, then shoot the driver in the back of the noggin. Take the upper route after defeating the second Bulldozer so you can fight the third and collect an E. Another Hornet appears when you slide across the Jaws above, so get through here quickly. You'll face a familiar foe next: the first enemy you fought underground in Magnet Man's realm. You can't really slide under him here because of the stepped terrain; hop him and stay behind him so you can avoid his fire and shoot him in the back. When he dies, the ground will open up and deposit you before a huge Robot. Let it hop over you and get out of here on the right. Time to face Hard Man. Fire Magnets, and slide *out* from under him when he leaps up; if he lands on you, you'll be pulverized. The code to get past him is C4 E6 F5.

Top Man: Hard Man's power will positively cream him. The opening screen is a bit difficult: when the Nuts and Screws join, they're deadly. Don't stick around to shoot them: just slide ahead, stopping only to blast the little leaping Helmets. Below, stand on the fourth step to shoot the

Tops and the mini-Top Man there. Shortly, you'll face the Robot Cat, which is a killer: it releases two metal balls of yarn that roll around. You've got to hop them as they come and go at you . . . which means you'll be leaping constantly. Establish an inverted U pattern from the base of the Cat's perch to just left of the Girder, and you'll be able to avoid the Balls while keeping up fire at the Cat Another mini-Top Man and another Cat await: this one releases Balls and then metal Mice; fortunately, you've got more room to maneuver here. Leap the Balls and let them roll away, then stand to the left of the Girder and blast away at the Cat. Next level, wait until the Hardhat charges you, then go up the right side and across the top. Just don't touch the Spikes below or you'll perish! Ride the Tops across the abyss and face Top Man. *Get out of the left corner:* he'll cause a row of Tops to materialize, and they'll bash you hard there, making you part of the wall! Stay in the center, rush to the side opposite Top Man when the Tops fly down at you, return to the center and hit him with Hard Man's weapon, leap him when he charges, turn to face him, and repeat. Four hits'll do it. The code to get past him is A3 C4 E6 F5.

Shadow Man: With Top Spin, this fiend's easy pickin's. Drop down either Pit, but face in while falling to shoot at the Gun in the middle. Get away quickly by dropping again, or the projectiles will do serious damage. Helmets and a Bulldozer await, as well as a third showdown with your fire enemy. This time, though, you can slide under him with ease. The Walking Eyes are easy to beat, but when the overhead Domes attack, take a quick look around: the lights are about to go out! You'll be able to see your enemies but not the walkway. (Fortunately there are no Pits here, so all you have to do is forge ahead!) Leap up and blast the Dome to get the lights back . . . or simply backtrack and scroll them off. Descend, and when you come to the Lava Streams, jump into the Pit for invincibility as described in *Heroes* above. Shadow Man's room is near. To beat him, wait till he's fired his knives, then smash him with your Top Spin. Get behind him and repeat; four hits will do it. The code to get by him is A3 C4 C5 D6 F5. Armed with Shadow Blades *and* Rush Marine, it's time to destroy . . .

Spark Man: Go up and proceed slowly; you'll have to get past Electrical Screens for the few moments they're down —follow them and leap when they're crawling away from you—and position yourself between the Sparks fired by hovering Plugs. Bolo waits for you above—get on the step below him, leaping and shooting between Bolos—and proceed across the Elevators, which start to move as soon as you step on them. Same old adversaries ahead, until you drop down a Pit that lasts for several screens. As you head right along the bottom, watch out for the Trash Compactors: if you don't slide through in a hurry, they'll dump a ton of trash in your way or, worse, on you. If you're merely blocked, resort to Magnet power to get out. More Elevators ahead; if you fall off, use super jump. When you meet Spark Man, wait till he jumps onto the high point in the middle of the platform. Go to the step below it, on the left, and leap up to shoot at him with the Shadow Blades. Jump back off the step only to duck his fire, then get back on. Seven surprisingly easy hits and he's dead. The password to bring you past here is A3 C4 C5 F4 (blue) F5. Three bosses to go, starting with . .

Snake Man: Though the best weapon to use against him is the one that belongs to Needle Man, Needle Man is most vulnerable to the weapon of Gemini Man, who's most easy to beat with the Search Snake of Snake Man. Since Snake Man is the easiest of those three to beat with another weapon, he should be eliminated first. Be alert for an immediate attack by a foe that bounds in from the right; shoot the Snake heads as soon as they scroll into view—otherwise they'll shoot at you. Two hits will kill any head. When you climb the Ladder, there are three progressively higher Snake heads, all firing at once: kill the bottom one immediately, then leap up and take out the higher ones between their bursts. In the room above is a *huge* Snake head firing projectiles; stand on top of the Ladder and leap these while shooting at the head. Its death will also stop the body from wriggling. Upside-down Snake heads lie ahead: super jump up and down in the Pit before them, shooting them each time you rise. Up next are more Snakes (easy) and Pole Vaulters (also easy: just scoot ahead when they leap, turn, and fire). When you meet the Bolo Men—there are two in successive rooms—go up the right top Ladder of the second Bolo room to get the power-ups in the room above, then come down, beat the green goon, and climb the top left Ladder. You'll have to fight another giant Snake head and more Pole Vaulters, but they shouldn't cause you much grief. Even better: if you fall into the Pit beyond the two Vaulters (right under the window), and do the super jump here when your energy gauge is near empty, you can become invincible. Climb to the sky and super jump your way across the Columns and through the drifting Cloud People. Enter Snake Man's Tower and keep up a constant fire as he runs at you *and* away from you. He's going to unleash little Snakes that wriggle toward you two at a time: leap over them, obviously trying not to land on Snake Man. To fight him, use the powers you took from Shadow Man or Hard Man. Fourteen hits from either will kill him. The code to get by here is A3 (blue) C4 E4 F4 (blue) F5.

Gemini Man: Leap and shoot down the Eyes before they can drop too many Fences, and while you wait for the Fences lower, blast the Penguins that waddle in from the right. (If there *are* no Penguins, just super jump over the Fences.) Then—ta-da! Your old recurring friend from the first level. This time, stand still under your power gauge and do nothing: he'll soon disappear, opening a passage beneath him. Drop down and shoot the Roe ahead from a distance: little Fish will emerge from some (power-ups from others), and you want to be far enough away to blast them before they touch you. When you reach the giant Penguins —right after the Dragonflies—just slide by them: it's not worth sticking around here and fighting them or the Fish that swim from their mouths. Take the hits and *go*! When you reach the water below them, look for the area where the overhead squares first appear. At the very start of this, you'll see two small blue squares next to a large red one, under the left side of a large multicolored row of squares. If you drop into the watery Pit here, you can become invincible. After you fight (or ignore) the giant Robot, it's time to tangle with Gemini Man. He splits in two, but if you stand in the left corner and just keep disgorging Snakes, both dudes'll die. When one or the other Gemini twin charges, simply take a step or two to the right to avoid them, then return to the left when they vault away. The code to get you beyond them is A3 (blue) B5 (blue) E4, F4 (blue), F5. Now it's time to turn your Gemini Laser on . . .

Needle Man: As you might expect, you're welcomed here by Needle-spitting Armadillos. Keep your distance from each one, shooting all the while. If they survive, they'll roll into a ball and attack—meaning you've got to be ready to jump. Except for the Cannons that fire Red Cannonballs, you've met all the foes who appear on the deck. The Cannons are easily destroyed with gunfire, as long as you blow them up fast . . . or, if not, stand out of range of the Cannonballs, which kind of just *blurp* out of them, landing close to the Cannon. Below, you'll face Spikes that come from the wall and then retreat; time your slides carefully here, and watch out for the Spike that comes down over the middle of the three small Ledges ahead. After you battle two Bolo Men and another giant Robot, you'll meet Needle Man. Don't let him close: he fires Needles *and* throws out a deadly Coil. Fire your Laser and keep moving away from the boss; four strikes and it's back to the pincushion for him.

You should be able to get through all of the old foes who

return; if not, skip them by inputting the code A1 A3 B2 B5 (all blue) C5 D3 (blue) E1 F4 (blue). Wiley's realm presents few difficulties early on. After you take a swim, use Hard Man's fist to knock down barriers. When you reach the Ledges above, you can slide across. In the room with the disappearing Blocks, climb the first three diagonally to the center, then slide under the barrier there to the next Block, and ascend. When you face the Robot that spits out animals, just kill the animals to destroy the Robot. Summon the Dog and ride it across the Spikes when you reach them, and when you fight the big bruiser who assembles and disassembles, get close and use Shadow Blade to hit it in the eye; slide to get away from its body parts as they move to the other side of the room and reassemble. When the giant is back together, resume your attack. Next room: beat the Robot and go up the rightside Ladder. The lights go out above; at the end, go down the Pit and fight the Bolo Man and two Robots. Elevators sliding horizontally above Spikes are the next serious obstacle, followed by a showdown with yourself! You have to beat three of you; only one is real, and the others will perish when it does. More often than not, it's the Mega Man in the center. The next serious enemy is a series of Robots throwing Blocks at you. Leap the Blocks and shoot the Robots. In the transporter room you'll be sent to face all the bosses from *this* game again; use Spark Man's powers on Magnet Man. Beat them, and it's Wiley time. Or is it? To go directly to this stage, input A1 A3 B2 B5 D3 (all blue) E1 E6 (red) F4 (blue).

When the big machine attacks, stay to the left and use Hard Knuckle to destroy the gun underneath. When that's destroyed, use the fist or, if that runs out, use Mega Man's normal weapon to kill the Wiley. Naturally, it *isn't* really Wiley: just a lookalike! There's another level to go! When you confront the new Wiley machine, get on the right Ledge and use Hard Knuckle to destroy the head—four hits will do it; if you're out of the fist, use Shadow Blades, which are nearly as effective. A new head will arrive, with

Wiley in it: don't be suckered in by the new Ledge that arrives with it. Get on the ground, under Wiley, and shoot upward using Top Spin. That will cream the real Wiley.

Rating: B

Gameplay is reminiscent of the earlier games, but there are enough new twists and challenges to make this a worthwhile successor! By the way—the scientist is spelled "Wily" in the instructions, and "Wiley" on the screen. We've used the latter, but it would've been nice if Capcom could've gotten the spelling *straight*!

Challenge: B+
Graphics: A (especially in the Wiley level)
Sound Effects: C
Simulation: C

NINJA GAIDEN II

Type: Martial arts chop-'em-up

Objective: In the last adventure, Ryu avenged his father's death at the hands of the evil Jaquio. This time, in an adventure subtitled "The Dark Sword of Chaos," Ryu must face the monstrous lord Ashtar, who was secretly behind the events in the first adventure. Now, Ashtar is attempting to rule the world by opening the Gate of Darkness . . . .

Layout: The game is viewed from the side as Ryu makes his way through seven dangerous stages. The picture scrolls horizontally and vertically, depending upon the screen. Each stage is composed of consecutive action areas.

Heroes: Ryu's control pad powers are walking, running, crouching, and climbing. His button powers are kicking and thrusting his sword. Many of these functions can be combined. Ryu can also shatter hovering Crystals to uncover power-ups which give him everything from a 1-Up to the ability to split his body into three fighting Ryus. He can also pick up additional weapons from Throwing Stars to Invincible Fire Wheels. All of these will be discussed in turn. A word about the climbing ability: the easiest way to make use of this is to do a backward jump, get to a roof/

Ledge/whatever behind you, then leap forward. It's much more difficult to go forward: you have to jump off whatever you're holding, then quickly push the pad in the direction of the Ledge *while you're spinning*, and hope you make it! (It's easier in the windy Stage Two.) Note: weapon power-ups you acquire will replace the one you had before it. If you haven't exhausted your previous power-up, you may not want to claim a new one; in some cases the new one won't be as powerful. Regardless, if you're attacking with Fire Wheel, make sure you don't crack any Crystals: the power-ups last only a few seconds, and may vanish before you can get to them.

Enemies: In addition to the seven bosses, there are 27 lesser foes Ryu will face during his odyssey. Some are human, some are not; some fly, some slither, some crawl on walls. They'll be talked about as Ryu encounters them in *Strategies*.

Menu: There is only the one-player game.

Scoring: Ryu is given points for every enemy he fells and each power-up he uncovers; hits from enemies are subtracted from Ryu's energy meter. Each area of the game is timed; if the clock expires, so does that life.

Strategies: Stage by stage, area by area, here's what you must do to keep Ryu alive:

Stage One, Area One: Clone Barbarians attack first, and are easily dealt with. Concentrate on getting the power-ups: climb the Tower on the right, hop to the first building—you'll find two Blue Ninja Powers there—jump left to the Tower, then leap off to the left to get the Fire Dragon Balls. After the building, there's a Windmill Throwing Star: again, get it by jumping off the Tower on the right. At this second Tower you'll be treated to the Killer Bats and their yo-yo-like motions; leap or duck, depending upon how many there are (which is determined by how long you're in the area). Atop the next roof, you'll find, from the left, Red Ninja Power, Fire Wheel, and a Red Bottle. Another Red Bottle is located below the one on the roof; the next rooftop offers Body Split with Blue Ninja below—get to this roof by climbing up the *right* side of the building, hopping to the building on the right, then jumping left to this rooftop. Fire Dragon Balls are on the next rooftop to the right; Fire Wheel is above the alley. Get it by going to the right and leaping left off the small Tower. Grab it quickly and pull Ryu back to the right, lest it—and/or he—plummet into the alley. Next building: you'll find a Red Ninja and Fire Wheel on top, Blue and Red Bottle on the bottom. A bunch of Spider Wights will drop on you at the next small Tower: use Fire Wheel against them, then get the Blue Ninja Crystals in the upper left and right. You'll find Body Split and a Red Bottle on the next roof, Dark Ninjas on the roof beyond. These enemies will crawl up the center part of the wall and *leap* at you: make sure you're on the upper level of the rooftop, standing over the open door. Pick off the one on the right, then get the one behind you if he's still there. When these are gone, more will arrive, firing Throwing Stars, so don't dawdle! Jump to the Ladder, go left on the rooftop, continue climbing down, and get the Blue Bottle, Blue Ninja, and Red Bottle below. Then go through the door and face Dando.

Stage One, Area Two: The lumbering Dando comes at you slowly—step by step, inch by inch—then charges. During the lumbering stage, get in as close as his outstretched arm will permit and stab him two times, then back away, turn, stab him twice again, then leap him when he runs at you. Turn (so will he!) and repeat until he's dead.

Stage Two, Area One: What martial arts videogame would be complete without the obligatory boxcar screen? Here it is, with five kinds of foes: the familiar Spider Wights, Clone Barbarians, and Dark Ninjas (on the fifth Boxcar only), and two new foes—the Harpies and Jacksons. The former butt you back, while the latter rush at you *fast.* Brace yourself and kill them both at once: if you fail, they'll usually turn and come at you again from behind, even if they've been scrolled off-screen! If the Harpy hits you off the top of a car, try to grab the side of the opposite boxcar rather than fall between them; that will save you time getting back up. The Crystals here contain, from the left, Blue Ninja, Fire Dragon, Blue Ninja, Blue Bottle, Blue Ninja, Fire Wheel, Red Ninja, Blue Bottle, Body Split, Fire Dragon, Blue Bottle, Invincible Fire Wheel, Body Split, Blue Ninja, Windmill Throwing Star, the first of the Medicine, Blue Ninja, Fire Wheel, Red Bottle, Blue Bottle, Blue Ninja, Windmill Throwing Star, Throwing Star, Fire Wheel, and Blue Ninja. Make sure you get that Fire Wheel and hold onto it, since you'll need it in . . .

Stage Two, Area Two: You land in the countryside amid a gentle snow. Or *is* it gentle? Within moments blizzard Winds are blowing you backward . . . then forward! In this area you must jump from Ledge to Ledge with care, with the Wind to your back. Otherwise, you won't clear many of the jumps. (If you get caught on the Walls of Ledges, you've got trouble: it's extremely difficult to get off many of these. You have to wait until the Wind is blowing against the Wall on which you're hanging, jump *into* that Wind, and let it blow you back to the top of the Ledge.) If you're really ambitious, make a note of when the Winds blow which way according to the clock—for example, at 238 they blow to the right for the first time. Start by running ahead, at top speed, and clearing the first Pit before the Winds start. Crouch and kill the Mongolian here, then ride the Winds to the next Ledge, where the Rockman hurls Boulders at you; either charge at once—if you're fast, he won't get to throw—or hug the Ledge under him and fire one of your weapons. They'll get him from there. Best of all: get the Windmill Throwing Star from the first Crystal, throw it, and *don't* catch it. It'll plug the next

Rockman, two Ledges beyond. You can get a Body Split from the second Crystal after the first Rockman. Watch out: both Rockmen's Boulders roll once they're thrown, so jump any coming your way lest they knock you off the Ledge! Jump to the Mongolian's Ledge and get rid of him; Slimes await Ryu next, spitting small, red globs of poison. These, too, can bop you backward and off the Ledge. (Even if you cling to the Cliff overhead, they'll nail you.) Use the Fire Wheel from the end of the Mongolian's Ledge to destroy the Slimes. Up ahead the main challenge is moving from Cliff to Cliff as you make your way up; often, you've got to move backward in order to go forward—like right after you climb the first Ladder! Make sure you get the Scroll high to the right of the long Columnlike Cliff (that Column is located to the right of the Ledge at the top/right of the Ladder): it will boost the power of your weapons considerably. The Sniper Joe to the right of the Crystal may give you some trouble, especially since there are Rolphers rolling at you from the right. Stand under the Column and, using the Fire Wheel from the Crystal there, blast them all, then claim the Scroll. (The Wind may complicate this if it's coming from the right, blowing your enemies toward you while impeding your shots. Time your attack so the Wind's at your back.) There's another Body Split in the Crystal after you jump off the Stairs, along with another Joe; if the Wind's against you, leap his shots till you can blast him. Fire Wheel is the best weapon to have here, so keep it. The Crystal past the next Column is a much-needed 1-Up, but to get it you'll have to cut through a Harpy and Jacksons. A single, well-timed Fire Wheel should do the trick against all of them. Climb the Column and leap to the right for the Body Split. Scale the Column again and go to the Ledge on the right. There's Medicine between the Cliffs ahead: get it, and the Blue Ninja ahead, then go back down to the bottom of the Column—you can try dropping down where you got the Medicine, if you feel lucky. Head right when the Wind's at your back, and get Medicine and a Red Bottle on the Ledge. To the right are a Blue Bottle and Windmill Throwing Star: also a Harpy, which'll pester you on the Ladder if you don't kill it. Climb and face the boss of this region, Baron Spider. He's on an overhead Ledge: fling Fire Wheels at him while you dodge the Spiders he drops. When you can, rush to the Ladder on his right, climb, and leap onto his Ledge. Stab him repeatedly. One way or the other he'll soon jump down, and you should follow him and stab away. He'll go back up in a few moments; repeat until he's been debugged . . . for good!

Stage Three, Area One: Now that you've done some mountain climbing, you've got to cross the ruins at the top. Trouble is, you can only see when there's Lightning. (Fortunately, the bolts still flash when you put the game on pause: do so, and you'll be able to scope out the terrain before proceeding . . . without losing any time *or* being attacked!) The first gap in the Ruins is easy to jump, the second one not so easy—definitely wait for Lightning to shine things up!—and the third one is guarded by Will-O-Wisps, with a Slime on the right Wall for bad measure. If you can run past the Slime, do so: it's not worth the energy to kill it! The Crystals over these first three regions contain two Blue Ninjas in a row, Fire Wheel, Throwing Star, and a Red Bottle. After the third jump there's a long Wall whose Crystals contain, from the left, Fire Dragon, Red Ninja, Body Split, and a Blue Bottle. The next jump is also a long one, with a Red Bottle on top. A real trial awaits you next: Column jumping! Leaping from the Wall, you'll cross five narrow Columns, with a Clone Barbarian and Rolpher waiting on the Wall to the right. Pause on the last Column, let the Barbarian head right, then jump and use the Windmill Throwing Star. *Don't* catch it, and it'll cut down all your enemies! Climb the three Wall-Stairs: the Crystal above the Wall section *below* the third step contains Medicine. A few short hops and you're out of here.

Stage Three, Area Two: If you've gotten this far, you don't need to have every detail reviewed; we'll discuss just the highlights. You're in a tower, and on the first floor you'll find a Red Bottle, Blue Ninja, Fire Wheel, and Red Ninja. The last two power-ups are musts. (You'll have to stay on the floor to get the Fire Wheel, rather than take the Stairs. It's worth the fight!) It's necessary to jump off the last Wall to get the Red Ninja, which is low to the ground; that, too, is worth the risk. After you get it, climb the Ladder to the right. At the top, jump left to the Ledge, swap your Fire Wheel for the Fire Dragon in the first Crystal, then turn it on the enemies ahead. The Crystals beyond it contain Blue Ninja, Throwing Star, Fire Wheel, and Body Split. Over the next Ledge is Fire Dragon, with a Sniper Joe underneath: leap, duck, and blast him! Climb the Ladder and scope out the Stairs ahead. Descend five steps on the left side, kill the Harpy, go two steps up on the right and terminate the Jackson, then duck the Tarantula's venom and stab it. After the next set of four Stairs, there's a Scroll—in the bottom Crystal; the upper one has a Windmill Throwing Star; stand on the Ledge below to break the Crystal. Return to the step you were on and continue to the right, killing the Harpy if you haven't done so already. The next two Crystals are a Body Split and Medicine. Climb the Ladder, head left, and climb the Stairs. The first Crystal, a Fire Wheel, is easy to get—and *do* get it: you'll need it in just a moment; the second, a Blue Ninja, hovers between these Stairs and the next. Hit *and* collect it in mid jump. Ahead of the second set of Stairs is a 1-Up: unfortunately, to get it you've got to avoid the Razor-Rings of the Bomber Head Clone below. Your best bet is to fry them both with the Fire Wheel you picked up on the Stairs. If you'd rather engage in hand-to-hand combat, jump down, kill the sucker, *then* use Fire Wheel on the 1-Up. Continue to the left, getting both Bottles up ahead. Up the Ladder you go, with a Clone Malth waiting for you after you hop the Pit. Draw him over by pacing to and fro, wait until he fires, then vault over him and stab him in the back. Go right *under* the Ledge, collecting the Blue Ninja and Body Split. Jacksons will pursue, but to no avail: leap to the Wall ahead of you, climb to the Ledge above, and head left. Get the Medicine from the first Crystal, the Red Ninja from the second. If you're well-stocked with Fire Wheel, use it to kill the Clone Malth ahead and the Jackson behind, then take the two Stairs on the left to get to the Ladder overhead.

Stage Three, Area Three: The boss here is incongruously named Funky Dynamite, and you'll have a blast with him! He's invulnerable on the ground, which means you have to hit him when he's bouncing: do so with Fire Wheel. If you *don't* have this power, you'll have to leap and stab him . . . with a very good chance that you'll take a hit every time you give one. If you've got to take this tack, you'd better have a Body Split or two. Naturally, you don't want to be in the way when ole F.D. launches his flaming TNT!

Stage Four, Area One: Made it through the tower, did you? Now you've got to journey *under* the place, through flame-filled corridors. A Goblin's Eye will assail you right after the second Crystal (Blue Ninja, like the first); luckily, the outgoing orb will hesitate before attacking, giving you a chance to plug it. There are two more Crystals (Fire Wheel and Body Split); a few paces beyond, at the first fiery Pit, a Psychic Brain will rise up and spit flame your way—the first of many to do so in this stage! Fire Wheel it before leaping. When you reach the next Pit, pause by the Column to its left and destroy the Oblis. These pteranodonlike creatures are fast and will force you to take a brimstone bath if you don't ground them. Jump to the Wall across the Pit, come back to the left Column, hop over the Pit, and continue. Leap down to the next Ledge and get the all-important Invincible Fire Wheel from the Crystal: once you have it, race ahead. You should make it to the Ladder on the right with no problem. At the top of the Ladder, wait until the Will-O-Wisp is between you and the Ledge on the left—almost directly under the stalactite—then stab it as you jump down to the Ledge on the left. Go from there to the next Ledge over, leap up to the Wall, climb, and go right to the Ladder; if you're quick, the Goblin's Eye won't be any trouble here. At the top it's reunion time with a Rockman: use Fire Wheel and hurry to the right. The Crystal at the edge of the Ledge contains Medicine; the one hovering beyond it is a Scroll. *Don't* try to get the Scroll as you jump right. Rather, get to the Ledge and jump left. It's easier to grab the Wall on the left than vice versa. Body Split's above the next Ledge, trouble's on the one beyond. Use Invincible Fire Wheel as you race to the Columns—the most challenging part of the game. It's *extremely* difficult to land on top of each. The good news is that if you miss, you can still grab the sides; the bad news is you're a sitting duck there. Moreover, the only way off is to jump over the fiery Pits and try to swing back onto the Columns . . . not an easy move without the Winds from Stage Two to help! There are 16 Columns in all, and you'll be a nervous wreck by the time you reach the Ladder at the end of the stage! Climb, enter the door, and take a breather before starting . . .

Stage Four, Area Two: If you thought the Wind was bad, wait'll you get a load of the goo you've got to wade through here! Never mind the Clone Basquer up ahead: get the Blue Ninja, Blue Bottle, and Blue Ninja. You'll need the boost! Leap the first Pit and cross the flooded surface: see where the ooze is pouring from the Wall? Unleash your Windmill Throwing Star there and press ahead without catching it. The weapon will keep the coast clear while you leap to the Wall on the other side of the Pit, and climb down. At the bottom of the Wall is a super-dangerous maneuver: you have to jump down and *under* the Wall to the Ledge below. (You can make it: press the pad right/down.) Get the Fire Dragon underneath, since it'll let you clear out the area beyond. Shimmy up to the Ledge above, then take out (if you haven't already) the Clone Barbarian on the next Ledge over. Turn quickly after you jump and do the same to the Hustlin' Jim behind you. The next section is something of a maze; to get through it, here's what you do. Go right until you reach the Ladder, head down, jump left at the bottom, and walk left to the three small Ledges—going to the one on the bottom left, then jumping diagonally up to the right, then left, then to the top right—pausing on the upper left Ledge to kill a Harpy, and the upper right Ledge to slay a Clone Barbarian. Go to the Ledge where the Barbarian was and head left. Continue left, leap the Pit—*don't* go down here—to the dry Ledge beyond, and take the Ladder down. Go right at the bottom and stop under the Ledge after the second goo-Fall. You can't get it from here, of course, so go right, *past* the twin Falls, then up two small Ledges. Hop to the Ledge on the left—past the Falls—then drop to the Ledge with the 1-Up. (You may want to kill the Kuo-Tao first, lest he club you!) After you claim it, you can cause it to reappear by reclimbing the Ladder on the left and coming back down; depends whether you feel it's worth the bother. Likewise, there are many Crystals that can be reached by going back to the small Ledges on the right, ascending, going left to the Ledge where one of the Falls originates, continuing left, and going to the big Ledge above. It's worth doing if you want the adventure; otherwise, the power-ups (Blue Ninjas, a Blue Bottle, Fire Wheel) aren't really worth it. Better just to go back down, follow the small Ledges out the right—obtaining a Body Split above the first Ledge, Medicine next, and Red Ninja after that—and continuing your mission. Hop Wall to Wall to the top of the Ledge, then pass the Falls and face a real challenge: you've got to leap the Pit and grasp the Wall on the opposite side . . . *despite* the Falls raging down it! When you get near enough to the Wall hanging down behind you, jump back to it, then hop right. Cross this Ledge, hop to the little one ahead, and *immediately* blast the Pumpkin Head there. Otherwise, he'll knock you back to your doom. Hustlin' Jim will pursue you at once; when you reach the small Ledge, stop and kill him. Let the Pumpkin Heads coming at you plummet to their deaths, then continue. Pumpkin Head and Hustlin' Jims will plague you, but you shouldn't have much trouble with them.

Stage Four, Area Three: Naga Sotuva will attack you here. You can only kill the boss by striking its head, not its hands . . . which sweep at you with savage regularity. When you reach this area, stand on the one of the two middle Ledges —the one where the hand *isn't*. Jump up and stab the head until the hand reaches you, then leap to the opposite Ledge and resume your attack. It helps to have a Body Split or two when fighting Naga.

Stage Five, Area One: Again, just the trouble spots and important Crystals. Get the first Red Ninja on the high Ledge to the right by going up the left Wall and then to the right. Below, when you come to the Wall, go up, switch to the left Wall, and fire a weapon from there: you'll want to hit the Sniper Joe and Goblin's Eye before you get on that Ledge. On the right side of that Ledge, just wait patiently while the Goblin's Eye self-destructs. After descending and going left, you'll have to jump down a Spike-lined Pit, then pass under a Spike-lined Ledge. Not only that, Dark Carriers will attack under the latter. Don't panic: just crouch and kill them as if they were Spider Wights. Climb over the Wall and you'll have to deal with more Spikes and a Bomber Head Clone. Don't fight him until you come to the break in the Spikes. There, leap up so his Razor Ring will miss, then charge and kill him. (If you come at the thug slowly, he may not even throw the Ring, but back off the screen and leave you alone.) Leap to the first Ledge over the Fire Pit, then jump to the second Ledge—ready to fight Clone Malth. There's a Scroll in the Crystal beyond. Between the rows of Spikes ahead is a 1-Up Crystal. If you try to slash the Crystal as you fall, you may end up impaling yourself . . . and *still* not get the 1-Up. Hardly a good trade! Invincible Fire Wheel is a perfect way to get it *if* you will have enough left for what comes next—the crowd of Bomber Head Clones at the bottom. Ahead, over the small Ledge, you'll find Medicine—which you'll undoubtedly need by now. When you descend from the second small Ledge, you'll face Pumpkin Heads and Jacksons: don't get boxed-in in the corner, but hop onto the Ledge to the right, standing your ground just left of the Spikes and using your sword to slice at whoever comes your way.

Stage Five, Area Two: You've been through the fire, so now it's time to go ice skating! How close to the left side do you have to land on Ledges? *Very* close, or else you'll go sliding off the right. After jumping two Pits, blast the Slimes ahead before one of them has a chance to shift to the left Wall, which will make the area much more difficult to approach. Upon reaching the Mountain ahead, use Fire Wheel against the Tarantulas—and watch for one to attack from behind. The next section begins with a downward journey, but don't miss the 1-Up below the Ledge. To get it you're going to have to drop down and stab the Kuo-Tac quickly—not too difficult; he's slow—then cut the Crystal and catch the 1-Up before it drops. Beware the Harpy when you're on the small Ledges to the right: one hit from them while you're on the ice, and it's over the side. You'll come to three small Ledges side by side, and a small Ledge above: the Crystal to the right contains Invincible Fire Wheel. There's nothing new up ahead—only more short 'n' slippery Ledges with Hustlin' Jims and other foes on your tail.

Stage Five, Area Three: The fight with Ashtar looks more daunting than it really is. A circle of fireballs will collapse and the boss will appear; only then can he be hurt. After a few seconds the fireballs will fly out in the same way they flew in: watch the pattern, move to a safe spot, wait for them to recollect, stab Ashtar again, and repeat until he's Ashtarred and feathered.

Stage Six, Area One: The ruins of an ancient castle lie before you . . . a surreal landscape that consists of flat stretches broken by huge, broken pieces of Wall. The problem with these shapes is that Ryu must pass behind them—at which point you can't see him, though your adversaries can. You won't be in too much danger for the first three Walls; above you, the four Crystals are all Blue Ninjas. The fifth is a Body Split, which will be extremely useful when you're behind the Walls. After the third Wall turn and defeat any leftover enemies: if they follow you to the Ledge below, you'll suffer serious hits and run the risk of being shoved into the Pit beyond. Enter the Well to the right of the Pit: Wells are the only way to move from level to level here. After tangling with a Fire Snake and a Mongolian on the bottom, you'll come to an unusually large Wall. Hidden behind it are Ledges that you must use blindly. Step just behind the left edge of the Wall and hop up: you'll reach the first Ledge. Move ahead, and as soon as you pass the window leap again. You'll be on another Ledge, right by the busted window on the right: there's a Scroll in the Crystal ahead. If you leave the Ledges and swing your Sword, you'll also connect with a Crystal that will give you Medicine. After you leap a pit and deal with the Rockman there—or shoot him before you jump—be ready for the Goblin Eyes which will drop from above. After you whip them, stop on the high ground before the big stalactite and send up a burst of Fire Wheel: you'll dislodge a much-needed 1-Up.

Stage Six, Area Two: Rockmen, Fire Snakes, Killer Golems, and other baddies hound you on this mercifully flat terrain. The area seems to have been put here to let Ryu beef up his strength, for it's a smorgasbord of power-ups. From the left: Blue Bottle, Red Ninja, Body Split, Fire Wheel, Invincible Fire Wheel, Blue Bottle, Red Bottle, Blue Bottle, Body Split, Fire Dragon, Windmill Throwing Star, and Red Bottle.

Stage Six, Area Three: Your foes here are the twin bosses, the Kelbeross, you first encountered in *Ninja Gaiden*—

winged, poison-spitting, mean-as-mud dogs, only one of which can be hurt. Unfortunately, there's no way to tell from game to game which is the vulnerable one without attacking it and keeping an eye on its energy meter. Your best bet is to stand in the middle of the screen and attack the hopping hounds with your Sword. If you have Windmill Throwing Star, you can strike at them without being hurt: go to the right Wall, climb all the way up, then drop off and push the pad right. If you're lucky, you'll land in the doorway where the canine crushers can't get you. Naturally, if all you have is your Sword, this maneuver will be of no use whatsoever! Another helpful move is this: when the indestructible dog is beside the door on the left, fire off a weapon of any kind and try to knock the pup out the door. If you succeed, it won't return!

Stage Seven, Area One: What you thought you knew about your foes no longer holds true in all cases. Will-O-Wisps and Psychic Brains are faster, Fire Snakes are more plentiful. Rush ahead to start, and get the Blue Bottle on the first Ledge, Red Ninja on the second. You'll be followed up to this Ledge: turn and fight when you're powered-up. Drop down, go under the Spiked Column, climb the Ledge: there's a Blue Bottle above, Body Split beyond. After you cross the narrow Ledges, climb the Ladder, blast the Will-O-Wisps to the left, go up. Go right at the top: the Crystals over the Ledge contain Blue Bottle (lower) and Scroll. Kill the Fire Snake ahead and get the Body Split above it. Continue to the right: near the top of the small, ascending Ledges ahead watch out for the Will-O-Wisp, which comes *back* to life after you slay it. Head left on the top level and get a Body Split above the second step. To the left of the last Ledge is a Crystal with a 1-Up: you can reach it by leaping off the Ledge or by climbing the wall to its left and jumping off.

Stage Seven, Area Two: The course is pretty straightforward; the biggest problem is the number of enemies here, and the fact that they guard every Ledge or overlook each jump you have to make. The power-ups you'll get at the start will prove crucial: Blue Ninja, Body Split (below), Red Ninja (above), Windmill Throwing Star, Blue Bottle, Body Split, and Fire Wheel are the first seven. Use Fire Wheel liberally ahead. The next two Crystals are a Blue and Red Bottle, followed by an Invincible Fire Wheel: first take out the Fire Snake on the Ledge overhead, then get the Invincible Fire Wheel as you jump between the Walls. Continue left, climb, and go right: Fire Wheel is in the first Crystal to the right, with Blue Ninja beyond. Keep going right and then up and you'll reach the final phase, the confrontation with the ultimate evil. Surprisingly, the mastermind isn't as difficult to beat as the dogs were: stand to one side and fire or stab at the center. Tó paraphrase Patton—when you see who's there, you'll know what to do!

Rating: B

Sequels are difficult to judge. If the game maker changes the scenario too much, what's the point of making a sequel? But if the thrills are pretty much the same, why bother making it at all? The *Super Mario* games manage to balance these perfectly . . . the *Ninja Gaiden* sequel less so. It's fun, but if you won the first game, you'll beat this one too . . . without enjoying the sense of discovery you had the first time around!

Challenge: A−
Graphics: B− (though the opening screen gets an A+: it's awe-inspiring!)
Sound Effects: C
Simulation: C+

NINTENDO WORLD CUP

Type: Soccer match

Objective: The six players on each team move the Ball around the field, trying to get it past the Goalie while protecting their own Goal. Unlike real-life soccer, however, this game can be played on six different surfaces: grass, soil, sand, concrete, rock (rough and bumpy), and ice.

Layout: The player looks down at the field from approximately a 45-degree angle.

Heroes: Each player can run, pass, and kick in eight different directions. Every man, as well as each of the five teams, has strengths and weaknesses, discussed in *Strategies*. See *Scoring* for information about the Hit Point function.

Enemies: The other players—and, in some cases, the surface itself.

Menu: From one to four players can enjoy the game.

Scoring: Players earn points for getting the Ball into the Goal. Players themselves have to watch their Hit Points; if they're struck or upended too often by the Ball, they'll be benched until someone scores or the half ends. Each game is divided into two timed halves.

Strategies: Before examining the strengths and drawbacks of each team, here are general tactics to apply.

- The most effective way of bringing the Ball downfield (other than with a hefty kick, which can be imprecise and cost you control of the Ball) is to have two players run parallel to each other. Have them pass the Ball as they go; if an opponent tries to get between you, simply don't pass! Most of the time, however, your foe will be behind you, unable to catch up. The two men should stay relatively close, approximately a player's-width apart.

- If you're trying to reach a loose Ball before your opponent does, *don't* automatically run: some players—especially slower ones—can get there faster by jumping several times over.

- Run the Ball downfield, staying halfway between the Touch Line and an imaginary line drawn upfield from your side of the Penalty Area. When you're a few steps from the Penalty Area—slightly higher than the top of the Penalty Arc—pass to a player you'll have waiting on the *other* side of the Penalty Arc, where the Arc meets the Penalty Area. Your opponent's Goalie will have been drawn to the side on which the first player was approaching, thus leaving the other player free to kick diagonally into the Net.

- You can achieve the same surprise by bringing the Ball to the corner on your opponent's side. The Goalie will most likely swing over to guard against a corner kick; that's when you pass to another player and drill it in.

- This is a virtually foolproof move: even if you don't score (which you will, much of the time), you'll be getting the

Ball deep into enemy territory. Unlike real soccer, you can stand right in your opponent's Goal area even if the Ball is on the other side of the field. Have your partner—in a four-player game—or the computer get the Ball to you in the air, and bop it right into the Goal, preferably using a Bicycle Kick.

- Having mentioned the Bicycle Kick, let's talk a bit about the strongest Bicycle Kick you can make, one that should be taken close to your opponent's Goal. If the Ball comes to you in the air, send it to a teammate, holding the A button as you do. Your teammate will return the Ball at once; because of the A button, however, the Ball will have an extremely high arc. As a result, you'll be able to fire off an almost unstoppable Bicycle Kick.

- Always remember that a pass is *slower* than a shot. Thus, if you want to get the Ball downfield fast, shoot it toward a teammate. Just make sure the player is there to receive it, or your opponent may take possession!

Regarding each of the teams, here's how they stack up against one another:

England: Moderate speed is about the only asset this team has, meaning you'd better shoot the ball as often as possible or it'll be stolen. England's got the same basic drawbacks as . . .

France: This is one weak bunch of Europeans! Strengthwise they're the pits, and will spend almost as much time on the bench as in the field. They're also slow, and tend to turn over the Ball a great deal—especially if one player's dribbled for too long. In other words, keep passing. Take this team only if you want to give your opponent a real advantage. (Or use it for practice: if you can score using these guys, you can win using *anyone*.)

Germany: The best team, the Germans are stronger than Italy and U.S.A. on defense, slightly weaker on offense due to a lack of speed. However, you can compensate for that by bringing out the Goalie: you really won't need anyone in the Net, since the Ball will rarely get there! A fleet team playing the Germans can steal the ball, but they'd better take a Goal shot at once: the Germans will snatch it back in no time. The best defense against a German player is to try and tackle him as he's about to shoot—no easy task, given the Germans' strength. Super Shots against the Germans work less than half the time.

Italy: Faster than the Germans, the Italians are not *quite* as strong as them; they're the game's second best team. Take a lot of goal shots with this team, and rely on dribbling more than passing.

U.S.A.: Here's a team whose players have diverse talents, all of them extremely valuable. All around, this is the third best team. They're especially strong on Super Shots. The biggest drawback: the players are rather slow, which makes it impossible for them to catch or outrun other players—though the jump technique described above will help somewhat. This slowness can be very detrimental at the Goal, where defensive speed is crucial. To counter this, have the Goalie play more or less in the center of the net, able to get to either side as necessary. Don't fall for feints: if an opponent passes to try and get around him, edge *slightly* toward that side rather than committing fully. A final note: the fullback Davy has a Bicycle Kick Super Shot that homes in on the Goal like a moth to flame. Even if the other Goalie intercepts and boots a Davy kick back, have Davy ready to execute a follow-up in your opponent's half of the field. He's especially effective on the high-bouncing concrete surface.

Rating: A

Goal! was a terrific soccer cartridge, so why get this one? Because there's a greater diversity in the players, and the multiple surface option guarantees that you'll *never* get bored! The figures are a little cartoony—sort of like a field of Barney Rubbles—but that doesn't really detract from the play value.

Challenge: A
Graphics: B–
Sound Effects: B
Simulation: A

THE PUNISHER

Type: Superhero shoot-'em-up

Objective: The Punisher is determined to clean up the streets of New York and rid it of that infamous crime-master, the Kingpin.

Layout: The view is from behind the Punisher, looking out at his victims as the screen scrolls from right to left.

Hero: The Punisher comes equipped with a gun and ammo. Power-ups are uncovered by shooting up objects; these power-ups are pictured in the instructions and are acquired by being shot. By blasting copies of the *Daily Bugle* lying about, the Punisher can pick up important hints.

Enemies: In addition to the Kingpin, there's an endless parade of ordinary thugs, as well as five "lesser bosses." Some of the thugs appear to be innocent folk until they turn and fire at you; some of the pedestrians *are* innocent folk. In a way, these are enemies too: if you shoot them, you lose energy.

Menu: No room for two Punishers in this game!

Scoring: Points are scored for enemies mowed down and special objects shot.

Strategies: One general rule: if the screen's full of enemies, concentrate on the right side first; the left-side foes will be scrolled off the screen in short order—on t'other hand, if you're playing to accumulate points, you'll want to get the left-side killers first. Playing on the right has another advantage: you'll get power-ups sooner, enabling you to keep firing, protect yourself, etc.

Taken boss by boss:

Jigsaw: In Stage One, stay slightly to the left of center. Shoot up the Crates *and* Pilings for points and power-ups, and watch out for the four gunmen who drop from the sky after the Crates. It's tough to spot the Frogmen in the murky waters beyond, but you *can* see the green patches moments before the underwater killers emerge. Stay to the right when you reach the next pier; shoot up the corrugated wall of the Warehouse for points (second panel), then move to the center so you can dodge left or right to avoid attacks from both sides. Foes will fill the screen in quick succession on both sides—if they lie down, kill them fast: they'll roll to one side, aim, and fire. If you don't hit them at once, enemies will collect and overwhelm you with gunfire. Keep blasting the Crates and Pilings when you can. The leftmost Piling under the open door of the second Warehouse will give you a Vest, as will the Crate to the building's right. Shoot the Prison Tower Windows and lights for points and power-ups; when you reach the end of the scroll, just sweep left and right along the wall to kill the cons, and use a Grenade if things get crowded.

In Stage Two A few easy targets are followed by three killers who drop in tandem from the left side. Guess which side you should be on? (Hint: it's not the left.) After that, stay to the far right, picking off guys as they come onscreen, and swinging to the left to blast enemies there. When you reach the second Gate—a recessed prison door;

only some are labeled "Gate"—watch for enemies to run quickly from the left and right across the screen; fire ahead of these guys to kill them. When you reach the big Girder, look up for the con who fires upside-down at you from the top. Shoot above the third recessed cell door to get a Vest. Target the red area above the cell doors that follow for First Aid and points. After the "Gate" sign are a pair of TV Screens where enemies will keep falling from above; hit the red areas of the cells beyond for Grenades, Extra Shells, and points. Blast the two lower wall Vents after the next "Gate" sign for a Rifle and points. The red areas over the next cells will give you a Grenade (second cell) and Vest (third). The remainder of the stage consists mostly of foes running left and right.

In Stage Three, to fight Jigsaw, fire at him from the center—preferably, with Grenades—and feint quickly from side to side to draw his fire this way and that. Always return to the middle, though, or he'll punch you full of holes. When he's up close, stand in the center of the screen. You can punch his face twice for every one punch he throws. If you stand in the middle, punch, shift to the left—out of range of his fist—you can beat him . . . but it *is* difficult to duck his punches, 'cause the big guy's fast on his feet.

Sijo: In Stage One, shoot the first Manhole Cover for points, and shoot on the right side, which is where most of the early thugs drop to or originate from. Watch for the gunner behind the Fence after the second Manhole. Shoot the roof of the Car in front of it for points. Enter the Bonus World ahead, then exit and be prepared to stitch the screen with fire from left to right. You'll get a Rocket Launcher here. Hit the Manhole for points and get Extra Shells from the thug above it. One criminal after another drops from the right side after the One Way sign. Hit the Barrel beyond for points, then slide to the left to avoid a chucked Hand Grenade. Shoot to the right when you reach the Windows, swinging your gun up to pick off the Snipers in the building. You'll get two additional batches of Extra

Shells here. The Barrel after the building gives you points. The guy with the Rocket Launcher on the stoop of the building ahead is tough, so have a Grenade ready. The second Barrel after the building has points. At the next building, stay to the left once the first Window has scrolled off the screen: a Hopper will jump in from there, hopping to the right while shooting at you. Plug this lunatic at once. Another will follow, so stay to the left. You'll get First Aid and points from the next two Barrels. Next up, at the end of the level, three killers: they shoot a *lot*, and one of them ducks behind a building after firing. Pick the building-ducker off—he appears first—then swing to the left to draw over the fire of the others. Cut back to the right in a hurry, and blast the other two.

In Stage Two, shooting most of the Pipes here will give you points or power-ups. Move to the far right after killing the first two thugs on the right: they're followed by a massive attack of killers dropping down straight across the screen. The rightmost guy in *this* wave doesn't fire at once, so you'll be safe on the right if you cut them down pronto. Shoot the next Pipe, then take out the guy on the right quickly: another thug will appear behind the Pipe on the left side, catching you in a crossfire. The four-Pipe set ahead is filled with goodies. Keep blasting at the right, to kill Hoppers and a killer who pokes from inside the tunnel. The next two Pipes give power-ups and points; skip the next one, but hit the Pipe after that. There are a lot of killers, but no concerted attacks for the rest of the level—the remainder of which is best played in the center of the screen, dodging *slightly* to the left and right as necessary. Enter the Tunnel after the Bazooka soldier and go through the Bonus World.

In Stage Three, when the ninja's in the distance, stand in the center of the screen and shoot; you can avoid his return blade-fire by dashing to the left or right, then doubling back in that small gap between the waves of blades. When he comes in close, shift to the left, staying just out of range of his sword as he jumps and tries to cut you. He'll be still for a moment after each attack, at which point you can kick him in the face. Move immediately to the left after you strike, then move back in after he's slashed.

Assassin: In Stage One, shoot the Girder and the Crates . . . then brace yourself for four killers to fall from above. Take out the lone guy on the right first, then switch to the three on the left side. After you beat them, stay in the center, shooting to the right—most of your enemies come from here—and blasting left when necessary. Move to the far right when you pass the third Girder, and stay there to kill the men that run from the right, one after the other. After the five soldiers have run out, hurry to the left and pick off the wave that runs in from that side. When they're finished, go back to the center: watch for the Bazooka man after the next Elevator. Blast the Crates to his right after you've killed him, and enter the Bonus World within. Back in the real world, stay to the right: in the center, you'll be pinned in a constant series of crossfires. After you find the *Daily Bugle*, stay more or less to the center for the rest of the level.

There are more Pipes and sewers in Stage Two. Nothing here you haven't faced before.

In Stage Three, Assassin hovers above you on rocket boots. Concentrate, first, on shooting off his arms at the elbows: his hands fire waves of mini-Missiles, which are devastating and extremely difficult to avoid. When you've disarmed him, so to speak, he'll start firing from his chest. Those projectiles are easy to dodge by moving left or right: keep hurling Grenades at Assassin—any part of his body—and he's doomed.

Hitman: Stage One features city streets, similar to the first Sijo level. Shoot Hydrants, Stop Signs, Awnings, and Manholes for rewards. (Cars are not rich hunting grounds this time around!) There's a white Car between two Manholes: at the end of the alley beyond them is a Bonus World.

In Stage Two, another street. Power-ups and points

abound; shoot everything. Foes are actually sparser than in the previous round. The Bonus World is located in a Manhole after a Beam sign that follows a building with two Awnings, a striped Blockade beneath the right. (The sign, by the way, will give you a power-up.)

In Stage Three, Hitman's in a Helicopter. Stay in the center and shift left and right slightly to avoid its twin guns; race any way you *can* to avoid his poison Grenades. Keep up a steady fire on the aircraft: it's surprisingly vulnerable to your bullets *if* you can avoid being killed first! Naturally, as soon as Hitman opens the cockpit, destroy him!

Colonel Kliegg: The stages here are not much different from what you've shot your way through previously. For that matter, the Colonel is extremely reminiscent of Hitman. He'll come at you in his tank: shoot out the guns, then destroy him when he emerges.

Kingpin: Nintendo admits it: the last boss presents a serious disadvantage to anyone who doesn't own the NES Advantage. Grenades are useless against the head boss, and without turbo it's *extremely* difficult to pump enough bullets into the criminal to beat him. But that's what you have to do, so make sure your trigger finger's in good shape before you attack the rotund rascal.

Rating: C+

Pretty average game of this type. Action fans will have a blast—literally—although strategy takes a back seat to a quick trigger finger.

Challenge: C+
Graphics: C−
Sound Effects: C
Simulation: C+

SILVER SURFER

Type: Alien shoot-'em-up

Objective: The barriers between this universe and the Magik Domain are threatened by an infernal new machine: the Surfer must fight his way through six worlds to collect its parts and prevent the device from being assembled.

Layout: The action is viewed from the side or above, depending upon the screen. There are six worlds in all; the sixth can't be attacked until the other five are won. The player can choose to visit the five worlds in any order. (Note: the names of the worlds are apparently the same as the name of the boss; the instructions are not clear on this.)

Heroes: The Silver Surfer has the ability to ride his Surfboard up or down, slow or accelerate, and fire Bullets. By passing over F symbols, he can acquire the ability to fire multiple Bullets at once. By riding over B symbols, he gets a Smart Bomb which will destroy every foe on the screen; he can hold no more than five of these. Other symbols are S for extra speed, a silver S for 1-Ups, and Orbs which give him double weapons. (When you get an Orb, make certain you use it *above* the surface of the ground, Pipe, or whatever else you're on: the double weapon can pass below it—even though the Surfer can't—rendering it useless in a frontal attack.) The Surfer can take on two Orbs, max. The power-ups are always in the same place but, once exposed, only remain on-screen for a few seconds. The Surfer has the ability to shoot down enemy bullets; his own Bullets have only a half-screen range.

Enemies: These differ from world to world, from the super-fast Ducks and Jumping Fish of Reptyl to the evil bosses. Some fire Bullets, others just run at the Surfer. Many give him power-ups when killed. These enemies will be discussed below.

Menu: Two players can take the part of the Surfer on alternate turns.

Scoring: Points are awarded for every foe destroyed, beginning at 300 points for the Fish on Reptyl. Points are also earned for F or B symbols he collects *over* five.

Strategies: Taking the different worlds in turn, here's how to handle them:

Reptyl: (Note: green Walls can be shot down in this world.) The view is from the side as you begin on this planet. Descend to meet the Fish before they leap, leaving about a half inch between the Surfer and the riverbed. Blast away, jumping up to sink the Duck for big points before you enter the Pipe, then enter the underwater Pipe—taking care not to hit your head on the top or the Board on the bottom. You'll pick up an Orb almost at once, and a single F two Fish later. When you do, slide Surfer toward the left, so he'll have enough time to pick off the Reptylians that come in pairs from the two smaller Pipes ahead. Upon leaving the first Pipe, rise a *smidgen* and begin firing behind you to get the Fish there. The second one will give you an F. (You can also rise *above* those Fish coming from behind you. If you do so—under the Bridge, where there's room—make sure you slow down by pushing the pad to the left. When the fleet Fish pass under you, drop behind them and blast them. You'll still get the F.) Enter the third Pipe and fight a school—no, make that a school *district*—of Fish, and kill the Reptylian to obtain a third F.) When you exit, rise quickly and kill the lower of the two Reptylians to get another F. (If you remain in the water, be prepared for a fast-moving Duck attack—though you can avoid this if you stay very *low* in the water.) Fish will arrive next, so if you're not in the water, dive back in after the Ducks pass, and blast them. After the Fish've been dealt with, you'll have no choice but to take to the skies since the water ends! Go up, but only for a moment: duck back down into the next Pipe and continue, fighting more Fish and Reptylians. Slow down, staying to the far left of the screen or you won't have enough time to shoot these foes. The Pipe will terminate in a dead-end, so rise, blast the green Wall ahead, continue, and hang to the left. Drop into the water when the Fish turn to the right; shoot them, then pick up both an F and your first B. Rise—you can try to fight the firing Reptylian above, or simply wait until it scoots to the left and rise behind it—and avoid the Tongue Frog ahead by dropping in front of it when its tongue is retracted. You've got to race ahead to encounter this Frog and get past it; otherwise, you won't be able to get into the water before the next school of Fish arrive. That'll mean shifting your guns to downward-firing—a needless complication. (If you die here, you can skip this reptile altogether by flying in the top right corner of the screen—pressed tight in that corner. Just drop after the Pole and head right, still hugging the right, and that side of the screen will actually guide you down to safety, leaving you home-free before the Frog appears.) Slip back into the water and another Orb will be yours. Rise to avoid the Tonguester on the other side, then drop back down in the water. Hopping Frogs will attack here; no problem, if you stay well to the left. Reptylians (two) and Fish follow, after which you have to exit up yet again and elude another Tongue Frog. Descend carefully after the Frog, first picking off the Reptylian who comes at you on top, then the one who attacks slightly lower. Continue ahead, but stay on the top now, *rushing* to the right and blasting the Reptylian gunner. If you get in your shots quickly, the artillerylizard will perish before too many Fish leap at you or the flying Reptylians arrive. By the way, you've got no choice but to fight the creature: the screen stops scrolling and killing it's the only way out. It'll take a steady barrage to do the job. When you've defeated this sub-boss, you're finished with the first part of this world.

The second phase is an overhead view. You'll pick up an S in the upper left almost at once—and a good thing, too! Discs descend from the top of the screen, and entrenched Turrets blast away at you. Begin by shifting to the left—position yourself right over the U of 1 Up—and blast the Discs, collect the S, then pull back to the bottom of the screen and blast the Turret overhead. As soon as you're past it, move to the right, zigzagging your way around the Turret overhead while blasting the new wave of Discs that descend. Hit the red Sphere beyond them for an F. Stay slightly above the center of the screen: right before the foliage appears, slide to the left and destroy the topmost Missile Launcher for an Orb. Shift left slightly, so you're right above the Surfer's picture on the bottom, and blast the purple Turrets, then turn on the golden one above them. Back at the water, move right—over the leftmost number of the score—and hit the Turret there, stay where you are to avoid the Missiles coming from the side Turrets, then begin plugging the purple Turrets ahead. The red sphere you'll pass over here will give you an F when blasted —a B if you got the first F. At the next area of foliage, stay to the left, but hang back toward the bottom. There are two Turrets firing at you from the right: if you race ahead here, they'll get you. It's best just to maneuver between their projectiles. (You can *try* to slide over and blast them, but they're tough to get without them getting you first!)

Deal with the Discs on the left by keeping up a steady fire. The remainder of the level is more of the same, plus a little common sense; you should have no difficulties here.

Mophisto: Drop so you're equal to the bottom section of the Pillar ahead, and move forward quickly to the center of the screen: there, your Bullets will reach the Ghosts. Pick off those you can, then really lay into them when they cluster in circles. Stay low until you reach the Stairs. When the first Door opens, stay to the left, nailing the Knights and Ghosts as they emerge. Be *sure* to get the Knights: like the Fish of Reptyl, they leap up. You can beat them all by clearing a Door, hopping it quickly—instead of waiting for another creature to emerge—slowing to deal with the next Door, and so on. (Be careful not to get your Board caught between a Stone and the edge of the screen as it scrolls left.) If you'd prefer not to fight much here, wait until you pass the fourth Door, then go to the very top of the screen, far right. No one will touch you there. Just make absolutely certain you slip back to the center after you clear the Doors —you'll see the barred, circular window in the background. Otherwise, you'll fly right into the row of blue Electrodes! Actually, the Electrodes aren't your problem here. The Demons are. These winged killers are perched on a bar near the bottom of the screen: mow them down at once or they'll rise one after another, hover for a moment, then *dash* toward you. Smart Bombing them is best. The last Demon will give you an F. There are more Electrodes after the Demons, their ranks swelled by Mechanical Bats which charge from the right. Stay in the center of the screen on the far left, picking the fiends and the Electrodes off as they attack. *Don't* go to the top- or bottom-left corners, or the Bats will corner you there. When you've cleared the Bat wave, stay on the top of the screen. There will be two waves of Knights leaping at you from the ledge ahead, and they're easier to pick off than the vertical row of Electrodes below. (Though if you do go below, don't hit those faces in the wall, 'cause they can knock you off. Also, the last Electrode will give you an F.) Once you've cleared the first wave of Knights, move in to midscreen and attack the second—especially if you're not packing heavy artillery. If you stay to the left, you'll be scrolled off the screen before killing the third Knight in the second wave. You'll face Electrodes rolling around in a circle beyond. Destroy them, then attack the second circle of Electrodes and collect the Orb inside the circle. Another wave of Mechanical Bats is followed by more Demons on the Ledge beyond. After that, you can go to the lower half of the screen and face Electrodes, or the upper half and face Doors with Ghosts. Opt for the upper half, and weave up and down as you plug the specters. There're no surprises hereafter.

Skrull Emperor: You start in an overhead-view section full of Missile Launchers, Turrets, Tanks, and more. (Note: you can only shoot down Missiles here, not Bullets. Also, you can fly over Turrets only *after* they've been destroyed, not before.) Move to the left when the battle begins: position yourself over the Surfer's left eye in the picture below—that's the eye on your right—ride the screen halfway up, and keep firing to take out the Turret there, then slide right to the number of the player indicator and blast the Turret beyond; neither will get off a shot. Hit the small Turret above that one to the left for an F. Shift to the center and blast the three-way Turret beyond. Following the Turret section, you'll face Tanks on the left and right; doesn't matter which side you take here—if any, since you can glide right up the center without being hit—so let's take the left. Position Surfer over the p of the "1 Up" indicator, staying at the bottom of the screen and shooting *constantly* to destroy the Tank Missiles and, then, the Tank. The Tanks are further protected by Surfer-Seeking Missiles up ahead: these'll swing diagonally toward you after you trash the Tanks, so blast them when you see them. Another Tank lies ahead to the right, and after you hit it—or avoid it by flying around it entirely to the far right—stay on the right to destroy the three-way Turret beyond and the horizontally-firing Turret next. (It shoots to the left, so you'll be okay. It also gives up an F when destroyed, which is even better!) Stay on the right: there are three Turrets above, two of which fire Bullets diagonally to the bottom left. If you *can't* destroy all of them, and opt to swing around to the right, you won't be hurt . . . at least, not by them. Just watch out for the Turret pointing straight down beyond them on the far right! After this, a new foe: a Railroad Gun, which whips back and forth above you on a Track. That's easy enough to get by . . . but there's a Tank waiting in the middle after the Track, and Turrets firing from the right side diagonally down to the left. Ride up the right side, flush against the side, where you'll be safe from the Turret fire *and* able to blast the guns! Rotating Barbells crisscross above you—three of them, one above the other, moving at different times. Smart Bomb 'em if you have one. A battery of four Turrets is next, on the right: hit the ones on the far right for power-up—the one on the lower right—stay on that side to blast the small blue Turret above (another power-up), shoot the Turret over that one, then watch out for the three Railroad Guns in a row shooting down at you. Pick them off one at a time; which one you go for depends, obviously, on where you are and where they are. Get this far, and you've got the feel of this world.

When it comes time to make your way through the Skrull circuitry, ride with the "maze" and keep from being scrolled off the side, without letting up on your forward fire.

Possessor: Ah . . . outer space, native stomping grounds of the Silver Surfer! Boxes attack, and one of them will give you an S; move in on them—well below the middle of the screen, the front of your Board, flush with the p in Up—and back off only to avoid any you may have missed. Skulls whirl over in a circle; stay close to the very right side of the screen and blast them as they enter. If you miss any, scoot to the left, low, and jump up to get ones you didn't destroy in the first onslaught (if you hug the bottom of the screen, at the 1 Up, they won't touch you). The second set of circling Skulls—which should be dealt with the same way—will reward you with an F. There are two Cannon ahead: if you can only get one, make it the bottom Cannon. Stay low—about an inch above the tops of the objects on Pedestals below—hitting the Egg ships (they open to release their projectiles, then close) and the Mechanical Birds beyond. Keep an eye on the slow-moving Artillery Gun pointing down from overhead, and the two down-pointing Cannon beyond. Skulls begin popping up from open Spitters below, and are easily picked off; just be ready to dodge them when they explode, since many of them contain two pieces of shrapnel each which fly off diagonally toward the bottom. If you ride the very top of the screen, you can get the Skulls *and* avoid the shrapnel; be prepared to hit the brakes when a Skull rises directly beneath you, though! Another way to deal with the Skull-Spitters is to blast the first Skull ejected, then rush past the Spitter *or* drop down and shoot it. If you can maneuver down and blast a Spitter, any Skull it spewed out will also explode. (And you may just get a power-up . . . hint, hint!) Two more Cannon like the first ones are next: rush ahead and get to the right of the green Bust on the pedestal, shoot the Cannon on the bottom, then go for the one on top—the bottom one is more difficult to hit once it starts firing. There's an Orb directly behind the one on top, followed by more Skull-Spitter and a Cannon. Hit the Cannon before you arrive . . . and look for a 1-Up on the ground beyond it! A Column will rise from the ground nearly to the top; if you don't shoot big hunks out of it, your journey'll end right there. Beware the downward-pointing Cannon right after it, and the circle of Skulls that come screaming your way next. After that: two waves of Mechanical Birds, the second of which will give you an F *and* an Orb! Ahead: a

Cannon on the bottom, more Spitters, a Cannon on top, more Mechanical Birds, another Cannon, a second rising Column . . . you know the drill!

Firelord: An overhead view with a difference: stray from the Lava River and you're dead! The first batch of Greenies gives you an F, so sway to the right and blast them. A Pincer comes at you next, followed by a quintet of giant Hands, which are vulnerable only when they're wide open. Take each successive Hand out by edging to the left after you've hit the one before it. More Pincers are next on the plate, then additional Hands; the second Hand gives you an F. Swing right to get the next batch of Greenies, as well as the wave that follows it, after which there are some fast, big, nasty-looking Crustaceans intent on Surfer for dinner. At least the first one's kind enough to leave you with a power-up. Fortunately, none of these nemeses fires anything at you! Greenies return—slip into the nook to the *right* before they arrive and shoot them from there, otherwise they'll corner you—then face another clutch of Hands, yet another herd of Greenies, more Pincers, another Hand, a whole squadron of Crustaceans, Greenies, Pincers, Hands—a veritable *sea* of them (easily navigated-through if you don't feel like fighting them)—and that's it for this section.

The next section is a sideview as you head through a Cave. Pteranodons attack—hit them with a steady barrage of fire from the left of the screen (the last one leaves behind an F)—followed by Lavaball-spitting Craters. Pass these using stop-and-go, shoot the Pumpkin on the Ledge beyond, and collect the S from the Pumpkin right after that. The Lava Falls that follows descends in waves; wait for one wave to wash over, then accelerate. Stay to the left and shoot the Pumpkins as they hop from the Lava river—once a Pumpkin sinks back, it doesn't return—hit the solo Pteranodon (fast, before it spits fire at you) and Pumpkins that follow—you might want to Smart Bomb the last

Pumpkin, which will also eliminate the Lavaballs just beyond—then stay to the top of the Ledge and shoot the Plant People who charge. Lava will rain down again—stop-and-go right by—after which you may want to drop down and collect the Orb. Two Pteranodons hit you next (easy . . . plus you get an F from the second) followed by Cauldrons dripping Lava. Inch past the Lava—a Smart Bomb will *only* eliminate the drops on-screen, not the Cauldrons and successive drops. You've got more Pumpkins on your silvery hands next, after which there's a huge Skull dripping Lava. Smart Bomb this baby into oblivion—you'll chill it out long enough to get by. More Plant People (easy) and a Cauldron spitting Pumpkins at you from above (pretty easy) follow, after which you'd better take the high road: the Pteranodons are simpler to beat than the Lava drops below. You won't have any trouble hereafter, until you meet . . .

Beyonder: The last world is the realm of the Beyonder, and you're going to do a lot of zigzagging to avoid all the stationary obstacles here, while also blasting the baddies. When you reach the Beyonder himself, there are no safe spots from which to attack. The only way to win is by moving around and shooting continuously. Naturally, one of the best things you can do—regardless of the level—is to turn on the game, do nothing, and watch as it scrolls through its various sections. Or, if you'd like to start with a terrific advantage, you can do the following. While the title screen is on, push the pad of both controllers up. Use the code CKWJT4. You'll be asked to use another password . . . but, instead, hit the Start button. You'll begin the game with incredible firepower including the ability to shoot behind you!

If you're the impatient sort, you can use the following code to go surfing through the game with limitless continues: SJM3333. Hit Start when the game asks for a different password. One other password, KJTTJK, will grant you perhaps the greatest power of all: invincibility. You should also give the game a go with J8SCL9.

Rating: B

This is one of the most difficult games you can buy for the NES—but there's just too little diversity from world to world to make it a must-have.

Challenge: A
Graphics: B–
Sound Effects: D
Simulation: C (You won't feel like you're flying!)

SPOT

Type: Chess-type game.

Objective: You must move Spots around the Board in order to adjoin your opponent's Spots, thus changing their color to yours.

Layout: The view is from above as you look down at the Board. All of the spaces on the Board are open—unless the player opts to block them off in an options screen.

Heroes: The Spots can move in a variety of ways, as illustrated in the instructions. They can only "clone" themselves when they move one space in any direction. There are also bonus rounds—accessed by landing on spaces randomly chosen by the computer—which allow you free turns and other benefits.

Enemies: Your opponent's Spots have the same abilities as your own.

Menu: One to four players can play each other, or you can tangle with the computer.

Scoring: Each Spot a player places earns a point; points are subtracted when the color of Spots are changed. Be advised, though, *never* to give up, regardless of the score: it's possible to go from being down 31–17 on the second-to-last move, to winning 25–24!

Strategies: The strategies discussed herein apply to beating the computer. However, they can be used to defeat humans as well! The only difference is that the computer has a limited menu of responses to opening moves, which makes it easier to set the sucker up for a fall! The key in winning in *any* situation is to *get your opponent to attack*! Lure Spots toward you by making one-space moves, and you'll be in a much tighter formation, able to leapfrog when necessary. Another rule: in the early stages, clone rather than go for big (but invariably temporal) gains. Close up any holes amid masses of your Spots: better to let your opponent hit you hard on the outside—you can always reclaim Spots—than have her or him fill an opening *inside*, where you will lose a slew of Spots *and* be unable to attack.

Open by moving a Spot from the upper left one space to the right. The computer will usually respond by moving a Spot on the bottom left to the right. If so, continue moving Spots right one space at a time. If the computer shadows your moves, you may win with as few as 13 pieces on the board. When you come within striking distance of the computer's right-side Spot, that Spot will attack. *Good!* It will clone, thus enabling you to strike down two Spots with your one. Meanwhile, on the bottom, the computer only ends up with your one Spot. You're already well ahead! What you must do next is gain control of the center of the Board, which is accomplished by building two columns down, one along the second row from the left and another down the second row from the right. You've already got the start on the right: add one more Spot to that side, then go to the left and fill in two there. That will leave you within striking distance of virtually the entire Board. When you've done that, you should have two T shapes on either side of the board. Start filling in the sides to the left of the left column. You'll be attacked within a move or two: when that happens, leapfrog ahead to reclaim whatever the computer seizes. Your goal: to build a pyramid with the point in the top left, filling out toward the bottom right. (If the computer throws you a curve and makes that impossible, move in reinforcements from the right.)

Sometimes the computer will respond to the opening move differently. If it moves to the right on the bottom after your opening move, *then* moves from the upper right to the left, move your Spot on the bottom to the left one space. Regardless of the computer's next move, go up from the last space to which you moved so that you have an L shape on the bottom. The computer will almost always attack that, and you'll be able to leapfrog over the Spots it sends at you, capturing them all. It'll attack again from the left, and you can take the remaining two Spots down there in turn. That'll make it 9–2 and you'll have no trouble from there, since the top two Spots invariably attack to the left. If the computer comes at you from the bottom left, keep going right. The computer will still charge at your Spots, enabling you to take them. The score should be 8–1 within a few moves. Move in from all sides to keep the computer boxed in on the lower left. If you start the game by moving down from the upper left, you'll probably be attacked from the upper right: deal with that in exactly the same fashion.

Rating: A–

Spot is a ton of fun, and, like *Tetris*, provides an intellectual challenge. Fans of *Othello* will be especially delighted with the twists, given the familiar theme. The one minor quibble: the computer could be a *tad* more diverse in its opening moves.

Challenge: A–
Graphics: A (the Spots are superbly animated)
Sound Effects: B+ (the different musical themes are cute at first, then quickly become redundant)
Simulation: A (looks and acts like a real gameboard)

STARTROPICS

Type: Adventure quest

Objective: Young Mike's uncle, Dr. Jones, has been abducted while doing research on C-Island. Your mission is to search the South Pacific "paradise" and rescue him.

Layout: The map screens and room screens both are viewed from overhead. Don't be misled by the opening screen: there are five main Islands and a slew of smaller ones to explore in this game.

Heroes: When he begins his adventure, Mike can jump, walk, and talk. The Chief will give him a Yo-Yo, after which weapons and power-ups are increasingly more difficult to come by. See *Strategies* for details. As for power-ups—Stars, Hearts, and Medicine—they only last on the screen for a few seconds, so get them quickly! A note about the Baseball Bat: the great thing about this weapon is that you don't have to be facing a foe to clobber it. Anything in the arc of your swing—front, sides, or back—is going to be bopped!

Enemies: These range from easy-to-kill Jellies to murderous Skulls! See *Strategies* for fuller discussions of your foes.

Menu: There's only the one-player game.

Scoring: Points are awarded for a combination of kills and energy expended. More important than amassing points, however, are getting weapons and energy.

Strategies: Start out by heading left, entering the village, and chatting with the Chief. He'll give you a Yo-Yo. Talk to *all* the natives . . . otherwise, you won't be able to get past the guard and into the Tunnel in the upper right corner of the village. Enter and face the Jellies. Since these creatures only move from side to side, you'll beat them handily. Kill them all—you can't proceed unless you do—in this room and the next. In the room after, jump to the right, Yo-Yo the Jellies there, uncover the Stars, and hit the Tile on the bottom right to reveal the Gate Switch. Hop over to it and the Gate will open. The Rattus ahead takes two hits to kill. There are Rattus in the next chamber; head right, then up, then leap the Tiles to the left. The lower Tile of the three-some at the Gate reveals the Gate Switch. Rattus and Jellies creep beyond: clear the room and continue. When you reach the next room, don't bother going to the chambers on the right or left—the Gate Switches can be revealed by jumping on the two Tiles parallel to those in front of you. The Switch you really need will be revealed by jumping to the Tile in the upper left. Next room: get on the upper right Tile of the bottom group to open the Chest. Now you've got 25 Shooting Stars, which have considerable range. Lower right Tile on top will get you the Switch. New foes here join the Rattus: Noctos. Yo-Yo the room clear and continue. Looper is added to the cast of characters, so return to Stars before you enter; this sucker is *fast*! Two stars will kill the snake. (If you don't want to be hurt, activate the Looper by stepping in its path, then stepping *out* of its way. You can shoot it as it retreats or passes.) Head up and left and cross the *lower* Tiles on top to open the Gate *and* the Chest in the lower left. Hit the Tile to the right of the Gate—at the vertex of the upside-down right angle of Tiles—activate the Switch, and return to the right. Head down the corridor: you'll get Medicine from the room on the right. The bottom Tile on the right will give you a Switch to the right. Go up for more Medicine, get it and *leave:* the Switch to the next room will lead you to death. When you emerge, the Loopers will be back . . . so be ready to hit them. (The one in the corridor is easy: just come out firing. To beat the second, wait at the end of the corridor, put a finger on each side of the pad, and rapidly tap left-right. That will activate the snake, put Mike where he's safe, and allow you to fire as the Looper passes. Repeat and it's bye-bye snake.) Return to the Gate, open it again—now that you know where the Switch is—and enter the next room to face Loopers and Noctos. One Nocto will charge: nail it when it flies to the right. Since you've got room here, take out the Noctos without activating the Loopers, then step in the path of the latter to get them going, and run that plan as you've done before, hitting them in the back as they retreat. Next chamber: time for the C-Serpent. Immediately jump *two* Tiles ahead to get in range, then Shoot Stars into its mouth when it opens, jumping its Fireballs as necessary. (Or taking the hits if you still have Medicine.) You'll have an extremely difficult time trying to kill the Serpent from just *one* Tile up.

Exit, throw the Switch on the next screen, cross the Bridge, and cross the Island to the top and then right. Have a chat with Baboo on the Beach. He'll give you the ID code to start Dr. Jones's Submarine—1492 . . . an appropriate code for a sea trip! Cross the Beach to the left, head down, and you'll find the Laboratory where the Submarine is based. Once control is turned over to you, search the seas for a solitary Dolphin. (Look to the bottom/right.) She'll tell you about her lost son; promise to find him, then continue right until you reach an Island. Enter the Tunnel in the lower left, park in the Harbor on the Beach, and exit the Submarine. Enter the Lighthouse to the left. After talking to the Keeper, return to the Submarine and head to the lower right . . . yes, right. Pass *through* the green strip of land, continue down/right, and pass through the land there as well. Moor in the Harbor there, get out and go to the House. The Dolphin will send you to get a Bottle on the Beach: go to the section of Beach below the house, head right and up, and walk to the left *through* the Mountains. The bottle will give you an important Dr. Jones code: 1776. (Patriotic lot of programmers, aren't they?) Now, notice the Big Heart above? Get it by returning to the Submarine, heading up, submerging, and sailing *under* the two rows of Mountains ahead. Pass through the Tunnel above, exit the Submarine, walk down the narrow strip of land, and cross right through the three Mountains. You'll be able to walk through them to the Heart. Your energy has now been boosted considerably—which will be rather important in the next phase of play! Walk to the Tunnel entrance in the upper right and prepare to face the hordes of Octo!

As soon as you enter the new section, a Mud-o-Fish will rush at you from the right. Three Yo-Yo hits will destroy it. Another will attack as you continue right. Jump to the Island on the right and get the Baseball Bat; switch to the Bat and pass through the Tunnel. Go to the upper right and whack the two Noctos there, then head left to the Sinking Tile, bashing the trio of Noctos before crossing, and making sure you get on and off the Tile before it goes down! (Not so easy with the Looper on the other side. Time your jump for when the snake's headed the other way. More Sinking Tiles follow, then a quartet of Mud-o-Fish; you can outrace the second—it *usually* doesn't leap to Tiles! The next Island is Nocto-infested; clear them out to open the Gate overhead. Spinistar will attack from the upper right: better to outrun this fiend by racing to the upper left path before it charges. You'll have to do some Tile-jumping again, with Octots patrolling 'em; jump to the Sinking Tile when the Octots aren't on the two upper or lower Tiles, then move ahead whenever they vacate a Tile. Make for the small Island on the left. Pick off all the Octots as you work your way to the top—use the Yo-Yo instead of the Bat, and be careful, since the Octots can leap onto your Island—then access the Switch using the center

Tile in the row of three just to the right of the Islands. Inside, you'll be faced with a Looper on the right. You can ignore that one, unless you want to whack it for fun. Head left, killing the Loopers, and enter the last corridor. Dead-end, right? Wrongo! Walk through the right wall—where the shadow hits the floor—and into the chamber with the Nocto and goodies. Trigger the Tile in the lower right, then walk through the upper right wall of the chamber. This will take you to the room on the right. Blast the Nocto, hit the Switch, and exit. Those annoying Spinistars are in the next section. Bat 'em all, preferably when they're dormant—if you're super fast, you can actually race up the center and get all four with two Bat-swings—then pass through the Gate. Goody: more Tiles. You'll be attacked by Puffs here: don't waste time trying to fight them. Just leap the Tiles *quickly*, beat the Octots at the other end, and enter the Gate. You'll get Hearts in the chamber beyond; the third Tile up on the right will give you the Switch. Five Noctos flap their ugly way through the next chamber. If you hit the right critter—the one on the lower left—you won't have to beat any others to open the Gate! That'll save you precious Bat-swings. Another Spinistar room as before is followed by—an empty chamber? You bet it is! Head left and fight the two Noctos and Loopers in here—or just the first Looper which charges: that's all it takes to open up the gate at the bottom. Inside, you'll find Medicine. The lower right Tile on the right gives you the Switch. Fight the Spinistars again—or just run past them—then head through the Wall where the shadow lies on the right. A new treasure room! The top and right Tiles give you the Switches you'll need here. And what *is* the treasure? A Snowman Doll, which you'll need in just a few moments to fight Octo. Yo-Yo the Octots here—don't waste time or a Puff will huff at you from the middle; start by rushing to the left, nailing the Octot there, and continuing around *fast*, clockwise—kill the Octot in the next room, and head forward to fight the boss . . . Octo! Octo's going to pelt you with Ink Balls, so hop from Tile to Tile and avoid them until Octo is in range. When he moves in close, hit the "freeze" button (the Snowman Doll) and Yo-Yo the brute to death. You'll need two full uses of the Snowman Doll—meaning hit the monster the *instant* you freeze it, both times. The baby Dolphin has been liberated . . . so return to your Submarine and follow mama Dolphin as she leads you to the next segment of your adventure.

Alas, you're caught in a storm. Your Submarine is wrecked, and you find yourself on an unknown island. Head down the Beach, then right to a Hut. Here, your Hearts will be filled completely and you'll be told where to go to find someone to fix your smashed ship. Walk right to the Tunnel. Got some new baddies here: a trio of Dodos. Three Yo-Yos'll do it for each one. (Best vantage point: rush to a position above the second Heart from the left, even with the top ledge of the projection in the bottom right. All three Dodos will charge from above, one after the other, allowing you to pick them off.) The next room up has a Chest guarded by two Dodos. Go right, just beside the lower edge of the water, and the Dodo above will usually come straight down at you. The other's a cinch. The upper left Tile will give you the Switch that opens the Chest (with a Bola inside) . . . but you still have to kill the Dodos to open the Gate. More new enemies: Ninja Monkeys. It takes two Bola hits to destroy a Ninja Monkey. Enter firing the Bola; you'll get the one right in front of you. Turn right and fire at once, killing the enemy there. Move right, and fire left or ahead; there're only two of the little guys left. The next room serves up six of the hairy hoppers, with the strips of land running up and down instead of left and right as in the previous chamber. Edge up the center strip, shooting as you go; stop before the closed Gate, turn around and fire down. You'll hit the apes as they cross from side to side, but more important, up there you can't be approached from the sides! The next room has a Chest with Loopers on three sides. Blast the one ahead with Bolas (two hits); the weapon will pass right through the Chest. The Chest is opened with the Tiles beside you;

when you trigger them, the Loopers on the sides will be free to charge left/right. You can still kill them with the up and back technique you've used so often. Destroying them will open the door; the other Tiles in this room give you nothing. Big challenge now: a *row* of Sinking Tiles. Watch them to get the pattern, then clear the first two and go to the non-Sinking Tile on the right. Power-ups will appear in the middle; get them and continue up through the Gate. The next chamber has two Dodos on the left . . . and another new fiend, Bonehead. There are two of those on the right and they're *really* thick-skinned, despite their appearances: you'll need four Bolas *each* to stop them! Hurry to the lower right corner—at the foot of the projection, not on top of it—and fire off eight fast shots, then turn on the Dodos. Get a good look at the next room as *soon* as you enter: the lights go out and the Noctos attack. (Fortunately, you can see the bats!) If you don't remember where the land masses are, you'll have a problem even if you beat the Noctos: the lights don't come back on! It's strongly recommended that you pause the game the instant you enter. If you don't get a good view, remember: you have to go up, left, down, then straight. Actually, it's not too difficult to get around. Just walk until you can't go any farther; you won't fall into the water. Ahh . . . but do you *want* to go into the next room on the left? Answer: no. It'll take you back out onto the Island. (If you want to get another glimpse of the dark room, though, you can go to the one on the left then come back in. You'll have to fight the fliers again . . . but what the heck?) What you really need to do in here is jump on the Tile on the right side, directly above the third Heart from the right. That'll switch on the lights! The one above it will give you a Switch; then you're outta there! (Fear not: you can jump on the "lights" Tile again. You won't turn off the juice!) You'll find Stairs in the room above: climb them, and you're through the Tunnel!

Walk straight up to the village and talk with the natives. (Answer "Mira" when given a choice by a lovely young lady you'll meet.) Keep going to the right and up; pass through the maze of vegetation to reach the Bridge that crosses to the lower section of the village: it's the only way to get to the Chief. He'll tell you about his sleeping daughter, Bananette, and the potion that will revive her. Return to where you entered the village, and go to the back of the Chief's hut: walk through the Wall on the left side—directly opposite the doorway of the hut above—and visit the sleeping girl. Go, now, to the upper right region of the village: talk to the stoic fellow there, and he'll let you out of the village. Continue to the right and—you guessed it!—enter another Tunnel. When you're inside there'll be two rows of three Loopers on either side. Step up to trigger them in toward each other, then do an end run, going around the side. You should take one hit, max, en route to the top. So there you are, in the next room—facing two Boneheads with your Yo-Yo. (Be advised: these odd birds can cross water!) Hurry to the upper left side of the cross—at the vertex of that right angle; in other words, where the top and left streams meet—and fire your Yo-Yo to the right. That'll stop the Bonehead there from jumping across, and will also kill him. Linger in that spot just long enough to draw the other Bonehead down the top stream, then run to the left Wall, turn, and face the Bonehead. (If you don't linger, and the bird comes at you from above, you're cooked.) Exit via the Gate on the left. Yum! Another dark room, this one guarded by a Looper. You'll get past the snake okay—but after that, the room keeps scrolling in the *dark!* There's a row of Loopers ahead, but they can't get to you. However, they're walking on *something*, right? Get in front of the second Looper from the bottom; that's the only one you can reach with your Yo-Yo. When you've killed it, simply leap ahead! You'll have to kill the snakes here by stepping between them as before to activate them, stepping back to the right, and killing them. That done, note the Octot beyond. See where it's jumping? That's where you have to go. Walk up where the Loopers were standing, kill the Octot when it's near, then hop to that Tile. Then to the one on the left. Then up one. Cheers:

the lights are back! And what's that on the opposite shore? A Baseball Bat *and* a Slingshot.

Next room over: three Flies. Go to the middle stretch of land, just below the door, and Bat them—they're fast, but one club'll do each Fly in. Here or in any Fly room, if you kill a Fly over water—or, later, Lava—and they leave a power-up behind, you may not be able to jump for it . . . but you *can* swing a Bat or throw a Yo-Yo to scoop it up. Anyway, hit the Tiles in the Fly room, left one first. More Sinking Tiles, almost the same as before, are in the room above. Start crossing the *instant* the lowest one rises after being submerged, and don't stop until you're on the top one. Jump to the Tile on the upper left to uncover two Hearts, then finish off. You'll find yourself, next, in an empty room with Stairs. Go down, take the Stairs in the next room, and head to the right. The only foes in the next room are Volcanic Craters, which spew Fireballs wherever you happen to be standing. The Tile in the upper left reveals the Switch. Make sure you hit the Try-Your-Luck Sign in the upper left as well: it'll give you a 1-Up or 2-Up, or take a life away. The odds are good ones; take a chance on it! There are three more Flies in the next room; before attacking them, go left and hit the second Tile from the left. It'll uncover a Stop Clock: hop to it, freeze the Flies—preferably when they're close together, since the Stop Clock paralyzes or just slows them for only ten seconds—and kill them. (Be careful, though: if you touch them, even while they're frozen, you'll be hurt.) In the room on top you'll face Mad Muddies, who spit fiery Mudballs at you. Cross this chamber quickly on the top of the island in the middle, jump to the Tile on the far right—revealing the Switch—and hurry out on top. The next room has Flies and Mad Muddies; go up the Tiles on the *right*. The left side ends halfway through the room. (You can Slingshot the Muddies or bash them with the Bat when they're close . . . but why bother? You can igore them, or, if they're in your way, simply leap over them.) At the top of the room are Sinking Tiles. If you don't take them rapidly, you're dead. Jump on the first one the *instant* it begins to rise from the Lava, then hurry to the left across the next two. In the next room head up the left side first, get the double Hearts, then turn around—you can leap over the Muddy that rises between the Tiles, if you don't feel like fighting. Go up the right side now. If all you have is your Yo-Yo, the game will be generous in this room. Step on the lower right Tile, keep an eye on the center Island, and a Bola will appear on the Island in the center. But wait! Do you want to go to that Island anyway? If you kill a Fly there, a wall will open on top. Pass through, have a look around—if the Flies don't get you—and decide if it was worth it! Then go back through the door (the Fly you swatted will have returned) and finish crossing the Tiles on the right. There's nothing on the Tiles at the top, or in the next room. Cross the corridor, and, in the next chamber face Magma. The key, actually, is *not* to face the molten monster. You have to de-energize the fiend. The Tile on the upper left gives you a Switch that destroys one Power Orb; the Tile on the lower right of the monster's base gives you the Switch to the other Power Orb. Hit both Switches and Magma's dead. Enter the chamber to the right, go down the two flights of Stairs, exit to the top, cross the last screen (no monsters here) and you're out of the Tunnel. Head up to the Castle, talk to the man out front, go around to the back of the place—on the inside of the River—enter the room there, then leave the Castle. *Don't* hit the Beach . . . not yet. Head to the left but go *up* into the Mountains. You'll find a hidden path there: take the Stairs and you'll add another Big Heart to your abilities. Exit the path to the top and follow the land to the left. Go into Ghost Village, head left, past the Pond, to the group of Headstones on the left. One of 'em's a fake—the middle one in the third horizontal row from the top. Stand on it and you'll find yourself in a new Tunnel . . . .

Where three Bonedogs welcome you. Either hop to one of the Tiles and pick them off, or wait a few seconds, then go to the lower left corner and let two of the canine bags o' bones attack from above. Yo-Yo each one three times. Go to the bottom right and do away with the other skeletal tailwagger. The Tiles here give you zilch, so exit on the left. A horde of Skulls is perched on the Tiles above, ready to take off and attack—reminiscent of the Octots; they won't present a problem. Run up to the top, turn left, and kill the nearest one. Jump onto the Tile, still facing left, and plug the second. Continue left, kill the third and fourth, then backtrack and go down. Kill the two Bonedogs as you go left, and jump up to the last Tile on the left. It will reveal a Switch that opens a Gate below. If you're low on Hearts, go up to the room there, get some, then reenter the Headstone. You can fill up your Heart meter again if you let the game save itself, reset, go back, and get more. When you have enough Hearts, go down after you kill the Skulls and Bonedogs, instead of going up. Enter this room and go straight ahead *immediately*, jumping the water—there are invisible Minies on either side, and you'll take hits if you don't vault over at once. Open the Gate and kill the three Muumus in the next room. They take a *lot* of blows to kill, and the best tack is to step to the right of the water, facing down the straightaway. One Muumu will attack at once, and steady Yo-Yo fire will destroy it. A second Muumu will come at you the same way. The third will either charge or is easy to chase down. Obtain the Rod of Sight from the Chest. Go through the Gate at the bottom and use a Rod here to reveal the four otherwise invisible Minies. Go down again into a Skull room—face right and wait: a Skull almost always arrives—and hit the Tile above the strip of land on the right. That will open a Gate to the right. Use the Rod here to reveal the four Minies, blast them, and exit to the right. Fill up on Hearts in the next room, return to the Minie room on the left—they're back, so be on guard—then exit to the bottom. Kill the Jelly in this room and exit—but *not* via the Stairs. Turn right at the Jelly and walk through the wall! In here are Hearts and a Sinking Tile. Cross the latter, hop right, then go up one Tile and left. That activates the Switch. Get the Hearts below by walking through the Wall to their right—you'll take a hit from a Minie here, but it's worth it—exiting the left Wall at the top, then coming back into the room. Next room to the right: a Cannon on the right fires at you, but won't hinder you much. Trigger the Switch, exit to the right, and face Noctos in a dark room. After you kill them, move ahead in the center of the room until you can proceed no more, then jump to the right. That will trigger a Switch—which becomes visible; hit it and exit to the bottom. Four Muumus and a Skull must be battled here—unless you happen to slay the one Muumu that opens the Gate; use the Gate at the bottom, and fight the lone Skull in the next Tile room. Seems a little easy, eh? Well . . . ignite a Rod to reveal the four Minies. Beat them, then jump on the Tile in the lower left to reveal a Lantern. Go right if you want to get Medicine and more Hearts—you may not need the latter, but the former couldn't hurt. Exit the Medicine room and head back to the Bat room, leap two Tiles (in the dark) and jump to the land on the *right*, head through the Wall, use a Lantern, pick up the Rod below, jump right and walk through the Wall on the right at the top of the Wall; on the other side, take two jumps down to trigger a Switch, jump right one, up one, and onto the Switch, jump up one to the land there, then head right through the Wall. There are Sinking Tiles on the other side, so use a Lantern here to make sure you don't blow it! What you'll be doing is jumping from the Sinking Tile on top to the solid Tile below to the Sinking Tile below that, then to land below it. Walk to the left till you can't go any more, up, right—again, till you can't move—then jump to land on the right, jump up, then walk right. The next room has a Mr. Armstrong to the right, heaving projectiles at you. He'll throw two, then sink, then reappear somewhere else, chuck another pair, etc. If you can't jump behind him and hit the hand there, you'll have to take the hits and charge, 'cause there's no getting out of this room without killing him. It'll take four Yo-Yo hits to kill him, which means you'll have to let him emerge twice to finish the job. Exit on the other side to a skull-shaped slab of land with two Muumus on top and a Cannon in the upper left and right. The fourth Tile from the left, on the bottom, triggers a Switch outta here . . . but you *don't* want to go that way. The next room is a dead-end with another Armstrong—if you end up there, hit the upper right Tile on the right to uncover the Switch and return to the previous room. After beating the Muumus, or simply running around them, go to the top of the screen and—leap of faith!—jump out over the water from any point. The screen will scroll land your way. There'll be a trio of Bonedogs on it, but would you have preferred to get wet? Beat the marrowy hounds, enter the Gate on top, and you've got two more Muumus to deal with. Fortunately, you can get a Clock by leaping on the left Tile . . . and you can also fight them *from* the Tiles on the left and right since the mummies can't cross water. Next room: two Hearts. Open the Gate with the third Tile up on the right. Nothing from the Tiles here, so head left; there's an Armstrong here and, from the Tile on the top left, a Rod. Return to the room on the right, use a Rod to reveal the Minies, kill them, and go to the right. Use the Rod, kill the Minies, and continue right. Nail the Bonedogs in the next room, jump on the third Tile from the left on top to get the Miracle Mirror, and continue right. Here, you'll face Wizards who appear and disappear . . . and will perish before the might of the Mirror as you bounce their Fireballs right back at them! Exit to the right and face a room full of Muumus; kill them all or pick the right one and you're out! Leave by the bottom, collect the Bola, activate the Switch, and exit below. Fight the Skulls *and* the Wizard here, hit the lower Tile on the far right to get yourself another Rod, leave to the left, and get set for a *big* battle: hit the Rod and you'll reveal Maxie and a team of Minies. Arm yourself with Bola, use the Medicine you got before when your power gets low, and just keep tossing Bolas into the ghost's open mouth. Exit to the left, use the Switch, and enter the room on top. Go to the top Tile, stomp on it repeatedly, and when the room fills with pond water you'll be spirited out. And, lo and behold, the pond has gone dry, enabling you to get the Crystal Ball! Return to the Fortuneteller—behind the Castle—and you'll be able, now, to enter the Castle.

Inside, talk to the warriors and then go to the chamber in the upper left. Climb the Stairs, and you'll acquire Shooting Star power! Descend, go to the upper right, and talk to the Head Warrior—who rebuffed you before! Now you can leave the Castle, cross the Beach, and enter the Tunnel at the end. Leap up and down ten times on the Switch and a land Bridge will form: cross, collect the Hearts on the other side, and say hello to some old Octot friends. Go left, then down, pick them all off, then jump left, off the Island. The Mud-o-Fishes will be easy pickin's, as will the Octots on the next Island over—beware the sneaky Mud-o-Fishes, though. When all are dead, the Gate will open. Cross the Bridge and you're out of the Tunnel. Walk to the left, then down. See the Mountain range above the lake? Walk left through the two Mountains from the top. Go to the hut beyond and talk to Po, then hustle to the Tunnel on the right. Lovely Loopers await, easily triggered and blasted—you only have to kill the ones on the bottom right. Exit right. Kill the Skulls here, but not where they hop: there's an Invisible Tile below the one in the upper right. Jump from it to the top Tile and get a Bat. Fight the Boneheads in the next room virtually as you did before—this time running to the right to kill the second one—and take a look at the Sinking Tiles in the chamber following it. You can't jump on the skull in the water—as opposed to the moving Skull on the Tiles—so don't even try. You've got to go around the Tiles before they sink, so *move* it, following the Skull to the bottom so it doesn't attack you. Naturally, the skull in the middle becomes a Switch when you hit the nearest Tile on the right; at least the Skull is kind enough to bop between you and the Switch so you can plug it. In the next room you'll find a Chest; get to it using the Invisible Tile between you and it. Your bravery will earn you a Bola. Exit to the top. Descend two flights of Stairs and cross the Sinking Tiles through the Lava. Pirate Ghouls attack you here: despite the fact that they *look* formidable, they're easy to beat. Hit the Tile next to the Sinking Tile above to get a Switch. Grrr . . . another Muddy and a Fly in the next room. You've got to kill the Muddy to continue. (Lure the Muddy out by crossing the Tiles on the left or right. Otherwise, the goo-ball will be tough to nail.) Exit to the top and you've got more Sinking Tiles. Make sure you get to the Tile in the upper left: it will reveal Hearts. After you expose them, hit the Clock—be sure the Heart Tile is more or less fully exposed: you'll go down with a half-submerged Tile. Next: Sinking Tiles and a Skull. The Tile top/left gives you a Switch: cross when the Skull is standing in front of the Gate. When you reach the land on the other side, hop left onto the Lava to reveal an Invisible Tile. Hop left and you'll get a Try-Your-Luck Sign. If you go up, you'll find a room filled with Pirate Ghouls. *Not* what you want! Don't go *up* in the Sinking Tile room. After you hit the Sign, to get back to the land on top, come back down two Sinking Tiles and head left. The Tiles there will give you a Switch; exit left. Acquire Medicine and Hearts, then return to the right. Cross the Tiles to the right and leave by that Gate. Kill the three Pirate Ghouls and continue right. (To draw them out, go to the far right and hop between those two Tiles there.) New enemies await in the next room: green Eyes. You've got to hit them to open their lids, at which point they make like the Flash and speed up. (Hit them from the *side*, though, or they'll rush at *you*!) You've only got a few seconds to zap them again, while their lids are open. Destroy all three and exit right, take the Stairs, exit up, fight the green Muddies in here—both usually give you power-ups—hit the Tile and exit up. Batter the Bull—the creature takes as many hits as a Muumu—trigger the Tile, exit up, and do the same in the Eye room. There are two Gates: exit up. Beat the next Bull, exit right, exit *right* from the next room, fight the Bull, go down a room, jump to any side at once to avoid the Looper, kill it and *stop right there*!

Don't go into the Gate. Head to the wall on the left and walk through at the center—no, there's no shadow indicating a passage . . . but it's there. Enter the Fountain room and leap on the waters. They'll hurl you to the top of the Mountain. There, you'll collect the Scroll and will be able to wake the Princess. Your Submarine will be repaired . . . and off you go!

Back at sea, head right to the Island and have a talk with the occupants. Head right and you'll be swallowed by a Whale. Talk to the lab assistant inside. You'll have to find the Lighter inside: take the upper right path, follow it around, down, and right. At the single Plank go up and submerge at the dark water. Go up, left, down *past* the dark water, left, and submerge. Go left, follow the water up—past the two single Planks—then turn left at the top. Come down around to the right, go down, skip the dark water, and stop in the pool there. Go to the top of the left Wall and sail right through it. Head down, get off the Submarine, and follow the path to the Lighter. Submerge at the dark water and you'll be back at the Raft. Talk to your companion, light a fire, and the Whale will spit you out. Then—and this is *totally* cool—put Dr. Jones's letter (attached to the instructions) in the sink and watch the secret message come up. Input the 747 MHz data, and you're on your way to the last section of the game!

Get off on the Island and have a talk with everyone in the village. Then go see the Chief. Head left from the settlement, talk to Parrot Peter, then reboard your Submarine. Travel to the left and down, enter the dark water, and sail up. Ride through the third Mountain from the top and moor there. Get a Worm from the fisherman in the Hut, then return to Peter and give it to him. You'll get a message: "Do me so far, do me?" Return to the Hut Island, walk down to the three Grasses on the bottom of the Island, turn left at the top one, and walk through the Mountain. This will bring you to the Tower. Enter and go to the Organ. Play the notes of Peter's message—starting with "Do" on the left—then walk through the Gate and go down the Stairs, then down the second set of Stairs. Walk through the Wall across from the Stairs and get a Big Heart. Exit to the bottom and you're on the Beach. Into the Tunnel you go . . .

The Jelly is a feint: the Wall on the *opposite* side, bottom, leads to a four-Heart chamber. (Different, obviously, from a four-chamber Heart!) The room here is full of Bats; only one of the red ones needs to die. (Run right at once and that one will chase you.) Exit left. The upper and lower Tiles give you more Hearts . . . but watch it! After the straight section in the middle, the Tile on top triggers an earthquake which will break up the Tiles. To get through, you must hit the trigger Tile in the upper left of the last vertical row—there are four Tiles; it's the top one. You'll have to jump some spaces, making your own shortcuts, to get through. (In other words, don't hit every Tile!) *Race* through the next two rooms, whose Walls fire Spears at you, then face the Silver Orb. Hit it with your Yo-Yo to send it rolling away, then hop it when it comes rolling back. (Make sure you hit the Tile near the door before crossing the corridor!) Next room: three doorways. Take the one on the bottom, stand just within the doorway to pick the green Loopers off, then kill the Bat and go to the Sign. Exit and take the Gate on the top. Kill the Rattus and walk to the upper right wall: you'll vanish into the floor and land in a room full of Stakes. They jab through the floor in straight lines, either side to side or up and down, so watch which way they're headed before you make your move—down and right is almost always the safest. Go to the Stairs in the lower left, climb them, and you'll be back in the Rattus room. Go to the hidden doorway in the top right section of the inner wall. That'll take you to the other side of the chamber: pass through the hidden door on the left. Looper-and-Bat room there: stand in the center and the snakes won't get you. Exit to the bottom and go left in the next room. (You'd have been in this room if you'd gone right in the three-Gate room. You could have gotten the Hearts that way . . . but you couldn't have made it to the exit on the left. If you *do* go in that room for Hearts, run in and out without stopping, or you'll be Speared!) You'll find yourself in a Tile room now, and you must be *patient*. Let the two Bats here come to you, 'cause when you move, it's earthquake time again! When they're dead, you'll notice with some alarm that the Gate hasn't opened. Fear not: the Trigger is on the bottom left. Run along the second row from the bottom. (You can do that without waiting to kill the Bats; chances are *very* good that they'll charge you from the front when you make this run.) In the corridor beyond, duck into the niche before the Bowling Ball squashes you flat. Move three niches next, then hit the Tile on top to get out, the one on bottom to get a Miracle Mirror. You'll need the latter against the two Fireball-spitting Pirate Ghouls in here. You can repel the Fireballs at any distance, though they only hurt the Ghouls when returned from less than half a screen length. Most important: don't let them catch you in a crossfire. Next room: a Rod in the middle of four Silver Orbs. Get right next to the Orb on the right before hitting it, otherwise you won't get the Rod and make it to the corridor of your choice before that Orb comes rocketing back. Which corridor do you want? The top is Sinking Tiles—including the one you're on. If you need Hearts, this is the place to go. Jump quickly upward to reveal the Switch: the Tiles on both sides give you Hearts. Exit and go to the bottom. Stand just inside the vertical corridor, facing down, shoot from there and jump. The Orb will pass under you. Hit the left Tile first. Enter and fight the green Loopers and Bats, then exit to the bottom. Fight the three Dodos, exit left, face another Bowling Ball. When dodging the Ball, don't go for Medicine in the next room *up*; you can't reach it yet. Instead, go *left*, hit the Tile in the room, leave by the top, and you're in a Bat room . . . with *lots* of Bats and Tiles—the non-Sinking sort! Hop your way through at once, without stopping, and none of the leathery fiends should hit you. Fight the two Bulls in the next room, use a Rod here, and exit to the left. (If you use the Tiles and exit right—which you won't have to fight the

Bulls in order to use—you'll uncover a Baseball Bat and Switch in the next chamber. This is the room on the *right* side of the chamber with the four Silver Orbs. If you go there, don't leave yet: hit a Rod and uncover the Minie. Exit to the bottom, get the Medicine, and leave.) After leaving the Bull room to the left, you'll find a chamber with two Silver Orbs. Next room to the left: Stakes! Run to the Tiles in the center and trigger the Switch *and* the Hearts . . . but watch out! The Stakes can come through the Tiles. Exit left and race ahead, grab the Hearts—more Stakes *follow* you—then jump the Spears as you wait to cross the Sinking Tile. After that: you've fought black and green Bowling Balls, so it's time for a red one. You can't get to the Hearts by outracing the Ball: you have to Yo-Yo it to pause it. Get the Hearts, rush back into the main corridor, and Yo-Yo the Ball again while it's still on your right. Continue stalling it as you head out the corridor. Exit left, then leave the next room at top. Look for the secret Gate on the right, then up on the top left. Hit the Tile and the Pirate Ship will sink. Sail to the next chapter!

Sail down/right and through the Island at the Eddy. Moor, enter the village, talk, set sail, and enter the dark water. Get a Big Heart from the small island. Sail through the maze—*not* the dark water—to the upper right and the Island with the Hut. After your visit, return to the dark water. Use it to go to the small Island with the Stairs leading to a Big Apple. Leave, visit the small Island with a single Tree, get out, look to the right, and you'll see an Island with an Eddy off shore. Sail into the Eddy. Enter the second dark water from the left, come down, enter the large dark water, go left to more dark water, go up, enter the Eddy left of the Island, follow the Submarine's directions, and submerge where the Sub tells you. Sail into the Tunnel, get out, and follow the corridor to the next set of chambers. Kill the four Loopers, enter the room and get the Anklets, which automatically increase your jumping ability, leap to the Tiles, exit at top, fight the six Muumus, exit left, cross the bottom Tiles to get the Anklet, then methodically kill the Octots and make your way through the Tile room.

Next: six Muumus surrounding a Chest, themselves acessible by Sinking Tiles. Get onto the middle Island when there's a gap in the Muumus and run ahead, turn, shoot, run ahead, etc. (Pick 'em off at the corners, before they turn.) On the top Sinking Tile, jump to the right for an Invisible Tile. Jump on another Invisible Tile to the right, hit the last Tile, and uncover Medicine. New foe in the next room: a Snail. Kill it, exit up . . . and face the wrath of its parent! (Get the Anklet in here before trying to reach the side Tiles. Anklet power vanishes after you leave each room.) Keep hopping from Tile to Tile until the thing charges, then blast it up close. Repeat; two barrages should do the trick—four, if you only have Yo-Yo. Next room to the left: nothing. Room beyond: three Snails. Next room: invisible Gate to the left *on top*—don't go in the invisible Gate with the shadow, just above left center. It's dark, but get the Anklet, jump on the Tile at the end, walk to the right—but *don't* leave the room or your Anklet will vanish—leap down to the strip of Land below, and hop on the Tile at the end to turn on the lights! Make your way through the room's many goodies—most notably, a Baseball. When you're done in here, leave by the right, reenter on the bottom left invisible Gate, and hit the last Tile in the room. Grab the Spikes, don them, hit A and B together and you'll dramatically kill all the Lobsters, enabling Mike to exit.

Next room: go along the top first to trigger the Anklet. Exit top after killing all the Snails and dodging the Cannon. The room above is fraught with Muumus and Tiles: let them come to you at the bottom to start, and kill them as you have before, only *faster*; you'll be slowed by the Tiles. The Tiles here give you nothing. Pair of Loopers up next, then the Wall Face boss: toss Baseballs when it opens its mouth, but make sure you jump its Spears! Beat the Face, and you're finished with this section.

Head toward the right and up in the maze, then go

down the Stairs for the Big Heart. When you exit the maze, go right through the Wall, then exit. Kill the three Rattus, go up and turn left at once to kill the first of the two Noctos. Quickly go right to nail the other. Why quickly? 'Cause knives are coming up through the floor, and they'll skewer you if you tarry! In the next room get the Asterisk and use it on the three sets of Loopers. (Nothing in the Tiles, alas.) Note: the *longer* you wait before pressing the B button when using the Asterisk, the longer it will go straight ahead before splitting. Next chamber: two sets of Loopers and a Purple Ball which behaves just like a Silver Orb. It'll cost you three Hearts to run through it, so you'd better learn to jump it! Next: Flies. Kill them with an Asterisk, hit the Tiles, exit to the left to collect the Hearts, then return to the Fly room and go up. Noctos next, and in the room after, Lizards and Fuzzies. Kill the Lizards *without* letting the Fuzzies hit you: they'll freeze your weapons for five seconds! Exit left and get the Hearts by going up on the right side—leap off the top of the screen—and heading down. When you get the Hearts, walk through the top of the Wall on the left. The boss in the next room fires projectiles in four directions: shoot your own weapons, making sure you're not in the way of the bullets!

And so it goes. You're not far from the conclusion of the game—which, if you've gotten this far, won't hold *too* many surprises (we don't want to spoil *all* the fun). The only thing you need to know is that the two giant Statues at the end of the game can only be beaten by Asterisks. Stay at the bottom center of the room to shoot, leaping to the side Tiles to avoid their fire.

If you're having trouble inside the spaceship, head up two screens, staying to the far right. Get the Ray Gun, go to the left side of the ship, fill up on Hearts, walk right one screen, then down one. Go to the right to get another Ray Gun, then go to left and enter the Warp. When you come to the four-Warp grid, use the one on the top. Go left, get Potion, then return to the Warp. Back on the grid, use the Warp on the right. When you re-materialize, use your Ray

Gun and cut a swath down. At the bottom, head left to the final Warp in this region. There's more spaceship to explore . . . but you're armed and dangerous and ready to rock 'n' roll!

Rating: B+

StarTropics is a magnificent Zeldalike addition to the videogaming library, perfect for players of all ages. One serious complaint: if you've advanced far in any level, you start *waaay* too far back again once you've lost all your lives. Give us a break, Nintendo!

Challenge: A
Graphics: B
Sound Effects: B– (great water effects)
Simulation: B

SUPER OFF ROAD

Type: Off-road Truck race

Objective: Steer your machine through obstacle-and mud-filled Courses.

Layout: Players look down at the Course from an angle of approximately 45 degrees. There are eight successively difficult Courses.

Heroes: The basic vehicle can be steered, accelerated, and braked. Power-up items, starting with the least expensive, are Nitro for a burst of speed; Tires for better traction; Shocks for better control over the obstacles; Accelcration to get you to top speed quicker; and Top Spccd, which increases the outside limits of speed your machine can attain.

Enemies: The other drivers . . . and the Course. There are Pits, Bouldcrs, Ramps, Hairpin Curves, Barricades, Bumps, and Water to slow you down.

Menu: Up to four Nintendo gamers can race against each other, either individually or in pairs of two.

Scoring: Winners earn money that can be used to soup up their machines.

Strategies: When it comes to adding to your car, the most important asset is *speed*. Hence, save up your earnings to buy Top Speed before purchasing anything else. After that, go for Tires, Accelerator, and Shocks. Since Nitro is relatively inexpensive, stock up on it with any extra money you have *after* you've bought Top Speed.

Before we look at the individual Courses, here are a few other general strategies. First, about Nitro. It's a useful tool, especially at the start: if you're in the front line, you can bolt ahead of the pack and not only take the lead, but use your Truck to impede the progress of your opponents. Conversely, if you're behind other cars, they will usually cluster toward the inside of the Course so they can hold the turns. Don't try to muscle your way past one or two Trucks by going on the inside; wait for a straightaway, then hit the Nitro and pass on the outside. With Nitro, obstacles such as Ramps can work for or against you. If you Nitro over one, you can get enough height and distance to leap Trucks ahead of you; unfortunately, if you don't hit the Ramp in or near the center, you may go flying off in a wrong—and fatal—direction. Needless to say, Nitro should also be used for less flamboyant maneuvers, such as passing or covering straightaways rapidly. And keep this in mind: your opponents also have access to Nitro! If a driver saves a burst for the very end of a close race and you don't, guess who's gonna be left in the dust!

When you take the curves, do so in as tight a turn as possible. Wide turns not only eat up more time, they increase your chances of spinning out and/or colliding with a Barricade on the other side.

In team modes, don't hesitate to "play dirty": there's no reason one Trucker can't smash into one or more "enemies" so his or her teammate can roll to victory! Even better, use a feint: one player can pretend to be the kamikaze driver, slowing up as if she or he is about to crash, just to draw an opponent's attention. Then the partner can do the actual smashing-up, leaving the fake kamikaze free to finish the race.

Now, as to the specific Courses—

Fandango: This one's shaped like a capital I, and because of the compactness of the Course, not to mention the Pits, Boulders, and Hairpin Curves, there's precious little opportunity for Nitro. The only three places you can conceivably use it are going clockwise along the top of the I—hit Nitro right before the Boulder and ride over it—going counterclockwise after crossing the Bumps on the lower right side of the I (after coming out of the bottom right Curve; use Nitro and take a wide arc into the gentle but narrow Curve that follows), and going *up* the Ramps in either direction at the finish line. (If you use Nitro going down those Ramps, it's unlikely you'll hold the Curve beyond.)

Sidewinder: A C-shaped course awaits, and it's as pocked and lumpy as the surface of the moon! It'll help if you have good Tires for this one. There are three spots to use Nitro: when you hit the straightaway coming out of the Curve in the lower left, going counterclockwise; when you've just come out of the Curve in *either* direction in the upper right; and along the bottom straightaway in either direction. Whichever way you're headed along the bottom straightaway, hug the Barricade: there are no Boulders or Pits here, and you'll be able to save time by making tight turns around the Curves.

Wipeout: As you navigate this 8-shaped Course, you'll find just two spots to get a real boost out of Nitro: coming out of the upper right Curve or the lower left Curve toward the center. Hit the afterburners before heading down either ramp and you'll go flying across the middle of the Course.

Big Dukes: You'll be driving through a lopsided 8, but the big deal here are the Ramps in the center. They form a box, meaning that whichever way you're coming, you've got to jump from one ramp to another. Make sure your Shocks are in good repair for this one! Nitro should be used as follows: going *up* the Ramp on the right or left; coming out of the turn in the lower right, headed toward the finish line—boost up, then hug the Curve after the finish line tightly and rocket over the Ramp; and once you've come off the top Ramp. Using Nitro on that last one will jet you to the upper right Curve. Stick close to the Barricade and *stay* close: the obstacles inside will slow you down less than those on the outside. Resist the temptation to use Nitro on the upper section of the Course: the obstacles will send you rockin' and rollin' all over the place!

Blaster: More or less resembling an LC, *Blaster* has a straightaway along the the back of the C section, and you can use Nitro coming or going. *Don't* use it if there are Trucks ahead: if you have to swerve around one—a devious player could slow and sucker you into a trap!—your Nitro-boosted path could carry you over the Ramp Barricade and into oblivion. In the L section on the left, use Nitro when you're driving out of the L on top or bottom. The boost will carry you over the Ramp Barricade with ease. Also, you can use the Bumps at the top of the L section to your advantage. If you've bought better Shocks, you can cut over these at a decent clip, leaving your rivals behind.

Cliffhanger: A backward C with two straightaways means the going will be fast here. Nitro your way up the rightside Ramps—don't try it going down, though!—and when you cross the top straightaway in either direction. (Be careful here driving right to left with Nitro: the leftside turn is much tighter than the one on the right, and you may plow into the Barricade. Using Nitro when you're crossing to the right will not only get you across the top straightaway, but will carry you well down the right side.) *Very* experienced drivers can use Nitro when you're driving from left to right over the back-to-back Ramps below the upper straightaway: if you hit it just before going up the first Ramp (the one on the left), and cut down hard when you turn using the right-side Ramp Barricade, you can really pick up ground here. However, most players end up shooting straight up that right Ramp Barricade, missing the turn, so be careful!

Huevos Grande: Another C-shaped Course, this track has Water on the top and in the center. Force your foes into the Water on top—don't let them do likewise! If the coast is clear, you can drive through the center of the straightaway, avoiding the Water altogether. There are three good spots for Nitro: crossing the central Water from right to left—do the Nitro boost when you're *on* the Ramp to the right—and going up or down the straightaway on the left. Experienced drivers can try Nitro on the bottom straightaway, but the Ramp on the left and Pit on the right can throw you off-course.

Hurricane Gulch: The best way to describe this Course is a J on its side, with the straightaway on top. Use Nitro in the upper left corner when you're driving right, and in the upper right when headed left; in both cases, hit the button when you're on *top* of the Ramp about to scoot down. The Ramp on the left has a smaller Ramp on its inside face. You want to use Nitro just *before* you hit this smaller Ramp, then ride up it and over the Water. The left side is a real problem spot here, since there's a Barricade in the middle. When coming along this section from bottom to top, stay on the *left* side of the central Barricade. When going down this area, stay to the *right* of the central Barricade. (If you stay on the left side while driving from top to bottom, the Ramp on top will almost certainly send you smack into the outside Barricade, unless you're crawling. And if you *are* crawling, you'll never win on this Course!)

Rating: B

There are plenty of auto racing games available for the NES, and this one can't escape that element of déjà vu.

However, the Courses are corkers, and the fact that a quartet of racers can play at once is a definite advantage.

Challenge: B+
Graphics: B
Sound Effects: B
Simulation: B

TEENAGE MUTANT NINJA TURTLES II—THE ARCADE GAME

Type: Martial arts quest

Objective: Shredder has hired the best talent in the universe to try and slay the Turtles: a pair of bounty hunters who have never been defeated. The Turtles must fight their way to these bruisers, then defeat Shredder himself in his Technodrome.

Layout: The game scrolls horizontally as you fight through seven different scenes.

Heroes: You can choose from one of four Turtles, each of whom has different abilities. These are described in the instructions. Hits rob the Turtles of energy, which only Pizza can replenish. The Turtles also ride Skateboards in Scene Four: your 'board follows you automatically when you jump in this phase.

Enemies: You'll meet your enemies as follows (once they're introduced, they may appear on any subsequent screen): Scene One: Knife Foot, Katana Foot, Karate Foot, Roadkill Rodney, and Machine Gun Foot (Bowling Balls do *not* hurt your enemies); Rocksteady is the boss. Scene Two: Boomerang Foot, Hammer Foot, Dynamite Foot, Bebop, Mouser, and Tora; Professor Stockman is the boss. Scene Three: Frosty and Snowball Foot; Baxter Stockman (as a fly) is the boss. Scene Four: Spear Foot, Big Bomb Foot, Motorcycle Foot, Blackhawks; tire-throwing Tired Fighters are the bosses. Scene Five: Laser Poles, Flippers, Tubular Transport; Stone Warrior is the boss. Scene Six: Blade, Vincent Van Growl, Venom Scorpions; Shogun Warrior is the boss. Scene Seven: Blizzard Blowers, Lasers; Stone Warrior is the boss. The remainder of the bad-guy heavyweights, including Shredder, also await you here.

Menu: One or two players can fight simultaneously. (In the two-player mode, more enemies will attack in each wave than in a one-player game.)

Scoring: One point is awarded for each foe you kill.

Strategies: In general, try not to let enemies collect on your left and right. Leap in order to keep them on one side; that makes them easier to slay.

Scene One: The ordinary Foot soldiers are easy enough to knock apart. As for the Knife Foot soldiers, they cock their arms before throwing, so you have a second to jump and avoid their blades. When you reach the Stairs, jump over the first Bowling Ball and stay to the right of the screen. Keep your Turtle *behind* the three Roadkills at the end of the round: not only do they fire beams, they unleash electrical lassos which, if they connect, will drain your shelled hero of mucho energy. Meet them by standing at the door until they emerge, then facing left and whacking them. You'll take out one for sure; muscle another into the lower right corner and destroy it, then deal with the last one. Katana Foot soldiers and Machine Gun Foot soldiers attack when you reach April; kill the two Katanas, then move to the left and beat the gunners before they can fire. They're followed by the arrival of Rocksteady. Stand to the right of the bookcase for his dramatic arrival: when he steps from the Earth Digger, get in your hits and keep him to the right. If he knocks you back, leap up to draw his gunfire into the air, then charge him and kick again. He'll charge; when he does, leap and get behind him, and hit away!

Scene Two: Karate Foot soldiers attack first—the first one from the left, throwing a Manhole cover at you. Check out the Parking Meter here: when you hit it, it goes flying and is a very effective weapon against nearby foes. When you face the Dynamite Foot soldier next, don't try to destroy the explosives before they go off; just get out of the way! (Don't let them work you into a corner, or you'll have two or three sticks hurled at you simultaneously!) Fight the Karate Foot soldiers, then go to the floor above for the Pizza. Come down the street—Karates and Boomerangs leap from the window—but look out for the two Pizza Hut signs on the wall facing you at the bottom: there are Boomerang soldiers waiting behind both. (Nice little plugola for the restaurant chain, huh? You decide: a touch of realism or tacky product placement?) Make sure you leap the Boomerangs as they're thrown *and* when they come back at you. You'll tackle a few more Karate Foot and Boomerang Foot soldiers—watch out for the soldier who comes from the Manhole after the wrecked car—then face Bebop: use your jump kick both to get away from him, his gun (the Beam emerges as bullets and spreads out), *and* to land back down on his ugly face. If you get in close and hack at him, he'll pound you back. Also, don't fall in the Manhole until you've beaten him; it'll cost you a lot of energy! The Manhole contains numerous soldiers—the new ones here are Hammer Foot soldiers, who swing croquet-type mallets at you—as well as Mousers: when these creatures eat their way through the walls, get to the *right.* Hit them as they emerge, and they'll fly to the far right. Hit them again there and it's over for them. There are three waves of Mousers, interspersed with soldiers . . .

and, after the third wave, metal Bars that rise and fall from the top right of the screen. You've got to get past them while they're up to meet the last wave of Mousers and then Professor Stockman, who's riding around in a hovercraft. Hit the Mousers he drops, and slash at the vehicle when it's low. Also use repeated jump kicks to get up to the vehicle whenever it rises.

Scene Three: There's snow . . . lots of it. Keep an eye on the white ground for shadows of falling (and deadly) Boulders. After you fight the first bunch of Karate soldiers, get to the *very* bottom of the screen to avoid the Snow Plow that comes barreling from the right. Next, watch out for those little mounds: there just might be an open Manhole underneath! (Don't let enemies punch you into them either; the result will be the same as if you strolled in yourself!) You'll face three Frosties in a moment—at the ubiquitous Pizza Hut sign. The snowmen hop and shoot Turtle-seeking missiles. Since you can knock down their projectiles, it's a good idea to stay on the ground and smack at the explosives, then whack at the snowmen when they come down. Keep them both on the same side of the screen, even if you have to leap over them to accomplish that. (Note: if you try to beat them by jumping up and hitting them, you won't be able to deflect their bombs as effectively.) Hit the Frosties until they melt, then kill the robots that were inside the snow. You'll face a Snowball Foot next—his Snowballs are lethal, though you can knock them down, unless you're caught in a crossfire—more Karate Foot soldiers, then get down to the bottom of the screen again to avoid a second Snowplow. It's followed by Snowball Foot soldiers and at—guess what?—the Pizza Hut sign, four more Frosties, which come at you in pairs of two. After fresh Boulders fall from the sky, and a small army of Katana Foot soldiers attack, rush to the far right and get in your hits on Tora's back. He'll catch Boulders that fall from the sky and fling them at you, *and* turn his fists on you. Keep airborne as much as possible both to avoid his attack, and hit him in the head and chest. He's tough, and it's going to take a lot of blows to bring him down!

On to the parking lot: like the Parking Meters before, fight enemies using the Cones (golf at them) and Barrels (hit them and they'll explode a moment later—when you've had a chance to get away so you're not destroyed in the blast). After you fight Knife Foot and Karate Foot soldiers, there'll be a Machine Gun soldier assault. Before they arrive, though, make sure you're on the *bottom* of the screen: a parked blue car will tear out, straight toward the bottom. Leap to the left and you'll be okay. More soldiers attack, followed by a red car racing down, additional Machine Gunners, Katanas who rush from a van—use the Drum to blast 'em—and finally the winged Baxter. He's going to fly around hurling projectiles at you. You *can* leap up and hit him, but you may run into the Stars he's throwing. Best bet: stay on the ground and knock down the Stars, wait for him to charge you—which he'll do regularly—and hit him then. Jump up *only* after a wave of Stars, then brace for another wave after you've gotten in your hit.

Scene Four: After a few old friends, you'll fight Spear Foot soldiers; they're easy to defeat using your weapon. Stick to the bottom of the screen after you beat the first bunch of Spearsters, to keep from being plowed under by a car. Hammers have at you; when you've beaten them, rush to the right, turn left, and bash the Rodneys as they pop from the roadway. Dynamiters and other retreads return; after the next bunch of Spear throwers, head to the bottom to avoid another car. When you see the big Tire on top of the road, it means the Big Foot Bombers are coming. These big guys look more intimidating than they are. They hurl Cruise-size missiles at you, but if you lure the killers over—they'll only throw their bombs when they're near—and leap the missiles, the thugs will be virtually defenseless. Despite their size, you can pound these fellahs easily—and best of all, they don't rearm after tossing their one explosive. Motorcycle Foot soldiers will pass by next; stay on the very bottom of the screen and they won't notice you—except for the last one, which'll run right through you . . . a small price to pay for getting through this section otherwise unscathed. More familiar soldiers attack until you reach the Tired Fighters. The pile of Tires on the right is full of these guys; stay to the right and attack the first wave from behind as soon as they've tossed their radials. Non-Tire soldiers will run at you from the right; when you've killed them, hurry to the right since more Tire-throwers will emerge. When you've defeated them all, you'll mount a Skateboard and race through the streets while Blackhawk Helicopters zip by, shooting bullets and an occasional rocket at you. These come in pairs, the second after the first has been beaten—they never arrive together. Use the jump kick to bring them down. Machine Gunners on Skateboards will attack, followed by Boomerangers and another pair of choppers. Then, it's on to . . .

Scene Five: Smash the Mousers that dig up through the floor on the upper left, take care of the Karate soldiers, fight the Mousers emerging from the floor on the upper right, then hop up to the high floor on the right. (The first new foes, Laser Beams, cut down across the screen from the center. If you're not on the higher floor, you'll be decimated!) Naturally, you'll be attacked by soldiers up here—Knife, Machine Gun, then Karate—but you'll be able to deal with them. After you leave the upper floor, Spears throwers attack—don't let them knock you left into the Lasers—and then Flippers arrive. These are robots that fall from overhead, open their shells, sprout legs, and fire Lasers. Like the first level Roadkills, they only shoot forward; two hits will take each Flipper out. But be careful: they'll work like a pack of dogs to surround you. If that happens, jump kick outta there. Use the Barrels on the two sets of Karates who crash through the second and fourth Windows, respectively. Moments later, Tubular Transports pour from an Earth Digger. These insectlike Helicopters also shoot Lasers, but if you go to the upper right and stand facing the Digger, you'll be above their line of fire. Just stand there, slashing away, waiting for them to fly at you. The first two will do that . . . then you'll have to inch down to the center right to hit the third. When it's been destroyed, move down slowly, staying on the right, and slowly stalk the fourth to the left. A second wave will emerge; rush back to the upper right and repeat. (Sometimes this doesn't work. If you find yourself getting hit in the upper right, simply leap out of the line of fire, wait till the things stand still and hover for a moment, pick one out, destroy it, then get the heck out of the way. Repeat for each.)

No sooner have you defeated them—as well as more soldiers—than you come upon the Laser Poles, which flit up and down on the right, firing Beams (the left one to the left, the one on the right to the right). To beat them, simply jump between them and hit them repeatedly. When they've been deactivated, you'll fight the flame-throwing Stone Warrior. The strategy here is simple: make like a Ping-Pong ball, tracing a giant V course across the screen. Leap over the boss to avoid his burps of flame and hit him as you pass overhead. (If you stay in real close to the lug, he won't even fire at you. It's only when you get far away that he tries to singe you.) Jump back—kicking him again as you fly over—and repeat until he's been reduced to a Pebble Warrior. You'll get a slice of Pizza before you face the enemy, which is fortunate: it'll take a *lot* of hits to destroy him!

Scene Six: After the Karate Foot soldiers—stay in the upper right corner to fight them—you must deal with Blade fighters. Not only are their knives deadly, these hulks leap—meaning that they not only spit knives ahead when they're on the ground, they drop them when they're airborne. Jump when they do and hack at them as you pass in midair, then hit them when you land behind them. Stay in the upper right after you beat them and deal with the

Karates. When you reach the Windows, stay alert: the Karate Foot soldiers arrive in novel fashion by bursting up through the floor. The holes they leave are dangerous, so don't fall in. Watch out for the Japanese writing on the wall: shortly after that, Spikes will explode from the floor. Trigger them by taking slow, tentative steps ahead, then leaping to the left when the Spikes appear. When the floor changes from tile back to wood, expect an attack from Vincent Van Growl, a huge tiger. Whack him on the nose and he'll retreat a bit; rush in, hit him again, and he'll slip back a little more. Repeat until he vanishes. If you miss and he leaps at you, jump over him, turn, and resume your attack.

Within moments huge Venom Scorpions will scuttle your way. Their tails are lethal, of course, but they also spit Venom. You don't want to jump these creatures, or you'll face their tails. Instead, stand just below the center of the screen, on the right, and hit them over and over on the head. The boss here is the Shogun Warrior. This brute's got a new twist: his head twists right off and attacks you separately from his body. Jump kick the Shogun when his head is attached; when it becomes airborne, watch the pattern it describes—it's the same figure eight pattern over and over—leap it, then resume your assault on its owner. Needless to say, get the Pizza here!

Scene Seven: Boomerangers first, Laser Poles second—both firing left this time; jump behind them—a Laser Beam right after them (leap it), Katana Foot soldiers next—don't let them push you into the Beam—Karates after. Blizzard Blowers are next: these rise from the ground to freeze you, so stay to the bottom of the screen after you tangle with the Karate Foot soldiers and weave up and down to get through them. Tangle with the Knife chuckers, more Flippers, two more Laser Poles firing left—get the back one first, then move up to the front one—Machine Gunners, Katanas, another Laser Beam, more Katanas, and Blizzard Blowers. When you weave past these, you'll ride an elevator for a bit. Get to the bottom: Bowling Balls will roll from the top down. Watch them, and jump back to the top when they close in on the bottom, then return to the bottom and stay there. Get the Pizza, fight the Machine Gunners, Rodneys, Knife throwers, more Rodneys, Hammers, Karates, and then—back away from that red door, dude! Get to the bottom of the screen as Stone Warrior number two comes crashing through. This one fires hefty missiles from his gun, but otherwise is just like the one before. Beat him the same way, only don't hit those Beams across the door on the right: they'll fry you! Win here and those Beams will disappear; enter and fight Krang. Do the same jumping V attack, avoiding Krang's optical Beam in the process; watch out when he crouches, too, because that means he's about to fire his fist at you, low and parallel to the floor. (Incidentally, *don't* do a jump kick until *after* he's fired a Beam. If you happen to collide with it on your way down, it'll bounce you back, not only causing you to waste a jump, but draining your energy.) When he dies, Shredder will materialize . . . and then split in two! Jump kick at the Helmets to knock the one off the *real* Shredder: otherwise, you won't know who to kill. And if you fail to destroy the real Shredder, the clones will just keep reappearing! Whatever you do, stay *behind* the fiend: if you're caught in his ray, you'll be turned back into a Turtle and will lose a life.

If all else fails . . . here's a code that will start you with ten Turtles. During the title screen, push up, right, right, down, down, down, left, left, left, left, B, A, Start. If you want ten Turtles *and* stage select, input B, A, B, A, up, down, B, A, left, right, B, A, Start. (When you hit the last B, A, Start combination, press the buttons in that order but *hold* them down as you do so.) You'll have to work fast to get it all in before the title screen disappears . . . but it's worth it, *n'est ce pas*? (Note: the former may need to be tried several times before you get the hang of it, while the latter can be difficult to get to work. When it *does* work, you'll get a "Stage Select" prompt, which you can change by pressing the pad left or right. Hit the A button to go to the stage you choose. The menu offers ten stages; the game breaks several of the scenes into two parts. If you want to go to Scene Seven, you should ask for ten. Actually, with both ten-life options, you're really getting many more lives than that: when you continue, you'll start at the level you were at with nine *new* lives!)

Rating: C+

Not as much fun as the original, where the Turtles were more compact and *tougher*. The cast of characters is not as diverse as they might have been, and the bosses, though challenging, are much too similar.

Challenge: B−

Graphics: C (good . . . but there's a *lot* of image breakup when figures overlap, such as in the Stockman phase of Scene Two)

Sound Effects: B−

Simulation: C+

TETRIS

Type: Place odd shapes into neat piles

Objective: Imagine yourself at the bottom of a swimming pool with someone dropping bricks and other debris from above. That'll give you an idea what *Tetris* is like! Geometric shapes known as Tetrads fall from above. If you can maneuver them so that one or more segments form an unbroken horizontal Line, that Line will disappear and any Tetrads stacked above it will fall. However, if the screen fills up with Tetrads—which is what'll happen if you let them form *broken* Lines, that is, Lines with gaps in them—and a part of any piece touches the top, the game ends.

Layout: There's no scroll; just the screen and its hail of Tetrads.

Heroes: There are seven kinds of Tetrads: Z-Block, Z-Block Reverse, T-Block, L-Block, L-Block Reverse, Four-Square, and Four-Bar. You can rotate these so that the composite Blocks of any Tetrad are pointing up, down, or sideways, and you can shift the Tetrads to the left or right of the screen. Once they touch down on the base of the screen *or* on an unfinished Line of Tetrads, you have a second to slide the piece to the left or right . . . including beneath overhanging Blocks of other Tetrads if you wish. The game allows you to see what Tetrad is "on-deck" as one piece is falling. Tetrads fall one at a time, but speed up as you reach each new level.

Enemies: Only the mounting pile of Tetrads!

Menu: There are nine different speed levels to which you advance as you play. Unlike the Tengen version of *Tetris*—which is no longer for sale, though it can still be found at many rental locations—this version is for one player only. (The Tengen cartridge offered a split screen in which two players competed using the same Tetrads simultaneously.)

Scoring: Erasing Lines gets you points, but the real trick is to erase four at once; a.k.a., get a Tetris. Tetris scores increase by 1200 points each on subsequent levels.

Strategies: Only general strategies apply, since every screen will be different depending upon how you place the Tetrads. *Tetris* is pretty much a game of common sense—for instance, only a Four-Bar Tetrad can complete a Tetris—but there are still a few strategies that can be used in most situations:

- If you get one of the Z-Blocks at the start, move it to one side or the other and slide the next piece under its open end; for example, the base of an L-Block or L-Block Reverse will fit nicely underneath the Z-Block or Z-Block Reverse, respectively. T-Blocks can also be used in this manner, as can Four-Bars if you've got a lot of room to turn it on its side. If you get the Z-Blocks later in the round, when Tetrads are piling up, *don't* place them so there's an empty space beneath them unless you have absolutely no choice. That space will be trapped there, making it impossible for you to finish the Line. Push Z-Blocks to any flat surface at least two Blocks long and wait for the next L-Block.

- Try, always, to leave a Block sticking up *somewhere* on a flat surface. That will give you a place to rest a Z-Block, and will save you the trouble of having to stand a Z-Block on end and then slide another piece under it.

- Four-Squares and L-Blocks/L-Blocks Reverse are natural companions. If they come in that order, you can turn the base of the L-Blocks up and drop it on the left or right side of the Four-Square.

- If a T Block is descending, and a Z-Block is coming down next, remember that the former can be placed in many more places and positions than the latter. In other words, don't drop a T-Block into a space that is the only one on the screen that would have accommodated a Z-Block! That's how gaps get formed and Lines start piling up!

- When a Four-Bar Tetrad comes along, don't automatically drop it on end somewhere to complete a Line or two. *Resist* those impulses to clear away one, two, and three Lines, especially in the early going. It's better to drop a Four-Bar Tetrad horizontally, if you have a long enough area for it; build up the pile and use the *next* Four-Bar to polish off four lines at once and get a Tetris.

- There's nothing wrong with dropping Tetrads into spots and trapping open space beneath them . . . provided that by putting the Tetrad there, you will eliminate the lines it finishes—and thus that Tetrad—making the open space acessible again. For instance, it's okay to place a T-Block Tetrad in a space large enough for an upside-down L-Block, provided the entire T-Block disappears when the Lines do.

- One very valuable move with Four-Bars often works when you have a mess of a pile on the screen: if there are *two* four-Block-wide gaps one atop another, and they're covered by a partial Line, you can slide a Four-Bar through an opening by dropping it vertically, then quickly rotating it so that it's horizontal. In this way you can fill the bottommost of the four-Block gaps. Other Tetrads can be used in this fashion since they're wider than they are tall. However, only the Four-Bar can be slipped through an opening a single Block wide.

- If things are getting tight at the top of the screen, push Tetrads to the sides as much as possible. The higher the pile gets, the tougher it will be to do that. If you let the pile build in the middle, it'll be awfully difficult to slide Tetrads to the sides *and* rotate them later on.

- When you reach level nine, the name of the game is to notice what piece is coming next, see where you want to put it, rotate it *fast* as soon as it appears, and *then* shove it into place. Don't try moving it above where it belongs and then rotating it: turning a Tetrad takes room, and there's usually more of that the higher the piece is on the screen.

- Relative to the above, at the risk of stating the obvious, one of the worst moves you can make, a real dumb bunny of a maneuver, is to place a Four-Bar *upright* if your pile has reached the top half of the screen. You'll have a real problem shifting subsequent Tetrads around it. Another seriously bad move is to leave a one-Block-wide column—that is, a column for a Flat Tetrad—on the far left or right. If the center section builds up, you won't be able to get a Four-Bar Tetrad on end and over there . . . especially if the pile is eight or more unfinished Lines deep! A *good* move as the game speeds up is to fill in the sides first, simply because they *are* the toughest to get to.

- Don't waste a pair of Four-Bars in an opening where a Four-Square will do . . . unless, by so doing, you can get a Tetris. If you've got a two-Block-wide opening, and two Four-Bars on the way—one falling, one on deck—and the pile is still low, it's best to use the Four-Bars elsewhere: to start building up another area for your next Tetris, and wait for a pair of Four-Squares.

- If you see a Four-Square on deck, make sure you have a two-Block-wide surface on which to drop it! Otherwise, you'll trap empty space beneath it. If you don't have a place for it, try and use the Tetrad that's falling to *create* a spot for it . . . obviously, without trapping an open area beneath *it*.

- No place to put a Z-Block? That happens, on occasion. In that case, try to trap a space no more than a single Block—by putting it endwise into a slot better suited to an L-Block, for example. However, make sure that in making the best of an untimely Z-block, you don't botch your chances to finish up a Tetris. If you're on the verge of finishing up four Lines on the bottom, place the Z-Block somewhere on top to keep the corridor open for making that Tetris.

- Unless you're trying to construct the framework for a Tetris, do *not* try to change the shape of an inverted L-Block opening in the Lines by adding a Tetrad to the lip of the opening so that only a Four-Bar Tetrad will now fit. On some boards, waiting for a Four-Bar can take ages!

Rating: A

How can we give the game an A when its technical aspects are merely average? Truth is, the game doesn't *strive* for a spectacular, realistic look . . . it's stripped down for cerebral action! *Tetris* is an original and brilliant classic, with levels of difficulty to please every player.

Challenge: A
Graphics: C
Sound Effects: C
Simulation: C

TOTAL RECALL

Type: Science fiction quest

Objective: "They stole his mind," says the advertisement. "Now he wants it back." Maybe he could get a better one? Loutish Dennis Quaid is a construction worker . . . or is he? Is the brawny dude really an amnesiac secret agent who worked on the planet Mars? Your job is to travel around Quaid's home on Earth and the seediest spots on Mars to find out.

Layout: The screen scrolls from side to side as Quaid journeys around both planets. There are "On Foot" screens, as he walks around the two worlds, and an "In Transit" screen, in which he pilots a vehicle from Earth to Mars.

Heroes: Quaid can walk, crouch, jump, punch, and use the various weapons he finds as he travels. These are listed in the instructions and are discussed below. He will also find Energy Canisters during the game, as well as 1-Ups. At the controls of his Car, Quaid can fly forward or backward, rise or fall, fire weapons or drop Mines.

Enemies: There are many, from simple street thugs to your turncoat wife to Martian mutants.

Menu: Just the one-player game.

Scoring: Every clobbered enemy earns you points.

Strategies: Go right, fight the punks in the Alley, then enter the Theater on the right. Sit through the credits—if you do, you'll get a 1-Up!—and leave, duck to avoid the gunman in the Trashcan, make your way right, enter the next Alley, and after defeating the agents here, stand on the Trashcan, jump onto the Pipe to the left, and make your way along the network of Pipes to the lower Pipe on the right. Leap to the Ledge for mega-energy! Exit and you'll start fighting corrupt Police. It's always best to battle them while standing *nearly* all the way to the left or right—to the left if you're headed that way, ditto for the right. Just leave enough room for the ones who leap behind you to fit there: if you're all the way over and they land *on* you, you'll be hit. At the end of the street climb the Stairs, leaping the Bombs. Head left, beat up the crooked Police who attack. You'll fight them in front of two buildings: stand between the doors of both so you can hit them on whichever side they land. Enter the door where the hand is pointing down: that's your apartment; crouch near the door. When your "wife" enters from the right, firing her gun, hit her then stay behind her, punching her repeatedly in the back. Hit her enough and you'll get her gun: blast her—from a distance, since she can still kick—and leave before the gun-toting Richter arrives. (If he shows up before you leave, you'll have to run through his constant stream of fire to escape. It can be done . . . but it'll cost you aaaa *lot* of energy.)

In the fluoroscope phase, beat the first guy by crouching under the first diagonal overhead bar and crouch just under the yellow part. Shoot and kill the first "Skeleton"; the Orb overhead won't hit you here. After the first bag o' marrow is dead, kneel under the second beam, also under the yellow portion, and the detached Orb won't get you. When you've killed the second guy, keep up a repeated fire on the Orb to destroy it. You'll have two more bone-bodies to defeat, while avoiding the fire of the next Orb, which will detach and also come flying your way. (You can destroy it too, or avoid it:

there's only this Orb and one more above, so they won't bug you much.) Bust through the glass when the Skeletons are dead and head for the Subway.

There, crouch to hit the Dogs, rise and rush at each agent between bullets—they only attack one at a time—hit him, and as soon as he runs past, get behind him and hit him in the back twice. He'll drop his gun and all you have to do then is crouch. Every agent will always attack you, and you'll be able to defeat him. Squatting also ensures that you can beat off any Dogs that rush at you. If you happen to get hit, you'll have to tap the pad quickly from left to right to shake the animal off; otherwise they'll sap your energy quickly. One good bit of news, though: you can get to the Canisters on top by hopping to the couplings between cars, leaping to the top, and beating up the red-clad agents who attack there. A couple of punches will do-in these unarmed dudes. You can then collect the Canisters at your leisure. You'll fight four agents in all on the platform below, and a steady stream of Dogs. Enter the train door indicated by the hand.

When you reach the Cement Factory, climb up the right side, get the gun, then come back down. Go up the leftside Ladders. On the third floor, you'll face five Crushers coming down at you. Get through these using stop-and-go—you'll have to stand more to the right between each Crusher than you think: if you position yourself dead-center between them, you'll be hit. At the end of the room climb down. Go right at the bottom and fight the two Bums. Climb all the way to the top, walk left, stop-and-go through the new Crushers, go left, fight the Bums, and jump *over* the cooking fire. Go down. At the very bottom you have to fight the Hat Bum. Naturally, it's no ordinary chapeau he's wearing: it's a Boomerang Hat. To beat him, take a look at the two barred windows that are part of the background scenery. Stand between them, slightly toward the right, and kneel facing the Hat man. When he throws the Hat, it'll pass over you then swing back, directly toward your legs. Jump it, all the while keeping up a steady fire at the killer. It'll take 16 or 17 hits to get rid of him, but it's worth it! Return to the beginning of the Cement Factory after you win here . . . but be prepared to fight the people who were sitting quietly before. Leaderless now, they'll be in a fine snit! Leap the Cooking Pot to get out.

You'll find yourself at the Flight Terminal now. Stay away from the Windows here, and don't fire at them: a vacuum is the last thing you want to create! Leap to the first Beam, use your gun to hit the Orb, and proceed to the next room. Kill the sentry and destroy the Orb quickly, move to the third room (similar to the first), and then to the last (a blend of the first three). You shouldn't have much difficulty here. There are no "safe places"; shooting quickly and accurately are your only protection.

The Transit Hub is next, and you've got to pass through it three times to exit. Head to the right, grabbing Canisters and avoiding the light-colored Mines. You've an endless supply of bullets, so shoot everything that gets in your way. In the next section, you'll face Cats as tenacious as the Dogs you fought before—deal with them the same way—as well as angry Mutants. You can only exit the door at the end when someone else opens it, so be prepared to leap through. Once you're through, head right, shoot the Martian, enter the Drain, go right, and be ready to jump the Bone piles you encounter: if you happen to touch them, they'll become Skeletons and attack you. Stop-and-go through the Boulders, and *don't* enter the door. Go to the far right, leap, and shoot the Driver in the head when he appears in his Arnold-crushing vehicle. When the drill has been stilled, enter the Pyramid. Only quick shooting will get you through the ground-based and airborne foes, while good timing will allow you to survive the Electric Sparks ahead. When you finally reach the boss, work your way to his right—otherwise, your bullets will strike the Martian machine—stand face to face, and blast him.

The most important thing to know is the second secret of the Theater. Once you reach Mars, if you die there you can return with no problem. Simply enter the Theater and you'll warp right back to the Red Planet. (This won't work if you've shut off the game, though: *Total Recall* has no battery!)

Rating: D

Pretty boring game made from a pretty dumb movie. The fighting is imprecise because the figures are *clunky*, and the action is dull and repetitious.

Challenge: D+

Graphics: F+ (very cartoonish with no details; only the neat interscene graphics keep it from getting an F)

Sound Effects: C (okay music, but uninspired effects)

Simulation: D−

ZELDA II: THE ADVENTURE OF LINK

Type: Fantasy quest

Objective: Ganon's back, and once again he's lashed out at Zelda. Link, now sixteen years old, sets out to save her; to accomplish this, he must make his way through seven Palaces.

Layout: The view is from overhead as Link journeys from place to place, but changes to a sideview whenever he encounters Ganon's minions and must do battle with them. Unlike the first game in the series, *The Legend of Zelda*, Hyrule is now divided into two regions, West Hyrule and East Hyrule.

Heroes: Link is a more complex fellow these days, with three facets to his abilities: Attack, Magic, and Life. *Attack* refers to the power of his Sword—which he can wield while standing or squatting, and can learn to thrust up or down. Magic pertains to the supernatural talents he will acquire as he travels, while Life refers to his physical energy. As in the previous game, Fairies add to Link's Life gauge. Specific items that add to Link's abilities will be discussed in *Strategies* as necessary.

Enemies: From living Skeletons to evil Knights, Hyrule is overpopulated with rotten souls similar to those in the first game. They will be referred to as we go along.

Menu: There is only the one-player game.

Scoring: You earn strength and abilities as you travel.

Strategies: For the most part it's self-evident how to fight foes in this game, so we won't go into battle tactics *unless* special maneuvers are called for. Also, you should make a map of your travels. You'll have to retrace your steps numerous times, which'll be easier if you can spot landmarks along the way. When you begin the adventure, you're in the Castle in West Hyrule. Exit to the right and follow the road to the upper right. When it levels off, head down until you reach the village of Rauru, a little clump of structures to your left. Talk it up with the people there for clues, and make sure that in *every* town you visit, you talk to a lady in orange clothes—she'll fill your Magic Containers—and another in red (if you go inside with her, she'll replenish your Life Containers). In Rauru be sure to stop at the fifth building, located after the Bridge. Go downstairs and get the Magic Shield

Leave Rauru heading back up the road. To the upper left of the straight section of road—where it levels off—you'll find a Forest. Enter and claim the Treasure Bag, thus boosting Link's Life Level. Travel to the right until you come to a Cave—the exit will be visible first; continue on a bit to find the entrance. Enter and proceed with caution: it's quite dark, and you never know when a foe will sneak up on you—a Lowder, for instance, though if you watch carefully, you can just make out its feet. When you exit, head to the upper right and you'll find yourself at the first Palace.

Palace One: Enter the Palace (a.k.a. Parapa Palace), take the Elevator to the right down to the second level, and head left until you reach the Key. Take it and go right, past the Elevator that brought you here, past the next Elevator to a third lift; a Fairy beyond it will restore your Life, after which you must ride the Elevator up, head right, and claim a pair of Keys. You should also use your Sword against the Statue after the third Key: it will respond with a magic-boost! When you're finished here, return to level below, head toward the Elevator on the left and ride it down. Go left, racing across the Bridge; it'll collapse after a moment, so don't tarry! Collect the Candle at the far end of the corridor, then go right, ride the Elevator back up one level, head right, and take the last Elevator down. Walk right and fight the Temple Guardian Horsehead: defeat the equine evildoer by staying on the left side of the screen and leaping up when the creature is within range, stabbing it in the head. Its death will reward you with your first Crystal: place it in its setting in the area to the right.

You're finished in the Palace, but before you go to Palace Two there are power-up items to get. If you follow the road on the *right* below the Palace, taking it straight down, you'll come to a patch of Grass—you can't miss it, since the road *ends* there! Inside is a Heart Container. It's also suggested that you make a side trip to the Castle where you began the quest: below it, to the left, is a Cave with a Magic Container. Get that too, and then visit the village of Ruto. To begin that journey, go to the Forest where you won your first Treasure Bag and follow the road to the left, then diagonally toward the upper left. Where the road levels off again, leave it and head straight up: you'll find the Cave of Stone Statues there and, in it, a Trophy that will be useful in Ruto. Continue due left into Ruto, making sure that you stop in the fourth building. There, use the Trophy to acquire Magic Jump. Head straight down from Ruto and enter the Cave; make sure you say hi to the Fairy when you emerge. You'll find her in the small Forest just to your right. Not far below her is a 1-Up—a Link doll about which we'll tell you more before you enter Palace Six. Keep going straight down until you reach Saria, a.k.a. the Water Town. En route, right before entering the village, you'll cross a Bridge: you might want to spend some time on it now, killing Bago-Bagos to boost Link's Attack, Life, and Magic abilities. In Saria, there's a Mirror beneath the table in the third house; once you've found it, the woman who owns it will be so grateful she'll send you to the second house for a special Life boost. Idle chitchat with the villagers will tip you off to one more important stop: the log cabin home of the bearded Bagu. Follow the road to the upper right when you leave the village and you'll find him nestled where the Trees have been hewn—look for this area in the *second* group of Trees. Bagu will make it possible for you to cross water, which is a vital asset as you set off on a hefty hike in search of the Hammer. Return to Saria, have a talk with the Sentry at the Bridge, cross, and go straight down. Before long you'll reach Death Mountain. The series of Caves can be daunting, so pay attention! They're populated by all kinds of monsters, but the real problem is taking them in the correct order. Imagine Death Mountain as a giant clock with the first Cave—the lone opening in the foothills on top—as twelve o'clock. You will not even be entering the center Cave—where the clock hands would be attached—or either of the two Caves, each located at the ten o'clock, nine o'clock, and seven o'clock positions. Nor will you enter the innermost Cave at the four o'clock position. So, go into that first Cave in the foothills. Upon exiting, head clockwise to the Cave below you, to the right. Exit, scoot clockwise to the Cave below to the right, exit, move counterclockwise to the Cave on the right. (Note: stay on the *bottom* level in this next Cave.) Exit and go clockwise to the entrance in the lower right. Exit, and it doesn't matter *which* way you go to the entrance in the lower right. Ditto exiting this Cave, though the next entrance is now in the lower left. Exit, go clockwise to the entrance below you to the left, exit and walk clockwise to the Cave in the lower right. When you leave this Cave, go left to the Cave wherein lies the Hammer! When you exit this Cave—the way you came in—use the Hammer on the Stone beside the Cave: you'll be rewarded with a Magic

Container. To return, you needn't retrace your steps through all the Caves. Instead, go to the far right, enter the Cave there, and you'll exit onto a road that leads straight up. Make your way back to Saria, then follow the yellow (brick?) road as it heads left and up. Your destination is Rauru—you've been here before—and, in particular, the pesky Stone that forms a roadblock. Whack the Stone with the Hammer and you'll not only clear the path, you'll earn another Life Container! When you're through hammering, head back down the road, return to Bagu's residence, and continue to the left. A short trek beyond it you'll come to the Cave of Sacred Water. The name of the place should tell you what you came for! After obtaining it, search the Swamp to the lower left: there's a 1-Up hidden here! When you're finished in this area, head right and get back to the road—pausing in the Cave overhead: there's a Treasure Bag in there that will give you 200 experience points. You should also make a trip to the Swamp below the Cave and to the left: the Red Jar there will be of enormous help! Anyway, when you reach the road, go down and follow it to the right. Stroll into the town of Mido, which is just above the road. You'll find the Magic Fairy in the third house after the Church. Speaking of the Church, double back and take a Magic Jump up to the steeple. Inside, your swordsmanship will be improved with the addition of down-stab ability! When you're finished in Mido, head to the left, go up the road a bit, then turn left at the Swamp and slog through. It's slow going, but vital: it's the only way you can reach Midoro, the Swamp Palace.

Palace Two: It's suggested that you use the Magic Shield now and then in tough spots—such as the battle with Helmethead and other tough foes. To begin with, use your Sword against the Statue at the entrance and you'll almost always get a Magic Container. After entering, take the Elevator down *three* levels and go right: there's a Key at the end of this very short corridor. Return to the Elevator, go up a level and head left: you'll find another Key at the end of a slightly longer corridor. (You can reverse the order in which you get these Keys; it's your call.) Go back to the Elevator and take it up another level. Head left and get the Key here, continue on to the Elevator, and ride it down to the next level. Go left: after hacking your way to the end of the level, you'll be able to claim the Handy Glove, a miraculous anti-Stone weapon. Be certain to leap and stab the Statue on the high ledge just outside this chamber as you leave: you'll get a Magic Container. Return to the Elevator that brought you down here and take it *down* a level. Go right and, protected by your Magic Shield, best the enemies you meet. Do *not* take the Elevator you pass as you go . . . not yet, anyway. At the end of the level use your Handy Glove to smash the Stones blocking the Key, get it, then return to the Elevator you passed. Ride it down, go right—keeping an eye out for a mass of Stones. If you smash them on the right, you'll uncover a Magic Jar. (But Link's now in a *pit*, you say! No problem. Just hack away at the Stones on the left and build yourself a Staircase!) When you come to the three Stone ledges from which there's seemingly no way off, simply have Link stand on them. They'll crumble beneath his feet: when he lands on the last one, hop to the right *pronto*. Get the Treasure Bag if you can, then continue right. When you meet up with Helmethead, the battleplan is simple: with Magic Jump and Magic Shield, leap up and use downthrust to remove his helmet. Repeat this maneuver three or four times on his exposed head, and he's a goner. (In fact, here's a little challenge for you: see if you can kill him without ever touching down, using your Sword like a pogo stick to bounce off his head over and over.) The Crystal is now yours.

Palace Three: It's time to take a self-guided tour of the Island Palace. Reach it by heading left, as though you were returning to Mido. Just before the village, turn down and enter the Graveyard. Go to the King's Grave in the middle of the cemetery—while you're here, looking for the Red Jar

—then walk exactly eight steps down from the King's Grave and Link will drop into a secret Cave. Go right until you come to a high Wall; use the Magic Fairy to fly Link past it, and in no time flat he'll be on the Island. Try to get a Magic Jar from the Statue by the entrance, then take the Elevator down and set off down the corridor. There are two Keys to find here: the first is hidden under Stones three rooms after the Elevator chamber, the second two rooms beyond that. Double back and take the Elevator down a level, go right, get the Key, and continue right, watching out for the blue Knight who flings Swords at Link's legs *and* head. The chamber after the Key room contains a Raft that Link will need later. After getting it, head left four chambers: you'll find a Key in the floor on the left side. When you chop away, make sure you do what you did previously—that is, cut down diagonally to create a Staircase so you can get out. Head right to the Elevator, take it down, and go right. Jump to the top ledge, kill the guard, and hack your way through the Wall. The foe on the other side—Ironknuckle—is mounted. Leap up when he charges, thrust your Sword down, and repeat until he's unhorsed. You'll be able to slay him then as you did the others. Go right to the Crystal setting, and leave in that direction.

Your work in West Hyrule is finished. Raft in hand, go to the Dock; you'll find it to the upper right of the Graveyard, at the end of the horizontal road. Upon arriving in East Hyrule, make tracks down and to the right. After a short trip you'll reach the town of Nabooru. Your initial destination here is the first Fountain, where you'll help a woman get a drink by thrusting your Sword into the Fountain. She'll be happy as a clam; go right with her to the first house, where you can get Fire. Make sure you replenish your Magic and Life before leaving here. Head up from the village to a Cave; thanks to the Fire, you'll have no trouble clearing it of enemies.

Upon exiting, go right until you reach the Bridge, then cross to the Maze. Go down, then left, and stay left until you can only go up. On the left side of the Wall up ahead is a secret Cave; in it is a Lost Child. You'll need the kid in a bit. Make your way to the left side of the Maze by going up—with the Palace on your right—left at the Wall and up the right passage, left at the Wall and down the first passage (going around the Wall below and continuing down), left *under* the first horizontal Wall to your left, down at the left Wall, right, down the first passage, through the break in the Wall below, left, up the passage, then down around the Wall. (There are other ways you can go; look for them, if you're of a mind to!) Here, you'll find another hole—only this one doesn't contain a Child. It has a Magic Container! When you've got it, retrace your path and leave the Maze for now, recrossing the Bridge and heading left over East Hyrule. At this point it might be a good idea to detour back to Nabrooru and fight foes outside the village to build up your Attack skills. In any case, head next to the village of Darunia. Go left, and on the second screen leap to the top of the third house. Slither down the chimney, and Link will get the power to do upthrusts. Leave and head left. At the first house on the next screen swap the Child for Reflect, a power that will be necessary at your next stop: the Palace of Maze Island.

Palace Four: Enter, take the Elevator down, go right, and catch the Elevator in the last chamber. Take it down one level and go right. The Bridge will evaporate under your feet, but Magic Jump will get you over. (If you *do* fall, don't sweat it: maneuver Link to the right, catch the floor of the next level, go right, and get the Winged Boots . . . but we get ahead of ourselves!) Get the Key on the right, and use your Sword on the Statue: you may be rewarded with a Red Jar. Go left and jump down into the Pit now, holding the pad to the right so Link lands on the floor. Get the Boots. Link now has the ability to walk on water! Head left and jump down the Pit, heading right on the bottom. The Bridge will collapse as you cross, so *move* it; get the Key on the other side. Go left three chambers to the last room on this level—repelling the Wizards with Reflect

Magic—and strike down at the Stones to get another Key. Go back to the Elevator and ascend three levels. Go left, past the Elevator, and stab overhead in the next room for a Key. There's another Key in the screen to the left of that, after which you should double back to the right and take the first Elevator down. Head right and get another Key on the right side of the chamber. Go all the way to the left, take the Elevator there down, and turn right. You'll have to face Carock, but you can beat him by squatting on either side of the screen and using Reflect and Magic Shield. You'll get the final Key when the guardian is history. Go right, and . . . you know the game plan from here!

Prior to hitting the Sea Palace, get yourself another Heart Container by crossing the sea off Nabooru, to the right. Walk due right until you are able to head up: you'll find the Container almost straight up from the Palace. After obtaining it, return to Nabooru and check out the desert below the road for Treasure Bag. You should also engage foes in the fields outside the town: don't enter the Palace without boosting your Magic, Life, and Attack at least to level seven. Go back across the waters until you find the opening that leads to . . .

Palace Five: Upon entering, take the elevator down and go right. The Fairy will get you over the Wall; go to the next screen to expose the Key, then double back to the left to get it. Cross the crumbling Bridge to the next Elevator, go down, then head left: there's a Key on a Stone overhead. Don't do anything, though, until the Stones have all fallen. When the avalanche has ended, cut through the Stones to take Stairs up to the Key, pausing only to deal with the Moas that attack—and earn big rewards for so doing: no reason you can't build up to level eight right here! Continue left to the Elevator, go down and head left, take the next Elevator down a level, go right, and use your extraordinary Magic Jump to get the Key up on the right. Go right two screens and, after defeating the guardian therein, you'll be faced with what *seems* to be a solid Wall. It isn't. Once you've killed Ironknuckle, you can walk right through it! In the next screen, take the Elevator down. Go left and pick up the Flute in the next room; you'll need it later—no kidding! Before leaving, stab the Statue to the right of the Flute for—hopefully!—a Magic Jar. Go right and up the Elevator, walk to the right a screen, take the Elevator there up to the next level and go left a screen. You'll find another Key on the Wall there. Get it, go right and back down the Elevator, then head left four rooms to the Elevator, which will take you up a level. Go left to the Elevator on the next screen, ride it down and walk left to get the Key on the far left of the next room, then return to the Elevator and take it up two levels. Go right a room and you'll face the fat, Mace-swinging Gooma. Jump up to avoid his attack, then stab him in his voluminous gut when you land. Repeat until the pug-ugly is no more.

Time for another journey through the countryside before laying siege to Dragon's Maze Palace, home of the evil Barba. First, go back to Nabooru—which is getting to be like a second home already—and travel straight down until you reach the Bridge. The spidery guard will allow you to cross if you blow the Flute. Keep going south, alert for stone-throwing attacks from secret Caves—if you zigzag and/or execute stop-and-go maneuvers, you'll be fine. Don't enter the Graveyard; when you see it, stay on the far side of the road. Follow the path to the bottom right and you'll come to another Bridge. Don't cross: instead, head to the upper right, enter the Cave at the top of the Forest, and exit. (It wouldn't hurt to search among the Trees just below the entrance: you'll find a Treasure Bag there.) In the second section of Forest, use your Hammer to hack down trees, and you'll reveal the hidden village Kasuto. Visit the second house and converse with the aged woman: she'll let you in and give you a Magic Container. Count off another six houses, enter, and make a beeline for the fire-place: that's where you'll get the Magic Spell. Press on to the outskirts of Kasuto and use the Magic Spell: a hidden Cave will materialize and you'll get a Magic Key within.

Now, go back to the Bridge. The Flute isn't what you'll need there: use the Magic Fairy to spirit you safely across. Keep heading toward the lower right until you reach the village of Old Kasuto. Enter the first door and get Thunder Magic . . . assuming, of course, you can fend off the invisible minions that will attack. Retrace your path until you reach three Stones. When you stand in their midst and put your lips to the Whistle, what do you think will appear? (No . . . not a mysterious Water World, Mario fans.) Before you enter the Palace, however, there's some business to take care of regarding 1-Ups. Remember the Link effigy we mentioned earlier? There are a total of five of them in Hyrule: one was outside a cave in West Hyrule, and there's another in each of the next two Palaces. The remaining pair are easily accessible (relatively speaking) in East Hyrule. Each likeness gives Link an extra life, and we didn't discuss them earlier because you might've been tempted to *use* them if you had them! That would have been a waste, Linkophiles, because you're going to need them *now*. So lace up your shoes and head for these two locations.

First, go to the bottom of the Beach to the bottom left of the road you used to cross over to Maze Island—the 1-Up is right near the Forest. Second, as you came down to Old Kasuto, you passed a Graveyard: go back to the road that wound around it, and head directly up from the top of the road, at the point where the Mountains and cemetery meet. You'll find the 1-Up on the right side of the Mountains, exactly halfway between Nabooru and Old Kasuto as the crow flies. (If you can live without this last one, don't get it yet: you'll be heading back to the Graveyard before you enter Palace Seven, so you can get it then.) When you've got the 1-Up(s), head back to the trio of rocks and start Whistling!

Palace Six: This is a virtually Keyless Palace, so if you don't have the Magic Key, you're in deep, deep swamp muck! Assuming you've got it, ride the Elevator past one level and get off at the second. Proceed slowly: the floor *looks* solid, but there's a hidden Pit right before the Ironknuckle. Magic Jump your way through. (Don't sweat it *too* much if you fall, though: the bottomless Pit actually scrolls back to this level. Just keep the pad pressed to the right so Link can land there when the level returns.) Continue going right, climb the Stairs, leap the Elevator, and you'll find yourself in a room of Columns. After the third Column, take a big Magic Jump: once again, the floor seems normal . . . but isn't. If you fall into *this* Pit, things won't be as easy as before. At the bottom you'll have to fight your way to the Elevator on the left and ride it back up, go left to the first Pit, and let it scroll you back two rooms to the left of the Column room. Once you're past that hole-y place, beat the Ironknuckle—knocking him off his horse as you've done before—and claim the Cross in the chamber beyond. With it, you'll be able to get a look at invisible adversaries! Go left, past the Column room, to the first Pit. Drop in, keeping the pad pressed to the right, and stop on the second level down. Head right, fighting foes and using the Fairy to carry you over the Lava pool. Three more rooms to the right and you'll be able to claim a little Link effigy . . . actually a 1-Up. Be careful, though: the room before it has another fragile span over a deep Pit: if you fall in, head left and get on the Elevator. There's also an Ironknuckle to fight here. After you get the doll, jump down the Pit to the left. Use the Fairy to break Link's fall at the next level, and fly right. When you reach the Statue room, position Link on the middle Column of the Lava Pit. Using Magic Jump and his Magic Shield, Link will be well-equipped to fight the serpentine Barba. The Dragon will emerge from the Lava: leap and stab the snakelike fiend in the head when it's rising *and* falling—two blows every time the monster shows its scaly puss! Upon Barba's demise, head right to the Statue to finish your mission here.

Getting to Palace Seven takes skill and stamina, and is accomplished as follows. Go to the bottom of the Graveyard—the one we told you before to avoid at all costs! You can get through relatively unscathed by luring your enemies out: leave the road until they show themselves, step back, and rush through when the coast is relatively clear. When you reach the Swamp at the bottom of the Graveyard, head left, continuing through the Mountain pass. When the Swamp turns, oozing upward, follow it. The way will zigzag a bit; when it straightens out, watch for a Moa attack. Use a Spell to transform it into a Boto, which is easier to slay. Continue up to the Cave entrance, prepared to battle some familiar fiends—Lowders and Achemans, most notably. Fire and Sword will take care of them. Upon emerging from the Cave, simply follow the narrow Swamp down, left, and then up; during the short leftward section, be prepared to use Spells or you probably won't survive. The Cave at the top of the Swamp leads directly to the Great Palace.

Palace Seven: Enter, descend using the Elevator to the right, and head left. Climb the Stairs, keep going left, and take the Elevator down. Travel right to the next Elevator, ride it down, then continue right. Cut your way through the Stones, keep going right, climb the Stairs, and hack away the Stones below so you can get to the Elevator. *Don't* ride the Elevator all the way down: certain sections of the Wall to the left are fake! Almost as soon as the Elevator starts down, you can walk right through the Wall and into a Statue room. Jump up to the Statue above and stab it. A Red Jar will appear; if it doesn't, exit, reenter, and stab it again. Do that as often as it takes until you get what you came for! Return to the Elevator and head down. Go right at the bottom and take the Elevator down. (You guessed it, fellow adventurer: the Great Palace is *deep*!) Head right, making sure you break the Stone above so you can access the upper right section of the Wall. Thrusting downward, drop Link onto the fourth Stone from the bottom: crouching here, you'll be able to deal with the enemy attack that will ensue. Resume your rightward trek, go down yet another Elevator, head right, break the Stone in the far right to get to the Elevator, descend again, and enter another false Wall on the left. Get the Red Jar, then return to the Elevator and continue down. On the next level, you'll find a 1-Up Link to the left and a Life-recharging Fairy to the right. Go down the Elevator between them and go left. In the second screen over, break the sixth Stone from the left to reveal a Pit: drop down and walk right. Cross the Bridge and go down the skinny Pit beneath it: when you hit bottom—and this is, at last, the bottom of the Palace—start stabbing Stones until you've uncovered a pair of Red Jars. When you've got them, go right to do battle with Thunderbird. Position yourself in the middle of the chamber and use both Magic Shield and Magic Jump on defense, and Magic Thunder on offense. Keep attacking the evil guardian's head; you'll know when you're making progress, as the gaudy dude will change colors from red to blue. Tough battle . . . but, unfortunately, not your last. When you're victorious, head right to fight the final enemy: your own Shadow! Stand erect and stab at the silhouette repeatedly with your Magic Shield as protection. The Shadow will leap over you; make sure you spin and face him as he does so, since you can get in some of your best shots at that time.

Once he's defeated, Zelda will awaken . . . and Link can take a well-deserved rest!

Rating: A

The game retains all the wonder and play-value of *The Legend of Zelda*, without simply rehashing that game. There are a lot of new twists, all of them imaginative and all of them daunting, and the magical elements are more pronounced and important. Even though some of the technical aspects of the game are less than perfect, the challenge more than makes up for that—hence the A.

Challenge: A
Graphics: B
Sound Effects: B–
Simulation: B+

NINTEN-DOS AND DON'TS

It's been a while since our last, sprawling *Ninten-Dos and Don'ts*, and we've got a lot of catching up to do on games old and new.

So why are we *jawboning*? Let's get *to* it . . .

Abadox: When the title screen appears, press A, A, up, B, B, down, A, B, Start, and you'll be indestructible.

Adventure Island II: To execute stage select, push the following when the title is on the screen: right, left, right, left. Then hit A, B, A, B. You'll get a "World Select Mode" prompt; by moving the pad up or down you can choose the one you want. Start the game by hitting the A button.

The Adventures of Lolo 2: To get to the last level and a showdown with the King, input VQTD.

To go to special, unadvertised rooooms, use the codes PROA, PROB, PROC, or PROD.

Air Fortress: Here are the codes to get you through the first two waves. First wave: ISTA, KA91(one), 6KAI, 8NYU, 2APP, O(letter O)S85, SUGA. Second wave: ABE4, 11(one, one)NA, 8AJI, TOBI, NDA4, MA1(one)K, DOMO, 7NDA. (A tip of the hat to Jeff Dixon.)

Alien Syndrome: Death is *not* the end! A trick that will gain you extra lives—but cost you friends—in a two player game, is this. Simultaneously push A and B when you die, and you'll snatch a life from the other player!

Astyanax: Go to the title screen and push up on the pad four times, then down, left, right, and up. Push Start. The game will begin . . . and you'll be impervious to the attacks of any foes. Be careful, though: you can still die if you fall off the screen.

If you'd prefer to skip levels altogether, hit the title screen and press the pad up, down, left, and right, then hit B four times. Push Start, and you'll bring up a menu that will allow you to choose your stage.

And if you simply want to use a continue mode, wait until you see "Game Over," then press A, B, Select, and Start. Gameplay will resume where you perished.

Back to the Future: To earn bonus points, wait until the action stops at the end of a street screen, then leap Marty as high as he'll go.

Back to the Future II & III: If you want to begin in 1875, do the following: while the title screen is on, hold down Select, A, and B to go to the password screen. Input the rather transparent code: FLUXCAPACITORISTHEPOWER.

Use Select to go back to the title screen and start the game in the Wild West.

Bases Loaded II: the Second Season: The code to take you halfway through D.C.'s season is: PUKVECW.

Bomberman: We *love* this underrated game—and if you can get your hands on a copy, you won't be disappointed. Anyway, if you use the code BACDIHCLOAFHABDNMOLG, you will access a level beyond where the game's *supposed* to end!

Boulderdash: Passwords to bring you to different worlds are:
Relic World: 225378
Ice World: 635870
Volcano World: 752053
Sand World: 840137
Ocean World: 840967

Bubble Bobble: Way back in our first book, we discussed this game at length. What we *didn't* give you was a code that allows you to access any level you wish by using the A and B buttons. The password is DDFFI.

Burai Fighter: Codes . . . we've got codes! They are, in succession: BALL, JOKE, DOLL, PAIL, GOAL, and GAME.

If you want to begin the game with your hero at full strength, use the code LOBB. Conversely, if you want to make the *game* more difficult, input the code GOOD. To get to the last three stages of each of the first two difficulty levels, use LIME, MILD, and NILE; and PLAN, MONK, and IDOL, respectively. To get to the final stage of the last difficulty level, input ICHI.

Captain Skyhawk: In order to skip any stage in this game—except the last boss—wait until the game is underway, then simultaneously push up and B on the *second* controller.

To become indestructible requires a bit more dexterity: while the letters are tumbling into place, push the pad up, right, down, left, and up a total of four times.

You can also start out with mucho power by pushing Start, watching as the title returns, then simultaneously pressing down and A.

Castlevania II: Simon's Quest: Give these advanced codes a try: FKNT KUSC TZSY UJJO and TDLI(letter i) HXDZ U48F 8TR1(one).

Cobra Triangle: When each stage gets under way, hold down the A button as the Triangle falls to the playing surface. You'll be able to rack up significant points here!

Code Name: Viper: To begin playing at level seven, punch in 081620. To go right to the end, input 217298.

Cosmic Epsilon: Stage select in this galactic gambol is achieved by getting to the title screen and pushing A, B, right, left, right, left, down, down, up, up. Use the pad to select the stage, then press Start.

There's also a continue mode to this game: when "Game Over" arrives to taunt you, push down Select and press Start. You'll resume play at the stage on which you died.

Crystalis: Prior to receiving Teleport, you can still whip through the game by doing the following: any time during the game, hold down A and B on controller one and A on controller two. You'll be whisked to another part of the game. If you *keep* pressing A on controller two, you'll continue to warp to different places.

Dash Galaxy in the Alien Asylum: To execute level select, do the following during the title screen: simultaneously push A and B, Select, upper left on the pad. Move the pad up or down to get to the level you want, then push start.

Deadly Towers: One of the toughest of the earlier Nintendo games, *Deadly Towers* can be beaten with greater ease by doing the following: start the game and allow yourself to be killed. Note the password and start the game again . . . only this time replace the first two characters of the code with EF or FE, then re-input the rest of the characters. You will start, now, with a suit of armor that is extremely powerful!

Dick Tracy: Codes that will solve the third through fifth cases are:

164–003–201

036–224–136
007–215–047

Dig Dug 2: To burrow your way to different levels, do the following: after the title screen has appeared, simultane ously press A, Start, and Select. Move the pad up or down, then use A or B to choose the stage.

Dino Riki: If you lose, don't despair! You can continue on that stage when "Game Over" appears by simultaneously holding the pad up and pressing Start.

Dirty Harry: For an unlimited number of lives, use the password CLYDE.

Dragon Spirit: In case you want to head into the fray with 20 extra lives—and who wouldn't?—fight the first battle, wait for the title screen to reappear, then hold A and B on controller two, and press Start on controller one. When the game resumes, you'll have a score of Dragons!

You may need some extra hands for this next maneuver. Switch on the game and, on controller two, simultaneously hold down A and B while pushing the pad up. Reset the game using the NES *console* while holding these, and you'll get the message "Sound Test" with OO beneath it. On controller two push B, up, up, B, down, down, and B. You'll see another number under the OO: using controller two, select the level you want by moving the pad left or right. When you reach the stage you're looking for, hit Start on controller one.

Dungeon Magic: Turn on the game, and let the story finish. Wait for the scene of the town to materialize on the bottom left, then press A on controller two *twice*, hit Start on controller one, and—bingo! You start the adventure with 100 extra Gold Coins.

Dynowarz: To reach successive levels, use the codes: 5431, 9892, 6315, 7452, 1697, and 6425.

8 Eyes: A few codes to get things rolling: ONAPPMBPPF, CKBPPAAPEE, and GBCPHAAHAD. The game repeats itself after you've won, though it gets more difficult each time you have to play through it. To access the more challenging levels directly, input the password TAXANTAXAN for a second go-round, or FINALSTAGE for the third version.

In any case, make sure when you reach the Jewel Room that you put the Jewels in the correct order: yellow, white, green, orange, blue, purple, red, and black.

Faxanadu: To get to the last phase of the game, use the following code: q8f?cn?,SwSYzGYLhqSthCEA

Incidentally, the King in this game can be manipulated to your advantage. To begin with, he'll give you 1500 Gold Coins. Spend the *entire* amount and then return to him with empty pockets. He'll fill 'em with 1500 more Coins! Keep doing this until you can't carry another item.

Flying Warriors: Here's a code you probably never would have guessed to get to the end (duh!): END.

G.I. Joe: Codes which will help you get through the game are:

3ZDX9ZOX1
N3GGN3BGB
5399N5XG2
5ZD3NN5X5
ZNS39N5XF

Gilligan's Island: Reach adventures two, three, and four using these passwords:

LJJGDMPC
ACCEDCAC
FAACPHFF

Gremlins 2: Passwords to get you through the game are:

GBQK (1–1)
BVKF (1–2)
DXNH (2–1)
CGMW (2–2)
NJTD (3–1)
ZFPJ (3–2)
SHMC (4–1)
VLBB (4–2)
NXRD (5–1)

Heavy Barrel: You can get three additional continues in this game thanks to a simple, and rather obvious, procedure. Select a two-player game, but play only one player, allowing the other player's warriors to perish. *Don't* push button A to bring player two back to life until player one has used up all of its continues. Then switch to player two and keep on fighting the good fight!

Heavy Shreddin': During the title screen, simultaneously hold down A and B while pushing left on the pad. When you start the game, you'll have 99 snowboarders in reserve!

Image Fight: To execute level select, push down the A and B buttons on *both* controllers. Push Start on controller one; after "Start Stage 1" appears, push the Select button to access the stage you want, then hit Start—both using controller one.

Ironsword: Whatever password you use, replace the fifth character with an N. This will give you additional lives!

Some passwords that you'll find useful: PPTHNT-MDHPPX, WBTMKZQZGPTX, and ZZTWBZXT-KDNB. To begin with *many* powerful weapons and extra lives, use the code NTTMNWLPPBDZ.

Finally, reader Donald Dunning suggests you try the code ZPJNGTXTKG.

Iron Tank: Nintendo-game master Donald Dunning strikes again, with this code to bring you to enemy headquarters:

2110944

Journey to Silius: To execute option select, do the following on the title screen: press B 23 times, then hit Start. The options menu will come up; use Select to pick the options, and the A and B buttons to work the numbers. When you've made your choices, shift the cursor to Exit and hit Start.

Kid Icarus: This one's among the oldest Nintendo games, but if you've still got one lying around, take this code for a spin: ICARUS FIGHTS MEDUSA ANGELS. Thanks to my pal Emory King III of Newbury, Ohio, for that. It's worth dusting off the cartridge to give this one a try!

Kid Kool: To earn a massive supply of 1-Ups—but not more than 255, or you'll lose 'em all!—here's all you have to do. Leap across the first Pond in 1–3. You'll hit a Pole on the opposite shore, and it'll vault you to the next screen. When it does, immediately push the pad to the left so you'll come down on top of the Pole. Keep bouncing on the Pole; when you've earned ten 1-Ups, go to the next Pond, leap in, and you'll restart before the Pole . . . enabling you to repeat the process.

Knight Rider: To jump right to the end of any level, pause the game while you're playing, then hold down A and B and push left and up on the pad. While doing that, use Select to go through all the weapons. When you've finished, restart the game.

Another procedure—one that allows you to go to any city—is to hold down A and B and reset the game while continuing to hold the buttons down. When Devon's "Select Mode" prompt appears, press up or down to change the stage numbers.

If you're the type who prefers using codes to various

button/pad combinations, NSMRNQIUKRISD will take you right to Phoenix with nine lives in reserve.

Kung-Fu Heroes: To continue the game after you've been defeated, push down A and simultaneously hit Start.

Lee Trevino's Fighting Golf: If you want to play left-handed, push the pad left and press A while choosing your player. The practical value is negligible . . . but it's kind of a kick just the same!

Lone Ranger: Enter the password 0810 7830 3251 2 (leave the rest blank). When Area Select 1 appears, use the pad to select any area you wish. (And check out your weapons and moneybag: not bad, huh?)

Low 'G' Man: Codes to get you from levels two through five (first two are pretty cute):

MICH
ELLE
ISAC
BILL

The Magic of Scheherazade: Go to any level you want by inputting W and the number of the level. The game will tell you that the code is wrong . . . but input it again, and then again. It'll work after three tries.

You can also take a look at the conclusion of the game simply by using the code END.

Mega Man II: Go directly to the nefarious Dr. Wily by entering these gridpoints: A1, B2, B4, C1, D1, D3, E3, E5, and C5.

By the way, a nifty trick can be executed on the round-select screen. While any baddy is glowing, hold down A and B and push Start. The stars in the background will be transformed into birds! It won't help your gameplay *one iota* . . . but you'll experience a nutty sense of accomplishment just the same!

Mendel Palace: Any time during the game, hold Start, Select, and hit Reset. the title screen will appear and you'll be able to play hidden levels!

Metal Fighter: On the title screen, hold down A and B and hit the Select button: press Select to choose your level—two pushes for the second level, three for three, etc.—then punch the Start button and you're off!

Metal Gear: For those of you still playing this classic, here's a code that'll give you the full inventory of weapons: 5XZ1(one)C GZZZG UOOOU UYRZZ NTOZ3.

A pair of codes which bring you nearly to the end of your quest are: WZRJZ QZZZD UJ51(one)O UI(cap i)QZZ NZRZE—and GHHII JJKKL LMMNN OOPPQ QQRRSS.

Finally, a code that will take you beyond the evil ruler to the very end: T1111 11611 11111 11111 11116

Metroid: Nintendogamer Bryan Baggett suggests the following high-powered code:

nNtd7K boo-W7 9tz0(zero)pW u00(zeroes)GTN.

Metal Storm: To get to advanced levels, here are the codes to use. Level four: FMM-FFC7-B5Z. Level five: M67-WL35-WQ5. Level six: 9JT-LQ3K-QGM. Special thanks to Rahman Warner for her help.

Mission: Impossible: The final mission can be reached by inputting: QBYZ.

Upon reaching the computer, use the code: MTKN.

Monster Party: Here's a code that'll bring you to the climactic showdown: DTv gs. iNT

Narc: During the title screen, simultaneously push A, B, Select, and up on the pad. Now hit Start: you'll be granted a pair of continues.

NES Play Action Football: To pit Chicago against San Francisco in the Power Bowl, input:

OIG9DQT5C8

For an advanced game in which San Francisco battles Miami, use:

B7H5DSD5FC

Rad Racer II: Steer your way through level select by going to the title screen and pressing B one time *less* than the level you wish to go to—that is, push twice to go to three—then holding the pad diagonally up and left and simultaneously pushing Start.

If you want to increase the difficulty level of the game—like it *needs* that?—you can opt to race with no lights on during the night races. Hold the pad to the upper left and press B eight times, then hit Start. Enjoy the dark . . . 'cause you may not survive it for long!

Rambo: To make Rambo invincible, use the following code: H800(zeroes) l(letter l)bW2 kG4Q KwKc 66Wh QbW2 0(zero)F1(one)D G1(one)9D.

Don't be alarmed when you start the game and your hero starts losing energy: when it reaches zero, Rambo will continue to fight!

RoboCop: When the continues allowed by the game are *dis*continued, don't despair, cyborg! You can continue by doing the following when "Game Over" rears its ugly consonants. Push and hold A, B, and Select, then—still holding them—press Start. You'll be allowed to re-access the continue option. You can do this as often as you like.

RoboWarrior: Frankly, this little gambit may be more trouble than it's worth . . . but what the heck? You'll get your money's worth out of the cartridge! Amass a total of 62 Bombs, then destroy a Lurcher using your basic weapon. Go to the subscreen, shift the cursor to Energy Capsule, but *don't* access it. Go to the second controller, hold the pad to the upper left; while you're doing that, press A two times on controller *one*. That will give you unlimited goodies. Stay on controller one and simultaneously press the Select button and hold the pad to the upper left. That will give you the ability to change levels by using the A and B buttons.

Rolling Thunder: Passwords which will help you through level three are:

6692956
4516110
6396857
4249741
6916079

To go to the sixth section of level four, use:

7236972

Shadow of the Ninja: Overwhelmed by enemies? Hold down the B button for six seconds and you'll summon lightning that will destroy them all! It'll cost you energy . . . but that's better than the alternative!

To execute level select, do this during the title screen: select the number of players, then hit A, A, A, A, B, B, B, B, A, B, A, B, A, B, A, B. When the game makes a sound, press the following combinations to go to the level you wish:

1/2: B on controller two
1/3: A on two
1/4: A and B on two
2/1: B on one
2/2: B on *both* controllers
2/3: B on one, A on two
3/1: B on one, A and B on two
3/2: A on one

3/3: A on one, B on two
4/1: A on both
4/2: A on one, A and B on two
4/3: A and B on one
5/1: A and B on one, B on two
5/2: A and B on one, A on two

Note: while holding the buttons down as described above, you must push Start on controller one to begin the game at the level you wish.

Skate or Die 2: To wheel on up to higher levels from the *story* screens (not the Ramp), use controller two and press—sequentially, not at once—Start, A, Select, B. Use the pad to select the level you want to visit. (Incidentally, in the Mall, *don't* make all the deliveries as scheduled. The *even* numbered schedule is fine . . . but do Joe's Formal Wear, Rhinestone Jewelers, Wumpus World, Kafka's Candies—with or without big bugs?—Stiller's Outpost, and Pathos Fashions first, third, fifth, seventh, ninth, and eleventh, respectively. You'll earn multiple rewards for your initiative!)

On the two-screen Ramp, shift your board demon to the far side—the skater's left. As soon as the character puts hand to head, push Start twice and Select once. An alarm *should* sound; if it doesn't, perform the maneuver again. What the alarm means is that you can fall as often as you like but will always have Boards in reserve!

Snake, Rattle, 'N Roll: You can warp ahead in this game by doing the following: at the start of the first level, leap to the first single-square Island you encounter. Hop up and down, using your forked tongue, and you'll be spirited ahead.

You can also warp *way* ahead if, from the start of level one, you travel *only* in a line, hopping objects but never veering from a straight course. If you get to the end with at least 96 seconds left on the clock, a Rocket will arrive to carry you to level eight.

Snake's Revenge: For a full-powered assault on the final building, input the password: 5WN3 8#MV RML9 BRP! %!HT N67Z 3QZ8 26

Solar Jetman: Codes that will bring you to later levels are DHGMQQGBHGNB (nine), DGGWBPBBNBNB (ten), and DHGDQLNBTLNB (eleven).

Solomon's Key: It's been a while since we took a look at this game in any of our books, but there's one maneuver that is noteworthy for its novelty rather than strategic value.

In Room 17, take care not to lose any lives. There are Sparkling Balls on the eight Blocks in the bottom of the room; either eliminate or redirect the fiery fiend on the top right Block, get on that Block, create a Block to the right, and leap onto it. Jump up against the overhead Block 11 times. What do you get for all this effort? Mighty Bomb Jack, from the eponymous game, will make an appearance! We didn't say this was a profoundly significant ploy . . . just a fun one!

And to Mrs. Karen Ruch, who couldn't find the Constellation Symbol in Room 44: it's located four spaces below the door. The Golden Goose can be found against the right wall, halfway up.

Solstice: This game's a toughie, so it's a good idea to know how you can get a limitless supply of Wizards. If you find yourself in danger, go to the subscreen and press the following: B, Start, Start, B, B, Start, Start, B, B, Start, Start, Start, B, Start, B, B, B, Start, Start, Start, B, Start, B, Start, Start, B, Start, Start, B, B, Start, B, Start. You'll know whether or not you've entered the sequence correctly, since the screen will flash. Return to the game, then go back to the subscreen: not only will your supply of Hats be plentiful, you won't lose any when you die!

Star Soldier: At the title screen, push Select on controller one ten times. Then press the pad to the upper left while, on controller two, you push the pad to the bottom right. While you're holding both pads, use your nose—or have a friend do it; use a finger, that is, not push your nose down! —to hit Start on controller one. This procedure will give you an overwhelming arsenal to begin the game.

Super C: During the title screen, push the pad right, left, down, and up. Push A, B, and Start: you'll commence the action with ten warriors on the bench!

Super Mario Bros.: One of our Mario experts, Shashi Persaud, has been working on what many of you say is one of the toughest aspects of the game: finding that elusive Water World entrance. Shashi has found a method that seems to work. When you reach the end of level 1-2, bust the second and third overhead Blocks from the right, stand on the leftmost edge of the Pipe *facing* left, and jump *backward* against the right side of the screen.

Shashi also reports that you can "get small and shoot at the same time" by jumping on Bowser *and* the Axe at the same time at the end of level 1-4.

Meanwhile, reader Connie Minyard of Virginia not only made it to the Water World—"I stood at the left edge of the Pipe, pressed down, jumped, and then walked through the wall"—but also reports having heard rumors of a Chocolate Factory hidden in the game.

Finally, thanks to reader Adam Stead for his interesting letter about *Super Mario Bros*.

Super Mario Bros. 2: Reader Kathryn Hedrick shares the following for 4/3: "On the thin Ledge after the Staircase wall, if you're the Princess you can do a running jump and fly to the next Ledge. Go into the second door, and after you get the Crystal Ball you can enter Fryguy's chamber without having to deal with the enemies in the other doors."

Super Mario Bros. 3: West Virginia reader Leonard Hyde

wrote a lengthy epistle in which—among many, many other things—he suggested the following: "On 1-2, get the Starman near the end. Race ahead and kill the Para-Goomba. Go back to the pipe, jump over the first three Goombas that come out, and lead the Goomba parade down to the card to cash in for big points! Four Goombas on the screen add up to 15,000 points! If you leave the Para-Goomba alive and succeed in bopping off her wings, she will be the fifth Goomba . . . and a 1-Up!"

However, that's not the best part. Leonard says that on 1–3, if you enter the Mushroom House immediately after losing a life—still flashing with invulnerability—the game will give you an unlimited supply of P-Wings!

Super Pitfall: If you lose, wait until the title screen returns then press Select, hit A three times, and hit Select again. The cursor will shift closer to the bottom of the screen: leave it there, press Start, and you'll continue from where you died.

Sword Master: At the title screen, simultaneously hold the pad down and press Select. Hit Start and you'll have unlimited continues.

Tecmo Bowl: If you want to match a team against itself, here are some of the codes to use:

Cleveland:	49AFFBA9
New York:	269DFFA1
Chicago:	697BFFA5
Los Angeles:	969FDFA5
Dallas:	63AEFFA5
Miami:	46AFFDAB
Washington:	997FBFA5

Teenage Mutant Ninja Turtles: In a never-ending quest to bring you the world's coolest tips, we asked Ultra Software to think hard and come up with their *best* hints for winning this game. Well . . . advanced players won't take much joy in Ultra's advice, but beginners may be interested. They said, find the captured Turtle in level three by crossing the Foot Bridge and going into the first room of the building to the right. They also suggested investigating Building 13 on level four, and the center building's basement in level five.

Nothing earthshaking, there . . . but ours is not to question why, ours is but to report the news!

Thunderbirds: Reset the game while pushing the pad diagonally to the top left. Hit A, followed by B, and then Select: you can now choose your level.

Another neat maneuver is to pause the game during play, push the pad diagonally to the upper left, and simultaneously press A, B, and Select. Exit the pause function, and you'll be whisked to the end of that level!

Tombs and Treasures: To go directly to the end, input:

'n&+ T3qy bvL] h8iW
%-"4 PKJV =p-y k986

Vegas Dream: Here's the ultimate password: plug it in, and you'll see why!

G!E! K7!H 1(one)8UL QF
9T7K !!!! !!P1(one) A2
VGAU 8LVK RGAU 8L
5QK7 DQI(cap i)2 GLS4 I(cap i)P
3MWJ SHBU 9M22 22
22J3 ?MIT CWAN XM
TI(cap i)CW AN33 3333 G4

Actually, *any* password can be used to earn you millions of dollars. Simply input the code *reversing* the seventeenth and eighteenth characters. Your pockets will be filled to overflowing!

Wall Street Kid: Here's the ultimate financial district code:

MCAiB 10W0? SH40Q 2020E
0?%4? $4?%4 2V8MK CQ208
M30C0 C

Who Framed Roger Rabbit?: A code that will give you one very well-armed Roger is: LLHHHHHHODHHOHHHH-HHHGZ.

In case you're having trouble finding the pieces of the Will, look for two in Toontown, one in Los Angeles, and the other in a Cave in the Outskirts.

Willow: A couple of advanced codes for you: rtw fPP Bj9 mb? 1(one)Sq H7h and Mo! aCC vei Nxg I(cap i)5D knV

Another code you'll definitely want to try is tQW 5IT gxq Xev Vzf xvn. Once it's entered, hit the Select button and a pair of characters will appear on the screen. These are coordinates that indicate exactly where you are. To change them—and thus warp elsewhere—move the pad up and down while holding down A (to change the character on the right) and B (for the character on the left). After you've made whatever changes you wish, hit Select and you'll be whisked elsewhere. The combination OF will bring you to Nockmaar Castle. Note: this technique doesn't *always* work. Sometimes it'll give you on-screen gibberish that is interesting to look at but of no play-value.

A final code, which will give you an inventory full of goodies, is 8zs L4B W4K fyM 6JW 5Kq.

World Championship Wrestling: To bring yourself to within a pair of victories from the championship, use the code H5YT 1(one)YQ7 OHNZ.

Xexyz: Employ the password A2A4A6A8A0. This will allow you to skip the odd-numbered stages. If you enter the code BBA1357912, you'll fight all the bosses of the odd-numbered stages. Finally, input 5C2B5C8A1(one)E if you want to go to the end.